The Lucas Plan
a new trade unionism in the making?

Members of the Lucas Aerospace Combine Committee on the steps of Wortley Hall 1977: from the left, back row: Brian Sheppard, Dave Newton, unknown, J. Cavanah, unknown, Tom Gallagher, Les Halstead, unknown, Terry Ford, unknown.

Middle row: Brian Salisbury, Tommy Quirk, Mike Cooley, Trevor James, M. Cryer, Jim Hulme, Phil Asquith, Danny Broomhead, Ernie Webber.

Front row: Ron Mills, Mick Cooney (not to be confused with Jim Cooney or Mike Cooley), Jack Gunter, Pat McSharry, Sid Flemming, Danny Conroy, unknown.

The Lucas Plan
A new trade unionism in the making?

Hilary Wainwright and Dave Elliott

Cartoons by Larry

Allison & Busby
London · New York

First published 1982
by Allison and Busby Limited
6a Noel Street, London W1V 3RB, England
and distributed in the USA
by Schocken Books Inc
200 Madison Avenue, New York N.Y. 10016

British Library Cataloguing in Publication Data:

Wainwright, Hilary
    The Lucas struggle.
    1. Lucas Aerospace 2. Lucas Aerospace Combine Shop
    Stewards Committee 3. Diversification in
    industry – Great Britain
    I. Title   II. Elliott, Dave
    338.7'6291'0941   HD9711.5.G74L/

    ISBN 0-85031-429-1
    ISBN 0-85031-430-5 pbk

Set in 9/11 Plantin by Alan Sutton Publishers Ltd, Gloucester.
Printed and bound in Great Britain by
Richard Clay, (The Chaucer Press) Ltd,
Bungay, Suffolk.

Contents

Preface   1
Chronology   5
1   A new approach   7
I   Background Circumstances
2   Out of the white heat. . .   16
3   The failings of the old; the foundations of the new   26
II   Creating the Combine Committee
4   Roads leading to Wortley Hall   34
5   A new organization in the making   48
6   A new organization in action   64
7   Expertise and self-reliance   76
III Workers' Plan to Meet Social Needs
8   The origins of the alternative plan   81
9   Drawing up the Plan   88
10 A positive alternative to recession and redundancies   98
11 A question of power   113
12 Local victories: the Plan in action   122
IV   Beyond the Company
13 The Lucas Combine provides an example   140
14 An idea come of its time   159
15 Up against institutions whose time is past   172
16 A lost opportunity   183
V   No Combine is an Island
17 The Combine on the defensive   199
18 Making connections   217
VI   Conclusions
19 The limits of collective bargaining   231
20 A new trade unionism in the making?   243
Resources — further information and contacts   266
Notes   269
Technical glossary   273
Union names   273
Index   274

To Ernie Scarbrow
Secretary to the Lucas Aerospace Combine Committee 1969–80

Preface

In recent years two overwhelming fears have haunted people in Britain: the fear of unemployment and the fear of war. Both are the outcome of forces that often seem to be outside the control of so-called "ordinary people": technological and market pressures producing the constant threat of "redundancy"; and the momentum of the military machine carrying with it the threat of extermination. "Ordinary people", however, have been resisting both in extraordinary ways.

In 1975 and 1976, for instance, shop stewards working at Lucas Aerospace, a company heavily involved in arms production, drew up a detailed plan for socially useful products and new forms of employee development. They put forward this plan as an alternative to redundancies and to arms production. In doing so they demonstrated in a most practical way how people without any official power might reverse both the drive towards militarism and the growth of unemployment.

The Lucas Aerospace shop stewards were organized through a unique cross-plant, multi-union combine committee, representing 13,000 staff and shop-floor workers in the seventeen Lucas Aerospace factories. This organization and the Plan itself was a challenge not only to the priorities of management and the government but also to the trade-union establishment. The Lucas stewards faced hostility and indifference from all these quarters. The company refused to negotiate on the Plan, commenting: "We are very unresponsive to a deliberate attempt by a group of workers to achieve a *de facto* situation to achieve bargaining rights across one of our companies [sic]." The Labour government, after Tony Benn had been removed from the Department of Industry, accepted the company's view. However, the Plan received widespread support among workers in Lucas Aerospace, within the labour movement and from a wide spectrum of people throughout the country and internationally. The Lucas stewards and their supporters became a constant political irritant to the government. In the end the government had at least to be seen to do something to support the Plan and save jobs. But by then, 1978–9, it was too little, too late. The Tory government which followed provided just the right conditions for Lucas management to attack the Combine. The result has been serious defeats for trade unionism in Lucas Aerospace, as elsewhere. Even as we write, Lucas Aerospace are trying to sack 1,200 workers from their Burnley plant, despite record profits from the post-détente boom in defence orders. Nevertheless the ideas pioneered by the Lucas stewards, and the workers' self-confidence they inspired, have put down roots which cannot be so easily destroyed.

The purpose of this book is to explain this remarkable initiative. We look into its background, explore the extent and the nature of the support for it, and try to understand the obstacles and hostility it faced. We look behind some of the myths that have grown up around the Lucas story and assess its wider significance for the future of trade unionism and socialism. The Combine Committee encouraged us to write this book not primarily as an archive or as an academic commentary but as a resource for others who are gathering their collective strength to resist unemployment and war. For this reason we have been concerned to highlight the weaknesses and failings of the Combine Committee as well as the successes, so that others can learn from its mistakes.

The story of the Lucas Plan raises, tantalizingly, many of the major political, economic and technological issues of our day. We were tempted to follow up them all. We decided however to stay as close as possible to the story itself and only to indicate the wider issues that it raises. Where possible we have given references to enable readers to follow up these wider themes themselves.

There is one issue, however, which lies hidden behind the main action. It too requires a book of its own; a book about what a feminist theatre group once called "class struggle widows". Almost all the leading participants are men (see Chapter 4). Most of these men are married with families. Their involvement in the Combine, on top of their local trade-union activities, has meant time and energy away from their wives and children. In some cases the women married to these stewards are themselves actively involved in similar activities. In the majority of cases, however, they are not involved in trade-union and political activity; in some cases they have been indifferent or even unsympathetic and have sometimes become more so as their husbands' commitment left them without support or company. The Combine, like most trade-union organizations in the male-dominated sections of industry, did not openly discuss the problem and explore ways of providing more support for delegates' families. These problems are increasingly being discussed informally, partly because some stewards' relationships have cracked under the strain, partly because feminism manages to sneak in everywhere, and partly because gradually a few more women have become involved in the Combine Committee. No doubt it will be these women who will make sure that the informal talk influences the Combine's ways of organizing.

This book grew out of a project funded by the Social Science Research Council. In 1977 the Lucas Aerospace Combine Committee approached the SSRC asking for research assistance under the SSRC's Open Door Scheme — a scheme designed to give industrial, trade-union and community groups access to academic research facilities. Dr David Elliott of the Open University Technology Policy Group, who had already been involved with the Combine as a technical advisor, was asked to establish the project, and in January 1980 Hilary Wainwright began work as the full-time Research Fellow for a twenty-month period. She worked with the Combine and with CAITS — the research organization set up jointly by North-East London Polytechnic and the LASSCC — on several problems which their Plan was facing. During this time Hilary visited all the Lucas Aerospace sites, talked with all the shop stewards' committees and attended Combine meetings. When the SSRC funding (£15,000) came to an end, the Open University Faculty of Technology provided funds for the completion of the project and the writing of the book. In this latter period Hilary visited all the sites again for more structured interviews with shop stewards and, to a lesser extent, workers without any trade-union position. She also interviewed ex-Labour ministers, trade-union officials, MPs, academics and trade-union activists elsewhere, who had been involved in one way or another. Dave contributed work on the more technological aspects of the story and Hilary carried out the final writing. Drafts of the book were circulated to Combine delegates at two different stages of the book's progress for further criticism and amendment. The drafts were discussed at several Combine meetings. One member of the Combine, Phil Asquith from Burnley, was delegated to liaise with us.

Throughout the project the needs of the Combine Committee have influenced the research programme. In many ways then this project is part of a new development in research practice: research geared to the strategic needs of a trade-union group. Perhaps inevitably, the fact that the SSRC project was undertaken for the Combine Committee has meant that Lucas Aerospace management have refused to answer any questions arising from the research; although management-oriented research projects usually find trade unionists willing to answer questions. However several members of middle management have been willing to talk to us, as has one ex-manager. We have tried to piece together a view of management's strategy but our understanding of the internal workings of the company's management are not as full as we would have wished.

There are many people we want to thank both for help in improving the content and for making the project extremely enjoyable. First, we want to thank all the stewards and their families who were so hospitable and helpful when Hilary visited the different sites. Two shop stewards who left Lucas Aerospace before we started our work have also gone out of their way to help. One is Frank Wood, who was sacked in 1971 partly, no doubt, because of the organizing he did in Birmingham which prepared the way for the Combine at that central site. The other is Jack Gunter, who used to be AUEW convenor in Lucas Aerospace, Birmingham, and was one of those who first took hold of the idea of an alternative plan and sharpened its political strategy. We also want to thank Mike George, Jane Barker, Dave Pelly, Dot Lewis, Tammy Walker, Bill Evans and Richard Fletcher at CAITS for use of their files when they were trying to keep them in order, for answering questions while they were in the middle of some other work and for reading and helpfully commenting on parts of manuscript. We have had especially helpful comments from Michael Green, Tony Fry and Paul Willis of the Design Collective in Birmingham (see Chapter 20 for details of this collective), and Shirley Cooley, Chris Goodey, Doreen Massey, Jeff Rooker MP, Robin Roy, Chris Smith, Phil Stern and Sue Ward have read particular chapters and made useful corrections. Thanks especially to Tony Fry for his elegant diagrams and maps. We have also been helped by several individuals involved in the disarmament movement or working with rank-and-file trade unionists in other countries. We would like to thank Dave MacFadden, Natalie Shiras and Marilyn Kjellen-Rogers from the Mid Peninsula Conversion Project (California) and Peter de Vries from Holland for their information and encouragement. Special thanks to Sylvia Celentano, Alison Cook and Sally McIver for typing different drafts and to Lynne Amidon for help in compiling the index and making useful comments on the manuscript. Roy Bhaskar, John and Joan Bohanna, Ruth Elliott, Mary Kaldor, Sheila Rowbotham, Lynne Segal and Joyce Wainwright have either read or discussed the story and the ideas interminably — or so it must seem to them. Thanks for their support and encouragement. However, neither they nor any of the other people who have helped bear final responsibility for what is to follow.

A final point: at the end of the book there is a glossary of technical terms and a list of the unions and other organizations mentioned in the text.

H.W. and D.E., April 1982.

The Lucas Story: a brief chronology of events

1967–69	The Labour government's Industrial Reorganization Corporation encourages Lucas to rationalize aerospace components industry. Lucas Ltd takes over AEI aircraft group, English Electric aircraft component section and several other companies.
Dec. 1969	Combine Committee founded with four sites involved.
July 1970	Conservative government.
Jan 1971	Rolls Royce crash. 2,000 redundancies at Lucas Aerospace.
Mar. 1971	Lucas Aerospace formed as a unified subsidiary company.
July–Sept. 1972	Burnley strike.
Dec. 1972	Beginning of pensions campaign.
Jan. 1973	All thirteen Lucas Aerospace sites affiliated to the Combine Committee.
Apr. 1973–	
Jan. 1974	Campaign against 800 redundancies.
Feb. 1974	Labour government.
Nov. 1974	Delegation to Tony Benn at the Dept. of Industry.
Jan. 1975–	
Jan. 1976	The Plan is drawn up.
June 1975	A local plan is drawn up as basis of resistance to redundancies in Hemel Hempstead.
Oct. 1975	A local plan is drawn up as basis of resistance to redundancies at Birmingham.
Nov. 1975	First approach made to Labour government for support.
Jan. 1976	Full Plan publically launched.
May. 1976	Company refuses to negotiate over the Plan.
July 1976–7	Campaign of teach-ins and leaflets at Lucas sites, pressure on individual unions for support, political campaign outside Lucas, nationally and internationally.
Jan 1977	Burnley management sanction heat-pump prototype project.
Feb. 1977	Redundancy fears following company announcement of "labour surplus".
March 1977	Combine Committee and Lucas executive in separate meetings with Labour MPs at House of Commons.
June 1977	Combine Committee seeks CSEU recognition.
Aug. 1977	Deadline for redundancies passes; no redundancies made.
Sept. 1977	Several manual shop stewards' committees split from Combine Committee. James Blythe appointed General Manager; tours the sites to draw rationalization plans.
Oct. 1977	Centre for Alternative Industrial and Technological Systems (CAITS) created at North East London Polytechnic.
March 1978	Company announce two-year reorganization plan with net loss of 1,400 jobs.
1978	Combine co-ordinates industrial sanctions against redundancies.
Sept. 1978	National Executive of Shipbuilding and Engineering Unions start negotiations with government and Lucas Aerospace.
Feb. 1979	Outcome of negotiations £8m for Lucas. Redundancies delayed. Joint working party on new products established.
May 1979	Conservative government.
June–Dec. 1979	Attempts to sack Combine Committee secretary.

--

Jan. 1980	Trade Union representatives withdraw from joint working party in protest.
Jan. 1980	Joint Forum of Combine Committees created.
May 1980	Sheffield local council start discussions with the Combine Committee about alternative plans.
1981	Unit for the development of Alternative Products created at Coventry Polytechnic.
May 1981	The Greater London Council and the West Midlands County Council take up idea of workers' plans for socially useful production as part of the new Labour administration's industrial strategy.
June 1981	Combine Committees and Trades Councils launch declaration and campaign on "Popular Planning for Social Need".
June 1981	Mike Cooley sacked.
Feb. 1982	2,000 redundancies announced at Burnley.

1 A new approach

"There is talk of crisis wherever you turn. I think we have to stand back from that crisis for a few moments and see where we are in relation to it. For it is the present economy that has a crisis. We don't. We're just as skilled as we were; miners can still dig coal, bricklayers build houses, and we can still design and produce things," argued Mike Cooley, a design engineer from a North London factory of Lucas Aerospace.

Jack Gunter, a shop-floor worker from a Lucas Aerospace factory in Birmingham, drew some conclusions: "We now have a two-fold job: we need to change the concept of what we mean by nationalization; and we need to prepare a plan about the sort of organization and company we want."

A meeting of the Lucas Aerospace Combine Committee was in progress. It was January 1975; the Labour government had been in office for ten months. Sixty or so shop stewards from the design offices and the work-shops of all seventeen Lucas Aerospace factories had gathered for the weekend in the comfortable surroundings of Wortley Hall, a stately home turned trade-union meeting place, overlooking the South Yorkshire Pennines. They were trying to work out a strategy to reverse the drastic decline of jobs in Lucas.

Between 1970 and 1975 Lucas Aerospace management had eliminated five thousand jobs out of eighteen thousand. The Combine Committee had fought some tough and bitter industrial battles over these jobs. In the long run, however, whatever the immediate victories, management had always been able to carry through their plans. The shop stewards were looking for more lasting solutions. They were looking for some way to control or at least influence decisions about investment and employment. The manifesto on which the Labour government had been elected had promised to nationalize the aerospace industry. Would nationalization of Lucas Aerospace provide more secure employment? In the three months previous to the January meeting the Combine Committee had tested out the proposal both with the government and with their own members.

In the previous November a Combine Committee delegation of thirty-four had crowded into Tony Benn's office at the Department of Industry — much to the irritation of senior civil servants and some national trade-union officials. The aim of the delegation was to press for Lucas Aerospace to be included in the nationalization of the aircraft industry. Equally important, the Combine had gone to spell out what they meant by national-ization. In their quarterly newspaper, *Combine News*, they put their case like this:

> Many of our members have deep reservations about nationalization. Indeed, the Combine's central concern is job security and a work situation in which our members can utilize fully their skill and ability in the interests of the community. Only in so far as nationalization could provide these things is it of any interest to the Combine.

Tony Benn had said that he did not have the power to include Lucas Aerospace in the nationalization proposals. He went on to suggest that the Combine Committee should be involved in drawing up a corporate strategy for Lucas Aerospace. He told the stewards, "We should be thinking of ways of producing our way through a slump. We must be prepared to diversify and we cannot ignore intermediate technology." He offered the possibility of a meeting between the company, the Combine and the government to discuss an alternative proposal along these lines, drawn up by the Combine.

The Combine Committee meeting in January 1975 was discussing the delegation's report back. The main question was: is there the support among the membership to press further for nationalization, or should the Combine Committee develop a new approach which would defend jobs and improve work conditions more effectively in the short run and at the same time prepare the ground for a genuinely democratic form of social ownership? There were other questions: how should they respond to Benn's suggestion? Could they draw up alternative proposals themselves without involving management? These items had been discussed at all the seventeen shop stewards' committees several weeks beforehand, along with the rest of the meeting's agenda, which was the procedure for all Combine meetings. This procedure enabled the delegates from each site to report on the feelings of the workforce.

Few delegates were able to report much enthusiasm for nationalization among their members. Delegate after delegate stressed the need for a new approach. Pat McSharry, a TGWU shop steward from Shaftmoor Lane, the largest Birmingham factory, reported: "We've been running a wall newspaper and nationalization comes up on it every week. The lads really have a go at us about this issue. It's made me realize that we can't look at it through the eyes of nationalization 1945 or the eyes of nationalization in the last ten years. We need to draw up a completely new concept." Delegates from Lancashire whose members had a more direct experience of at least one "nationalization 1945" — of the mines — emphasized the achievement of the earlier nationalizations. Mick Cooney, an AUEW steward from Burnley, argued:

> Although everyone will criticize it, the miners who work in the industry and knew the old set-up — one of our lads here tonight was in that situation — will tell you that it is now far, far better than it was. We have to build on that, with a new concept. We can't stand still. It's up to us to look for new forms. If we are going to sit back and leave it to the politicians to carry on, then, well, we deserve everything we get.

Then the meeting began to develop "the new concept". They talked in terms of an alternative plan, taking up Benn's suggestion. However, most delegates were sceptical about involving management in drawing up the plan. This question touched on a hot issue among trade-union activists at that time. Industrial democracy had been an important theme in the Labour Party's election campaign. But no one knew quite what it meant. There was suspicion of anything that seemed likely to undermine trade-union independence and make the unions carry the can for management's way of running things. The idea of drawing up a plan for Lucas Aerospace at first seemed to lead in this direction. Certainly older delegates like Danny Conroy, who had been part of the traditional Labour left for some thirty years, thought so: "If we were dependent on management in drawing up a plan we'd end up doing it on their terms. We would be cutting our own throats;" and at first he was doubtful of the workers' ability to draw up the plan on their own.

Others, especially among the younger stewards, were more confident: Mike Reynolds, an AUEW shop steward from Liverpool, put it forcefully:

> Let us draw up a plan without management. Let us start here from this Combine Committee; after all over the years it has grown and grown. It has ability not only in industrial disputes but also to tackle wider problems. Let's get down to working on how we'd draw up a plan, on our terms, to meet the needs of our community.

The meeting began to warm to the idea. Ernie Scarbrow, secretary of the Combine Committee, reported that he had sounded management out on the possibility of them giving facilities to the Combine Committee to work on their own proposals. Mason, the personnel director of Lucas Aerospace, had not been responsive. For some delegates that settled it: "If management don't like it, it must be a bloody good thing," said Albert Dougan, an ex-miner and a GMWU steward from Burnley with a reputation for speaking bluntly. Several delegates took the argument in favour of the alternative plan further: they warned that if the recession and more redundancies did occur (this was in 1975, remember) and they had not prepared an alternative, the members would hold them responsible. Another delegate reminded the meeting of all the money which the company received from government, without adequate accountability:

> What happened to the last lot of money? It led to redundancies as a result of Lucas's takeover of the Aerospace part of English Electric (in 1969).* It will be the same under the present Labour government, unless we fight for our own plan.

Most of the sceptics were won over by the argument that the plan would be based on the idea of socially useful products. In other words, it would not be done on management's terms. Although some of the proposals might be profitable for Lucas they would be chosen and designed primarily to meet social needs. Delegates gave examples from their own experience of needs,

---

* See Chapter 2.

which they as engineers could design and produce: for instance the need for more adaptable aids for the handicapped and for cheaper heating systems. Lucas Aerospace normally specializes in components for military aircraft but as Phil Asquith, who since his student days had been a strong supporter CND, commented: "We weren't going to be lobbying for more military orders like some of us had had to in the past."

As the discussion developed, through Saturday afternoon and into Sunday morning, one or two delegates still remained unconvinced. They thought the idea of the alternative plan was too political for the Combine Committee to take on. However, among the majority of delegates, enthusiasm for the idea of a workers' plan to save jobs at Lucas grew fast. Danny Conroy ended the discussion by proposing the following resolution seconded by Bill Deaton, the AUEW convenor at Hemel Hempstead:

> We reaffirm our policy that Lucas Aerospace be nationalized with full workers' control. We further instruct the executive committee to prepare a Corporate Plan for the protection of our workers until the full nationalization of Lucas Aerospace is achieved.

The resolution was carried with only one vote against. Soon after this decision at Wortley Hall, meetings about the alternative plan were held at every factory. The Combine executive drew up a questionnaire for all the factories, with two purposes: first to help the Combine to compile an inventory of the skills and equipment available in Lucas Aerospace. Secondly, to encourage workers to suggest how they could use these productive resources to meet social needs in their own communities and elsewhere.

The contribution of different groups of workers and different sites varied. But added together their contributions put to shame the academic experts to whom the Combine had written for advice. Only three out of eighty had responded with specific proposals. The discussions at the different factories produced, in total, 150 ideas.

The executive of the Combine Committee selected and developed five categories of proposals: medical equipment; transport vehicles and components; improved braking systerms; energy products and devices for undersea work. The criteria of social usefulness referred not only to products but to the production process itself. Thus the plan proposed production processes which would tend to conserve and recycle energy and materials rather than waste them, and would liberate rather than suppress human creativity. The shop stewards believed that any move towards industrial democracy would be a sham unless the nature of the labour process itself was changed.

In these and other ways which later chapters will discuss in detail, the Combine Comittee's plan suggested a framework by which people could connect their own and others' needs as producers with their needs as consumers. It suggested a way of overcoming the contemporary plight of so many who have to perform alienating tasks only to produce throwaway products that in effect exploit people as consumers.

A bold and radical plan then, although many trade unionists in Lucas Aerospace only realized quite how radical it was when they saw the reaction of management and the government. Many delegates had genuinely believed that management would be prepared to negotiate over it. But instead they refused even to discuss it with the Combine, insisting that it be discussed through "local consultative machinery". Terry Moran, an AUEW member from Burnley, was one of those who had high expectations: "I was horrified when management completely rejected it. We were actually offering to work collectively with them to create wealth for the country, and they rejected the offer." In his eyes, and those of many like him, management came out of the whole episode morally condemned. In that sense the plan had called the bluff of Lucas management's repeated claim to be socially responsible. As the Combine Committee put it later: "We believe this corporate plan will provide an opportunity for Lucas Aerospace to demonstrate whether it is really prepared to take its social responsiblity seriously or not."

It was not only Lucas management who failed to act according to their rhetoric: so too did the Labour government. The shop stewards at Lucas Aerospace had taken the 1974 Labour manifesto, with its commitment to "an irreversible shift of power towards working people", seriously enough to try to implement it in their own industry, in the expectation of government support. In the event (as will be seen), they were knocked back and like many others during that period became deeply disillusioned with orthodox Labour politics. Positive, enthusiastic responses, on the other hand, came from all over the world. Ernie Scarbrow's postbag for the first year after the public launch of the final plan proposals — January 1976 — contained up to fifty letters a week requesting information, speakers, interviews, advice. The local papers covering Lucas Aerospace sites — Bradford, Burnley, Birmingham and Liverpool — splashed news of the plan across their front pages. Hundreds of newspaper articles were written about the plan and several films and radio programmes were made; in the north-west of England there was a time when never a month went by without one or other of the Burnley stewards appearing on the BBC news programme "Look North".

Word about the Lucas Aerospace Combine did not have to rely on the media, however. The most important communication, leading to further initiatives and direct and continuing contact, was through public meetings. Large mass meetings of socialist trade unionists; small discussion circles of industrial chaplains during "a week of reflection"; crowds of young people on a CND demonstration; small meetings of shop stewards trying to formulate a strategy to fight a closure; socialist feminists meeting to discuss new approaches to politics; alternative technologists, discussing how their ideas could be implemented — Lucas Aerospace shop stewards have spoken to them all, in Europe, in the USA and in Australia, sometimes inspiring them, sometimes provoking them and sometimes just sharing ideas in a common discussion.

Clearly the desire of these trade unionists in Lucas Aerospace for a constructive alternative to the waste and degradation of the dole queue, and their readiness to challenge the enormous power of the multi-national corporations, struck a chord with thousands of others. What brought many of these people together was an initiative which breathes new life into the basic but often forgotten premise of socialism — production for social need. Through this process the Lucas Aerospace alternative plan has become a symbol. One purpose of this book is to try and understand just what it is a symbol of — for whom and why. The attempt to interpret some of the many diverse answers may help us understand the problems which trade unionists and socialists at present face. The early chapters will try to describe and explain the circumstances out of which this symbol was created. Later chapters will discuss the problems which have been and are being faced.

One aspect of the origins of the alternative plan which is sometimes underestimated is the history of the trade-union organization which produced it. No "lessons" can be learnt from the Lucas Aerospace experience without understanding the long, difficult process of establishing the confidence, the organization and the political awareness and honesty of which the plan was a product. Therefore part of this book is the story of the growth of the Lucas Combine Committee.

The discussion which took place in Wortley Hall in January 1975, five years after the formation of the Combine, illustrated the self-confidence that had already developed within the Combine Committee. There was no deference towards Tony Benn; they picked up his suggestion, but on their terms. Through the contributions ran a firm belief in the skills and power of the Lucas Aerospace workers and their right to determine how these skills should be exercised.

The democracy and integrity of the Combine showed up in the way they approached the problem of nationalization. It would have been all too easy for the delegates, most of whom personally believed in nationalization, to go through the motions of a rhetorical campaign, knowing full well that however many lobbies were organized, however many leaflets produced, the majority of workers at Lucas Aerospace would remain sceptical and not take the industrial action necessary to make the campaign for national-ization effective. Instead they listened to and argued with the membership. The membership's views on nationalization were mainly negative, but that led the Combine to examine the reasons and to think of a new approach rather than rely on the old rhetoric.

This self-confidence and ability to listen to and communicate with the membership was not gained overnight. As one steward had said, "Over the years our Combine has grown and grown." This growth began in 1969.

Gradually the Combine extended its credibility from several southern sites plus Bradford to the full eleven (with seventeen factories). It established a constitution and a newspaper with a print run of 10,000. The Combine involved staff representatives as well as shop-floor representatives. It won credibility by the support it could organize for plants in dispute or under threat: raising over £12,000 for the 1972 strike at Burnley; preventing any compulsory redundancies when management intended to impose 800, and providing moral and industrial back-up for many minor disputes throughout the company. It took the company by surprise over pensions; by sheer expertise and self-confidence it transformed the company's paternalistic pension scheme into a scheme that could provide decent deferred wages for staff and for manual workers, and at least the beginnings of employee control over the millions of pounds in the two pension funds.

The Combine Committee has always been unofficial as far as the trade-union leadership is concerned. Its multi-union, staff and manual, industrial structure cuts across the occupational and craft basis of British trade unions. As a result it has had little support from national unions in overcoming the problems it has faced. Sometimes the ideology and recruitment strategies of different national unions has tended to reinforce divisions between, for instance, office and shop-floor workers, thereby exacerbating the difficulties. At other times some union officials behaved as if they were positively hostile. Jeff Rooker, a Labour MP who witnessed some of the crucial negotiations at close quarters, summed up the worst of this in November 1981, in the 16th Aneurin Bevan Memorial Lecture:

> The workers at Lucas Aerospace actually saw their aspirations trampled under the feet of many of their full-time officials who used inadequate, out of date, trade-union structures to fight their own members. The management loved it.

Some individual unions have given support to the Combine Committee but none of them has been prepared openly to face up to the failings in official structure, policy and leadership which are so starkly revealed by the Lucas story.

Combine committees, lacking official trade-union support or management recognition, have come and gone. Even if a core of activists remains in being, their identity with workers in the factories easily fades, as old workers leave and new ones start, as plant leaderships change and as management pressures intensify. A well-known study by H.A. Turner[1] of shop stewards' organizations in the motor industry in the 1950s and '60s, for example, concludes that for these and other reasons combine committees are virtually impossible to sustain.

The Lucas Aerospace Combine Committee, though it has faced innumerable obstacles and also internal divisions, has continued its struggle for over ten years now. That in itself needs to be explained and learnt from. However, the Combine is now in a frail state, even though its ideas have become

part of the bloodstream of the trade unions and the disarmament movement. In part the Combine's problems are the result of internal failings: for
example, many delegates would admit that there have been times when
they could and should have done more to keep their members in touch
with the Combine Committee. In part the problems have been the result of
real inequalities between different groups of workers, leading to feelings of
resentment and suspicion which have in turn been played on by
management to produce divisions.

Many of the difficulties the Combine has faced flow from its being a
hybrid organization, both trade-union and in broad sense political, within a
labour movement that has a very rigid division of functions. When Lech
Walesa, the leader of the Polish movement Solidarity, was asked how far
Solidarity was a political movement he answered:

> There isn't a catalogue which lists what's political and what's not. I
> was taken to court for laughing politically, walking politically, so you
> can't divide things into political and non-political so easily. We think
> we are not a political group because we don't want to take over power.[2]

The general spirit of this fluidity between politics and trade unionism
applies to the Lucas Combine Committee. It too is not a political party in
the sense that it does not itself want to take over or achieve political power.
However, its functions as a trade-union organization directly expressing
and fighting for the needs of its members has led it, out of necessity, to
make proposals which go beyond the customary sphere of trade-union
activity. The stewards' plan to defend their members' jobs implies changes
in the priorities of government spending and purchasing. It implies a rejection of the adequacy of the capitalist market in co-ordinating resources with
needs. It seeks to release the massive resources locked up in arms production and it requires an opening-up of institutions of higher education and
technological research for use by trade-union and community groups. Yet
at the same time the base of the Combine Committee is a limited one: the
factory-based institutions of collective bargaining.

The experience of this tension by the Lucas Aerospace Combine, along
with other similarly hybrid trade-union based organizations, raises questions
about the limits of trade unionism. Can collective bargaining be extended
to develop and implement workers' alternative plans? Are new organizational forms needed to develop alternative plans, with a flexibility which
the institutions of collective bargaining cannot by their very nature achieve?
What kind of alliances are needed across unions, across workplace and
community organizations, and between the extraparliamentary and the
parliamentary representatives of working people to fight for an economy
based on meeting social needs?

One of the main reasons why this book has been written is because we
and the Combine Committee believe there is much about the Lucas
Aerospace workers' initiative which should be and can be generalized, if

the crisis of our present economy is not to overcome us. This does not mean simply supporting the Lucas Aerospace workers. As one steward said after a particularly supportive conference, "The last thing we want is a Lucas Aerospace appreciation society." Neither does generalizing the Lucas Aerospace initiative mean imitation. The principles of socially useful production and planning for social need do not necessarily mean alternative products. There were several specific factors which led the Lucas workers to express these principles in the particular way that they did. The generalization is the impact of the Lucas workers' initiative, by which the general principles are diffused and taken up creatively by others. Vital to this diffusion is an understanding of the special factors which enabled the Lucas workers to pioneer a new approach to unemployment, to government intervention in industry and to trade-union organization. Only then will we be in a position to disentangle the more general principles from the features of the Lucas Aerospace workers' initiatives which were unique. In other words we can best understand the general importance of the Lucas Plan if we first look carefully into the particular circumstances and particular groups of people who created it.

PART I: BACKGROUND CIRCUMSTANCES

2 Out of the white heat. . .

Lucas Aerospace is one company within the Lucas Industries group which includes CAV, Lucas Electrical, Lucas Batteries. Approximately 20 per cent of Lucas Industries resources are currently devoted to its aerospace activities.

Lucas Aerospace is Europe's largest desginer and manufacturer of aircraft systems and equipment, including fuel systems, flying control, instrumentation and electrical equipment. The company has been involved with work on Concorde, the Russian TU144 supersonic airliner, the A300B Airbus, the Lockheed Tristar, the RB211, the Anglo-French Jaguar, the European Multi-Role Combat Aircraft and more recently the Sting Ray missile system. About 43 per cent of its business is related to military aircraft, 7 per cent to other defence work. Approximately 45 per cent of its work comes from Rolls Royce and 27 per cent direct from the Ministry of Defence. It also has very small interests in medical technologies, and machine tools.

At the time of writing, in 1982, it operates fifteen factories in ten sites in three regions: around the Birmingham-Wolverhampton area, in the London region (Willesden, Hemel Hempstead and Luton) and in the north and north-west (Burnley, Bradford and Liverpool). The workforce, which totalled approximately 18,000 in 1970, had by 1977 been reduced to under 13,000. At present it stands at 12,000. Over one-third of the total workforce are skilled engineers, design technicians, draughtsmen and research staff — the vast majority of whom are unionized, as are virtually all the hourly-paid staff.

Origins

Lucas Aerospace was as much the child of Harold Wilson's Industrial Reorganization Corporation as of Joseph Lucas Limited. The contrast between the company's Labour parentage – and continued close relations – and its treatment of the workers has made its shop stewards doubt whether state intervention in their industry necessarily represents a step towards socialism. They were particularly angered by the £3 million which Lucas received from the IRC to rationalize the aerospace components industry without any public accountability or consultation with those at the receiving end of the rationalization.

Money was only a small part of the confidential encouragement which the IRC gave to Lucas to take over the majority of its competitors in the field of aircraft components and to consolidate them into a new corporate giant, Lucas Aerospace. Indeed, Harold Wilson was so concerned to reverse the decline in the profitability and efficiency of British companies that he gave the IRC "any powers necessary" to "stimulate British industrial companies to effective and profitable reform".[1] The IRC would carefully select a small number of the most efficient companies and build

them up at the expense of their rivals. One IRC report declared that "existing managements have no prescriptive rights and if they fail to deliver the goods they should make way for those who can".[2]

What was it about Lucas management that led Lord Keaton, chairman of IRC, and his team to consider Lucas to be one of those for whom others in the aircraft components field should make way?

In the past the name of Lucas has mainly been associated with motor vehicle components. By the late 1960s Lucas had become the chief producer of electrical components for the motor industry, although several motor companies were trying to end their dependency upon Lucas by encouraging Lucas's competitors or setting up "in-house" production. In 1970, the three subsidiary companies producing vehicle components, Lucas Electrical, Lucas Girling and Lucas CAV, between them managed over fifty factories, employing over 60,000 people. In the same year 85 per cent of Lucas employees were involved in making car components, accounting for over 80 per cent of the company's £300 million annual sales and providing nearly 90 per cent of its £10 million pre-tax profits. Aircraft equipment accounted for under 10 per cent of Lucas's activities. Several different industrial product companies made up the remaining percentage. The company's total assets in 1970 were £114,723, making it the 54th largest British-owned company. The company's headquarters are in Birmingham, where Joseph Lucas built and worked in his first bicycle-lamp workshop,

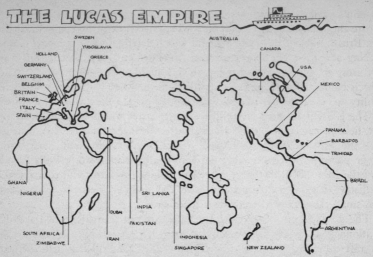

THE LUCAS EMPIRE

SWEDEN
YUGOSLAVIA
HOLLAND
GREECE
GERMANY
SWITZERLAND
BELGIUM
BRITAIN
FRANCE
ITALY
SPAIN
AUSTRALIA
CANADA
USA
MEXICO
PANAMA
BARBADOS
TRINIDAD
GHANA
NIGERIA
SRI LANKA
INDIA
DUBAI
PAKISTAN
BRAZIL
SOUTH AFRICA
ZIMBABWE
IRAN
INDONESIA
SINGAPORE
NEW ZEALAND
ARGENTINA

called "King of the Road", and where many Lucas factories are concentrated. Other factories are scattered from Burnley to London, from Rio de Janeiro to Sydney.

A well-established light engineering company then, heavily dependent on the motor industry. But in the competitive trading conditions that worried Harold Wilson and the IRC, the prospects for such a company were changing. Throughout the post-war years, vehicle components had been a highly profitable, booming industry. Between 1950 and 1965 the output of the Lucas Electrical Company, for instance, had doubled. Even during the depression of the 1920s and 1930s, Lucas had been growing, mainly through buying its weaker competitors. By the 1960s, however, the directors at Lucas could see ominous signs of a recession and over-capacity in the motor industry, especially in Britain.

In order to gain a firmer foothold in the international motor components market they began to expand their manufacturing operations abroad, especially in countries where the motor industry was still growing, first in Europe and later in Korea, Brazil and East Europe. Lucas carried out this expansion into new markets by takeovers and other arrangements, rather than by new investment.

As early as the mid-1950s the chairman's annual reports begin proudly reporting on newly-acquired European manufacturing facilities, and Lucas was consistently among those British companies urging Britain's entry into the Common Market. In 1961, twelve years before Britain signed the Treaty of Rome, the chairman of Lucas said that "any consideration of the future is dominated by the Common Market". Even before Britain's entry, Lucas had created in effect its own European market, acquiring ownership of or interests in at least five major European companies. It is ironic that the IRC, the creation of a government whose first priority was to restore

Britain's balance of payments, should have patronized and indeed helped to create the transnational corporations which had little or no commitment to the British balance of payments, and which extended their market by producing abroad rather than exporting from Britain. Nevertheless, this was precisely the type of management which found approval with the IRC: one which combined an aggressive approach to international markets with the ability to integrate newly acquired companies into their existing empire.

The government had no need to concern itself with Lucas's activities in the field of car components. Lucas had rationalized that industry, and in just the way the IRC would have wished. The government, along with other powerful forces, notably the aero-engine manufacturer Rolls Royce and the Ministry of Defence, wanted to rationalize the aircraft components industry. The IRC identified Lucas as the company best placed to bring the smaller component companies together.

The government, together with leading aircraft companies, had already "rationalized", or at least brought under monopoly control, the bulk of the aircraft industry. In the airframe sector, GEC and Vickers had merged their aircraft interests to form BAC. In the aero-engine sector, the government, on the recommendation of the Plowden Commission on the aircraft industry, had backed a takeover of Bristol Siddely by Rolls Royce. The result was an industry dominated by three major corporations, BAC, Hawker Siddely and Rolls Royce. For those who controlled the industry, the next logical step was to create a single company for engine components, offering the full range of aerospace engine systems. These include engine and fuel-control systems, power-generating equipment and various types of electronic, hydraulic and mechanical control systems. Such a company would be in an important position to win tenders from aircraft manufacturers throughout the world.

The directors of Joseph Lucas themselves were begining to think along similar lines. The company could not afford to stand still, as they were still recovering from the government's cancellation of the TSR2, the P1154 and the HS681 aerospace projects. Since the mid-1950s, governments were spending money more cautiously, demanding fixed price rather than the more traditional "cost-plus" contracts. At the same time Lucas was searching for a way to reduce its dependence on the motor industry. Investment overseas in yet more car components' operations would not be enough to cushion Lucas against the financial shocks which the motor industry engendered. With government seeking to support the expansion of the aircraft industry, it was clearly in Lucas's interest to reorganize the aircraft components sector by taking over its rivals. The chairman of Lucas, Sir Kenneth Corley, summed up the common interests of the IRC and Lucas when he said: "They [the IRC] made out a strong case for realigning the industry. They said there was only one engine manufacturer — Rolls Royce — and it would be more sensible to support one manufacturer of such things as fuel systems, control systems and so on. Of course we went half way to meet them, because we were keen to lessen our dependence on the motor industry. . . ." (*Times Business News*, 1972).

When the company historian Harold Nockolds describes how the vice-chairman of Rotax (Lucas's aircraft subsidiary at that time) "was given the assignment of bringing the various companies together",[3] he makes the takeover process sound remarkably effortless and painless. From the point of view of Lucas management it probably was; after all they had done it all before in the motor components industry. The Birmingham stockbrokers Albert Sharp & Co., close observers of Lucas, wrote that the aerospace takeovers were "A clear case of history repeating itself, with Lucas building up a dominant if not completely monopolistic position by acquiring competitors weakened by a demand slump parallel to the automobile electrics story of the twenties and thirties". In the car components industry it took Lucas three decades to acquire 80 per cent of the market, a position of power which many considered to be unfair and open to abuse. Lucas was referred to the Monopolies Commission in 1957 and 1963.* The aerospace takeovers went ahead far more quickly, amid the enthusiasm for monopolies which was gripping many industrialists, bankers and leading politicians in the late 1960s. Between 1968 and 1970 Lucas more than doubled its assets in the aerospace industry.

In 1967 Lucas owned two aircraft component companies and five major sites. Rotax produced electrical and starting systems at Willesden and Hemel Hempstead (a third site at Beaconsfield was closed down after the war) and the Gas Turbine Company produced engine fuel systems at Liverpool, Birmingham and Burnley. A small Lucas-owned company at Neasden, G.E. Bradley's, also worked closely with Rotax. Lucas acquired the AEI aircraft in Coventry in March 1968, and the Vactric Controls Equipment at Morden in June 1968. Moving into a bigger league, it negotiated with GEC and English Electric for EE's aircraft components section, adding to the Lucas empire in late 1969 sites at Bradford, Netherton (Merseyside) and Luton, plus a research and development centre at Shipley. Lucas turned next to another large components company, H.M. Hobson's of Wolverhampton. This takeover proved tricky and Hobson's shareholders voted on the offer. The 3,000 Hobson's workers, though, were simply part of the deal. By the end of 1970 they were part of Lucas. In the same year Lucas bought a small prototype machining company, Premier Precision of Bracknell near Reading. By 1970, Lucas Aerospace owned eight companies, eleven sites, and seventeen factories and had attained a dominant position in aircraft components. If Joseph Lucas were alive he would have named the new Birmingham headquarters of Lucas Aerospace "King of the Air".

---

* The Commission Report documents Lucas's monopoly position but concludes that this is in the public interest.

Rationalizations and redundancies

The IRC was not interested simply in building large industrial empires. The takeovers and mergers were preliminaries to the main task of industrial rationalization: cutting costs and increasing profitability. This would be achieved by imposing stringent financial controls on each enterprise; cutting out duplication; reducing overheads; exploiting economies of size by investing in capital-intensive machinery; concentrating and co-ordinating research and development facilities; centralizing the policy and training of supervisors and industrial relations staff in order to increase the output of the workers; and finally getting rid of products which did not fit commercially with the main product range. Management at Lucas Aerospace did not finally integrate the various companies until August 1971. Then the new management, having established financial control over their various acquisitions, began to identify the overheads to cut, the duplicated facilities to axe, and the new technologies to introduce. As the company historian puts it: "The first step was to discard any elements which lay outside the mainstream of aircraft work."

First, Vactric Controls and its workers were sold to another engineering company, Muirheads (which later closed the factory). The next step was to reduce the number of sites. Some closures had already occurred during the takeovers. Hobson's Integral factory at Wolverhampton had been closed and six hundred workers sacked as part of the takeover agreement. Moreover one of the factories on the Coventry site had been closed as part of the agreement with AEI.

The next target was Rotax itself. Management's plan was to close the Willesden factory and move the work to the new factory at Hemel Hempstead (built in 1952). According to the company history, all went according to plan. Nockolds writes: "The Rotax factory at Willesden was sold and the work transferred to Hemel Hempstead."[4] In fact, there was prolonged and militant resistance to the closure. In 1972 two hundred and fifty people still worked at the Willesden factory: a small group of office and shop-floor workers who, though beleaguered and vulnerable, were to play a major role in creating the national Combine Committee.

Rolls Royce collapse

At the beginning of 1971 Lucas was drawing up plans for streamlining the workforce in its gas turbine division. Before the plans were ready, Rolls Royce collapsed in January 1971, as the result of a drop in the market for Rolls Royce's main product, the RB211 engine. The uncertainty about the future of the RB211 engine, for which Lucas was to supply the fuel systems, led the company to "bring forward — and somewhat to increase redundancies" (*Financial Times*, 16 February 1971). Almost overnight, over two thousand people in Birmingham, Wolverhampton and Liverpool lost their jobs. The Rolls Royce crash, seeming like a natural disaster for which Lucas management was not responsible, made resistance to these redundancies very difficult. Journalists witnessed "silent meetings" of

shocked employees. A TASS representative at Birmingham, Ron Mills, remembers "the tension in the office as people waited for their names to be called. People would come back white-faced and sometimes in tears. The officials felt powerless. It was all such a shock. Very traumatic." Traumatic for the workforce but, as it turned out, very handy for management. For they were able to carry out their first major rationalization without meeting serious trade-union resistance. Moverover, Lucas lost nothing financially. All Rolls Royce's debts to Lucas were repaid and the RB211 order was reinstated. An internal memo made no bones about the value to Lucas of the Rolls Royce crisis:

> Prompt and decisive action was taken to deal with this calamity and, with the recent reinstatement of a modified RB211 programme, it does now *look as though some benefit will come from the whole affair*, in so far as the original Gas Turbine Company's factories are now considerably leaner and readier to face the world than they were at the time of the crisis. [Lucas Aerospace Twenty-Fourth Annual Survey of Factories, Financial Year to 31 July 1971. Emphasis added.]

The financial press and the stockmarket were enthusiastic about the new Lucas. The *Evening Standard* commented on 15 December 1971:

> There is nothing the City likes more than the sight of a fighting comeback by one of the respected giants of Britain's industry. And that's one of the reasons why the men of Throgmorton Street have so warmly welcomed back to the fold the shares of the huge motor and acrospace equipment group, Lucas. Having scraped along at 156p earlier this year, they have surged forward thanks to a tremendous

about change in company fortunes and are now just below the peak level of 388p.

And word is that Lucas will do better yet. In fact the group looks poised for one of its biggest ever profit advances.

And the *Daily Telegraph* (9 November 1971) pointed to one of the reasons for this upturn in the fortunes of Lucas shareholders:

But not the smallest factor in the second-half recovery was of course a wave of economy measures which included factory closures.

Management make clear in their 1971 Annual Survey that these redundancies and closures were only the beginning of the rationalization process:

There remains an excess of manufacturing resources within the Lucas Aerospace Company and in some cases a duplication of types of manufacture, and a plan is under consideration by the Aerospace Executive for further rationalization during the next eighteen months. The total payroll strength of the Aerospace Company has in the meantime been brought down from 17,488 to 14,169, a reduction of 19%. . . . Further reductions, particularly in the Electrical Group, will be required in the present year.

Longer-run strategy

The two thousand or so redundancies immediately following the merger were only the beginning. It would be wrong to think that the main form of rationalization which the IRC hoped would follow the mergers was simply the elimination of duplicate facilities and labour. The rationale for the IRC's interventions was more long-term and structural than this.[5] IRC-backed mergers would, it was hoped, enable the chosen companies, Lucas and GEC for example, to invest in the most advanced technologies, to rationalize industrial relations, to engage in joint international projects and generally regain the competitive advantage for British industry. An examination of the competitive pressures in the aerospace industry helps to explain what effect this had on Lucas Aerospace.

The aerospace sector had throughout the 1960s been one of the few sectors of British manufacturing industry that was maintaining its competitive position — with considerable government support. Lucas Aerospace was in a particularly strong position; internationally they offered the aircraft industry the largest available range of aerospace engine equipment available from one single organization. However, changes were taking place in the UK and European aerospace industry which intensified the competitive pressures on Lucas and on the rest of the British aircraft industry. Growing concentration in the aircraft industry was changing the structure of its markets and leading to the adoption of new production methods. The small batch production and specialized products characteristic of the companies which made up Lucas Aerospace had been geared to meet the fragmented UK and European aircraft markets of the past. These production processes were becoming less and less economic as these markets became more unified. The oil price rises from 1973 onwards further strengthened the tendency towards concentration. The financial constraints on airlines meant that they needed aircraft systems which were more economic on fuel. This required the production of a whole new generation of planes, involving major expenditure, and several aerospace companies did not have the resources to respond to these pressures on their own. The result was a rapid increase in the concentration of companies and in the size of the companies that remained; it also meant companies going in for more joint projects. The determination of the EEC to build up the strength of the European aerospace industry, as against the US companies, reinforced the tendency towards joint European projects. At the same time there was a move towards protectionist purchasing policies by different European governments. As a result, component companies without a manufacturing base in, for example, Germany or France would be unlikely to receive orders from projects involving the German or French governments.

All this meant that from the moment Lucas Aerospace was formed and management began drawing up its long-term plans, it sought to move in the direction of more mass-production and a greater standardization of products. That meant concentrating resources in the product areas that management saw as having the potential for longer production runs and greater standardization. It also meant an acceleration in the rate at which computer-controlled machines would be introduced on the shop floor, in the offices and in the design rooms. In terms of policies towards particular factories it meant that management favoured concentrating investment in several large factories rather than sustaining a larger number of small ones. This much was told to the stockbrokers Albert Sharp & Co. They report that the company's intention was to carry out "further rationalization of the UK factory locations. The widely dispersed nature of the UK plants — eleven in all — is a natural result of the way the businesses were acquired. *Theoretically the management would like to concentrate on four sites only*, gaining the benefits of overhead elimination" [Lucas Industries Ltd, Sharp & Co., 1975. Emphasis added].

On a far larger scale than Lucas, GEC managed to carry through such a rationalization during the late 1960s and early '70s. Why not Lucas? It certainly tried. Yet, after ten years and three major closure attempts, ten out of eleven sites still exist. Numbers have been reduced from 18,000 in 1971 to 12,000 in 1981, but management have stated that their target was 8,000. In other words, management's attempts to impose closures and redundancies have partially failed. In part at least, the reason for this was the resistance put up by the Lucas Aerospace Combine Committee. The twelve years of the Lucas Aerospace Combine Committee have been years of spirited resistance to the rationalization programme which began with the formation of Lucas Aerospace. Although this has been a resistance to

the kind of restructuring fostered by the IRC the Combine has not been campaigning for a restoration of the status quo, for inefficient management and competitive failure. With its alternative plan it has been campaigning for a different kind of restructuring: restructuring in the interests of labour rather than of capital.

3 The failings of the old; the foundations of the new

Meanwhile at the union headquarters little was being done to reform the fifty-year-old structure of the engineering unions, to counter the growing power and size of corporations like Lucas. What was needed was a trade unionism which combined the strong regional — and therefore across-company — traditions of the British trade-union movement with new organizations which paralleled the power structures of the multi-plant multi-national conglomerates.

Ever since the first post-war spate of mergers and takeovers in the early 1950s, shop stewards in the motor industry, and the engineering industry more generally, had been trying to establish the kind of company-wide, and sometimes industry-wide, shop stewards' combine committees which could meet this need. In order for such *ad hoc* — but nonetheless occasionally very powerful — initiatives to be sustained they needed some kind of official trade-union support. This support need not have entailed recognition of combine committees as permanent negotiating bodies; more important was official backing for time off to attend meetings, assistance from (expanded) trade-union research departments, support in the event of victimization in the course of combine committees' activities and more generally the legitimacy among the members which comes from official support.

The Confederation of Shipbuilding and Engineering Unions

In the engineering industry such support for a multi-union shop stewards' combine committee would involve a change in the constitution and rules of the Confederation of Shipbuilding and Engineering Unions. This confederation is the official multi-union organization for engineering, through which all multi-union affairs beyond the level of the plant have to pass. The problems which shop stewards and sympathetic local officials have experienced in trying to change the CSEU bear depressing witness to the inertia of official trade-union structures in Britain.

The CSEU was formed in 1936 to achieve greater co-operation between the separate unions in engineering, especially for negotiating purposes. The largest engineering union, the AUEW, did not come into the CSEU until 1947, mainly because its leaders, following in the syndicalist tradition of Tom Mann and the Amalgamated Society of Engineers, had always hoped to achieve one union in engineering by complete amalgamation. The syndicalists argued that not only was a confederation a second best to this but it would slow down progress towards one union by institutionalizing the autonomy of each union, under the appearance of co-operation. The main function of the CSEU is, at a national level, to carry out annual negotiations with the Engineering Employers' Federation on minimum wage rates and working hours. The CSEU also acts as a channel through which the government discusses issues concerning the engineering and ship-building industries. And it is the organization which formally convenes multi-union negotiations with individual federated companies

(companies belonging to the Engineering Employers' Federation). It has a district committee structure which normally brings together the district officials of the affiliated unions. These district committees are accountable "upwards" to the CSEU national executive. In a few areas such as Manchester, Glasgow and Sheffield, the District "Confed" (as it is normally called) also brings together shop stewards from the industry. However, these areas are exceptional, although every district has the structures for such shop stewards' gatherings. At the bottom of the CSEU structure are multi-union shop stewards' committees at a plant level. Inter-plant shop stewards' committees, however, such as company-wide combine committees, are not recognized by the CSEU.

The CSEU has no doubt achieved the aim of co-operation between union officials for negotiating purposes. Sidney and Beatrice Webb would have been proud that what they originally recommended had worked out so smoothly, in spite of all the inter-union differences. Efficiency in settling disputes, however, is not the same as unity and power in protecting the members' interests and, in the long run, achieving democratic control over the industry. The shop stewards' combine committees created in the last twenty years with these latter purposes in mind would say that, at least as far as the CSEU executive is concerned, the fears of the early syndicalists were justified. Although the CSEU's constitution states that its objectives are to "secure the complete solidarity of the engineering and ship-building unions" and "to propagate the principle of control of industry by and for the benefit of the workers", in fact the principle of preserving the autonomy of constituent unions — or rather, union executives — has been an overriding constraint. This explains why the CSEU has never been prepared to build combine committees into its constitution; they would be a threat to this autonomy.

Consider the response to a very reasonable proposal from Harry Urwin (ex-assistant general secretary of the TGWU) in 1956 to establish an official combine committee structure which would more effectively protect the interests of workers in the motor industry. At that time Harry Urwin was both an official of the TGWU and secretary of the Coventry CSEU district committee. Coventry was an area that was particularly affected by the mergers and reorganization taking place in the car industry. The custom of the CSEU is such that a positive proposal only needs the determined opposition of one major union and it is dead. In the late '50s several union leaderships were very hostile to the growing shop stewards' movement and combine committees in particular. As a result Urwin's resolution was referred to the CSEU executive, never to be heard of again. Urwin later described the CSEU as "one of the most authoritarian institutions of the trade-union movement".[1]

The reason for this authoritarianism lies in the CSEU's "top down" form of unity. Its most powerful body, the executive, brings together union executives who first and foremost represent the separate interests of their unions, however closely their members in the factories might work together. A concern for preserving union autonomy is normally much greater at an executive level; their jobs, power base and identity depend on it. That is not to say that all is sweetness and harmony on the shop floor; but unity within shop-floor organizations, based on unity in action against the employer, has gone much further than the wary, conditional co-operation which exists between union executives. The CSEU constitution does not allow for, let alone build on, the uneven way in which unity develops in the course of industrial conflict. For instance, while shop stewards' combine committees have on occasion been able to unite on a high level of militancy, the "top-down" unity of the CSEU is based on the lowest common denominator of the different union executives. And depending on the leadership of the different unions this lowest common denominator can be very low indeed. In effect each executive has the power of veto over any positive initiative with which they disagree, or which they feel is best kept under their own control. For a majority of unions to support action against the wishes of a powerful individual union would be to risk the break-up of the CSEU and therefore of the traditional bargaining arrangements. This means the CSEU has little ability to take positive action or even to back the positive action of those of its members. The concern of individual executives to preserve their autonomy also leaves the CSEU without resources. The individual unions are not prepared to allow it adequate resources, for fear of the unified body becoming more powerful than its parts. Its income in 1978 was £127,000 — very little considering the AUEW and TGWU's joint annual income would add up to £30 million. It has only two full-time officers. Its research resources amount to one part-time researcher who lectures at Thames Polytechnic and services the engineering unions on at least six NEDO sector working parties.

In the boom years of the 1950s and early '60s these anachronistic features of the CSEU did not seem significant. In fact the Confed was often treated as a bit of a joke. For example it is said that a previous General Secretary, Henry George Barrett, OBE, used to read books about goldfish during negotiations! It was only from the late '60s onwards, when companies and the government began to carry through major reorganization, that the CSEU's negative power, for instance its power to block the initiatives of shop stewards to form company-wide organizations, became important. At that point the lack of officially supported combine committees united around alternative policies for their industry proved a major source of weakness; in effect it meant that a supposedly strong trade-union movement was unable to prevent the decimation of jobs in the engineering industry over the next ten years.

The trade-union response to Lucas Aerospace
For the Lucas Aerospace shop stewards it meant they had no official multi-union organization to turn to in the face of redundancies like those they suffered in 1971 and the thousands more that were to follow. At the head-

quarters of the national shop-floor unions there was little or no reaction to the formation of Lucas Aerospace. There were no signs of a recognition that the prospects, conditions and power of their members had changed with the creation of the new conglomerate.

The staff unions, however, in particular AUEW-TASS, were more responsive to the new problems presented by mergers and takeovers. For instance TASS initiated a strike against the GEC takeover of AEI and English Electric in order to draw public attention to the problem of the growing power of the corporations. For TASS, recruitment in the major corporations was a priority. By 1973 nearly 75 per cent of their membership were concentrated in thirty-eight major companies. Recruitment prospects in the Aerospace industry were especially high, for the aerospace industry along with the computer industry has the highest proportion of scientific and technical staff to shop-floor production workers. The figures for scientific and technical staff as a separate category are not available for different industries, but some indication of the proportions is given by the fact that in 1970 46 per cent of the workforce in aerospace were technical, administrative or clerical workers compared to 23.6 per cent in the car industry and 30 per cent as an average for manufacturing industry as a whole. In Lucas Aerospace over 30 per cent of the workforce fell into the category of technical and scientific staff alone.

Not surprisingly then, TASS was quick off the mark to start negotiations about recruitment with the new company. This was probably speeded up by the fact that three leading members of TASS at that time worked for Lucas. Ron Whitely, the TASS treasurer until 1976, worked at CAV, Barry Seager, a member of the TASS executive, worked at Lucas Electrical and Mike Cooley, president of AUEW-TASS in 1971, worked for Rotax, now the Willesden site of Lucas Aerospace. These three, plus a Birmingham-based TASS official, started discussions with the company about demarcation rights for TASS. At the same time TASS began to negotiate a new procedure agreement for negotiations with the company on wages and conditions. The result of these two parallel discussions was the creation of the National Negotiating Committee in 1974 through which TASS negotiated across Lucas Industries at a national level. The same negotiating arrangements applied also to APEX and ASTMS. Thus while the shop-floor unions negotiated on wages and conditions at plant level (and then through the EEF-CSEU procedure) the staff unions had their own separate national negotiations with Lucas Industries. This difference was to be a source of many difficulties in achieving the unity of staff and shop-floor workers within the Lucas Aerospace Combine Committee. For the time being, however, the important point here is that with the exception of TASS the CSEU unions did not even begin to confront the problems posed by the formation of Lucas Aerospace.

Foundations:
(i) Previous combines in Lucas

The Lucas shop stewards had to rely on their own resources. Part of the foundations from which they could build were the shop stewards' organizations at each of the sites. Their foundations were also past traditions, old networks of contact and lessons passed on from previous initiatives that had failed. Such historical factors fall into two categories: first, previous attempts to form combine committees in Lucas; and secondly trade-union traditions in the aerospace industry.

The first attempt by shop stewards of Lucas Industries Ltd to build a combine committee met with straightforward repression by the leadership of the AUEW. In the early 1960s shop stewards from several parts of Lucas, including aircraft components, held regular weekend meetings in Liverpool, although the main Birmingham factories gave little support. In fact it was senior convenors at Birmingham who played a major role in its downfall. At the King Street factory, the heart of the Lucas empire, independent trade unionism, let alone combine committees, were anathema to management and senior convenors alike. Here genuine bargaining had not taken place since before the Second World War war and differences were "resolved" through the Joint Production and Consultative Committee. The senior AUEW convenor, Jack Allen, viewed the young combine committee as a potential threat to the convenors' notoriously close relations with management. Indeed, the lack of a genuine trade-union organization at the most important factory in the company, which helped to hold wages in the group well below those of the average engineer, was one reason for the formation of the Combine Committee. Allen kept an eye on the Combine Committee and informed the AUEW executive, who soon made use of this information, by threatening to discipline any member of the AUEW who attended the Combine. (Combine committees in the motor industry were similarly outlawed.) The first Lucas Combine Committee consequently dispersed.

However, the need for a combine committee organization was real and some of the members of the first combine were among those who tried several years later in 1965 or 1966 to form a regional combine in the south of England. A group of stewards at several Lucas-owned companies in the south urged all workers in Rotax, CAV establishments in Acton, Rochester and Hemel Hempstead to form a combine committee.

The document that called for this in 1965 pointed to the way in which management was reducing piece rates under the cover of reorganization. It argued that the official trade-union structures were inadequate to deal with the new powers of central management, a theme which in time grew louder. The stewards felt that their shop-floor power would slip away unless a new multi-plant organization was built. A sense of urgency ran through the document:

> It is high time that the trade-union organization so carefully built up should be transformed into a living force used to safeguard our position and prevent inroads being made on our established conditions.

This call did not lead to any permanent organization, but it sowed the idea in people's minds.

(ii) Trade-union traditions in aerospace

Although the stewards from the Rotax and CAV factories were all employed by Lucas, they were in different divisions with different national managements; they worked on very different products and were affected by different market conditions. This made it more difficult — though not impossible — to unite all but the most committed shop stewards. Within the newly formed Lucas Aerospace all the shop stewards' committees were under one management and were affected by the same market conditions. The particular products differed within plants and from plant to plant — the existing product range of Lucas Aerospace is over 150 — but the production process in each case was very similar: short-batch production involving highly skilled precision work. Management would often attempt to move production of some products from plant to plant. Moreover the shop stewards' organizations in Lucas Aerospace share similar industrial trade-union traditions. These industrial traditions are one important element in shaping both the organization and the policies of the Lucas Aerospace Combine Committee. In spite of many differences between the airframe, the aero-engine and the components part of the aerospace industry, there is so much interchange and liaison between them and so many similarities in labour process and in markets and financial conditions that it does make sense to talk of traditions for the whole industry. A shop steward from BAC in Bristol illustrated this by saying he had more in common with his French colleagues working on components for Concorde than with trade unionists from other industries in Bristol! The main features of these traditions as they affect the Combine Committee in Lucas Aerospace are the following:

First there is a stronger tradition of co-operation between staff and shop-floor workers than is to be found in most industries. The roots of this lie in the production process itself. Because production is organized for short batches and special orders — thirty to forty would be considered a large order — there is not the rigid division of labour to be found in mass production. Relations between designers and producers are not formalized and distant as in mass production, where each production worker is operating according to precise instructions from a designer with whom he or she has had no direct contact. In aerospace, up to the mid-1970s at least, close contact between designers and shop-floor workers was normal: shop-floor workers trying out and suggesting modifications to designs which they would then discuss with the technical workers from the design office. Their skills are very different; the designers' skill involves the ability to specify measurements in mathematical terms, whereas the fitters' or welders' skills involve the ability to make very precise judgements on the basis of more tacit understanding built up from experience. Through their work together they tend to respect the differences. It is not surprising then that the first combine committee which from its origins brought together office workers and shop-floor workers should be in the aerospace industry.

A second feature of the aerospace industry which provided favourable conditions on which the Lucas Combine Committee could build is a long unbroken tradition of strong trade-union organizations within the factories and also across factories, regions and companies. Aerospace was one of the few industries where shop-floor organization was gaining rather than losing strength during the 1930s. In 1935, while most shop stewards' organizations in other industries were still recovering from the defeat of the General Strike and the demoralizing effects of the depression, the aerospace shop stewards were establishing an industry-wide trade-union committee: the National Council of Aerospace Shop Stewards, and a newspaper, the *New Propellor*, to co-ordinate their offensive on wages and conditions.[2] The reason why aerospace stewards were able at such a time to take the bold step of building a shop stewards' organization across an industry, independently of the official trade-union leadership, was that government contracts to their industry put them in a very strong bargaining position. The cost-plus basis of these contracts enabled employers to make concessions and pass on the cost to the government. The government for its part did not baulk at the cost. With war looming more and more threateningly on the horizon, they saw an expansion of aircraft capacity as unavoidable even in the earlier 1930s. As a result shop stewards could win victories, gain credibility and build strong organizations.

Another factor explaining the degree of co-ordination between aerospace shop stewards at that time was the domination of the industry by a small number of large companies. The tendency towards monpolization developed earlier in the aerospace industry than in any other industry, because of the obvious economies of size involved with such large and costly products.

The National Council of Aerospace Shop Stewards flourished until well into the 1940s. In doing so it started a tradition on which other forms of shop stewards' organization were to build, both on a company-wide level and across different sections of the industry.

A third feature of the aerospace industry, which helps to explain the Combine Committee's approach to the state, is that pressure for nationalization had long been central to the activities of the unions in aerospace and yet has only very belatedly been carried out. An industry which is so dependent on the government and so monopolistic in its structure was an obvious candidate for nationalization even on orthodox state-capitalist criteria. The only obstacle, however, was that unlike the other industries considered for nationalization after the Second World War, aerospace was a highly profitable industry. The Labour government's refusal to make aerospace part of the first wave of nationalizations meant that trade unionists in the industry were in a position to observe and develop criticisms of orthodox forms of nationalization. In a sense they benefited from the historical advantage of being late. As a result politically-conscious trade unionists in the industry were less optimistic than the early advocates of nationalization about the possibilities of socialism and workers' control coming about through simply extending the existing state.[3,4]

If historical lateness was an advantage in developing new industrial policies, early experience of redundancies in the aerospace industry put the Combine in a strong position when management implemented its rationalization plans in the 1970s. For another peculiar feature of the aerospace industry is that, although it is sometimes booming (because of defence spending) when other industries are collapsing under the pressures of recession, it is also vulnerable as much in boom years as during depressions to the sudden cancellation of orders. The result is that workers in the industry were forced to develop tactics for fighting redundancies at a time when other industries were basking in the short-lived sunshine of full employment. The aerospace workers were by no means always successful, but over the years and the cancelled projects many of them began to shape a kind of trade unionism more able to resist redundancies than, say, the kind of trade unionism which developed in the automotive industry.

The contrast between shop stewards' organizations in the car component side of Lucas and Lucas Aerospace illustrates the point. For by many criteria shop-floor organization in some parts of Lucas Electrical (the main car components subsidiary) was as strong if not stronger and more militant than in Lucas Aerospace. Since the early '70s management has attempted to rationalize both divisions. In aerospace, Lucas management have still not been able to carry out all the manning reductions and closures which they intended. In the car components companies of Lucas Industries, on the other hand, the stewards have as yet been unable to transform a trade unionism which could exploit booming markets into a trade unionism able to resist management's pressure to contract.

These traditions do not in themselves fully explain the character of the Lucas Aerospace Combine Committee; there is no one set of traditions which can provide such an explanation. How these traditions were developed depended on the individual qualities and cross-cutting regional and political traditions of the shop stewards who came together between 1969 and 1972 to form the Combine Committee.

PART II: CREATING THE COMBINE COMMITTEE

4 Roads leading to Wortley Hall

The shop stewards in Lucas Aerospace started to form their combine committee nearly two years before management had managed to unify the
organization of the different companies into a single Lucas Aerospace structure. Even after this integration, in 1971, there was continued in-fighting
between the management of the old English Electric factories and that of
Lucas. In many respects Lucas Aerospace management were in as much
disarray as, if not more than, the shop stewards. This gave the Combine
Committee a rare advantage.

The trade unions at the Willesden site prided themselves on always being
one step ahead of management. They had even established a tradition
whereby the shop stewards would meet every Monday to decide on "the
stir" for the week. They calculated that the only way to keep the initiative
over the personnel manager was to start something themselves. The same
philosophy led them to take the initiative in forming the combine. As soon
as they heard rumours of Lucas having secret talks with the IRC about the
takeover of the special products group of English Electric (EE) they made
contact with the shop stewards at the factories involved. The result was a
joint meeting on 13 December 1969, less than a month after takeover
negotiations were complete. This was the first meeting of what became the
Lucas Aerospace Combine Committee.

The meeting was arranged to coincide with the regular quarterly meeting
of the GEC-EE combine committee at Wortley Hall, Sheffield. The GEC-
EE combine were also meeting the AEI combine that weekend (GEC had
just taken over AEI). All three groups of stewards were grappling with the
same problem: how to regroup in the face of a rapid industrial
restructuring over which they had absolutely no control. After an initial
session where stewards from all three companies discussed this problem in
general terms, the stewards of the English Electric Special Product Group
(SPG) factories of Bradford and Coventry went off to a separate room with
the stewards from the Lucas Rotax factories of Willesden, Hemel
Hempstead and Morden.

This joint meeting of the Lucas stewards with the GEC combines gave
the Lucas stewards the advantage of learning from the mistakes of others.
The EE and AEI combines had been unprepared for the aggressive,
centrally directed style of management of GEC. The EE combine, of which
the SPG stewards had been part, was in one sense well established. It had
kept going since the mid-1950s, and by 1969 had the support of over
twenty English Electric factories. But is was really little more than an information exchange enabling stewards to have better information and more
confidence in their plant-level negotiations over wages and conditions. As
Ray Andrews, a senior steward at the Bradford English Electric factory at
the time (now AUEW District Secretary), put it: "We never really had a

strategy, or detailed knowledge of the company. Nor could we organize co-ordinated activity throughout the plants.". This kind of combine committee seemed adequate in the 1950s and '60s when companies like English Electric had minimal centralized financial controls or corporate strategy. However, in the face of Arnold Weinstock's* ability to play off different factories against each other in order to drive through a centrally-directed plan, it disintegrated.

The Lucas stewards learnt from this. Their main purpose in forming a combine committee was to prevent a repeat of the GEC rationalizations. They had an urgent sense of the need to create a cohesive force out of the diverse plant and union organizations which made up Lucas Aerospace. From the start the discussions of the Lucas Combine Committee placed an emphasis on strategic thinking and advance planning. For them an information exchange among senior stewards was not enough.

What was the character of the factory committees which in the course of three years were to become a cohesive national force? What regional trade-union traditions influenced them? What were the production processes that their members were involved in and what did this mean for the skill composition and sexual division of labour within the workforce? How united were the different unions and different factories on each site when they joined the Combine? Who were the leading members of the Combine, which site did they come from and what attitudes and traditions did they bring to the Combine? One way of starting to answer these questions is to introduce briefly the different shop stewards' committees as they joined the Combine, and attended their first Wortley Hall meeting.

---

* The managing director of the new GEC.

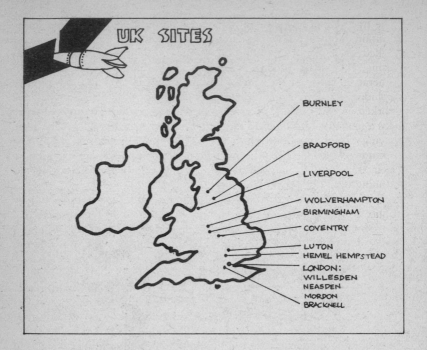

UK SITES

BURNLEY

BRADFORD

LIVERPOOL

WOLVERHAMPTON
BIRMINGHAM
COVENTRY

LUTON
HEMEL HEMPSTEAD
LONDON:
WILLESDEN
NEASDEN
MORDON
BRACKNELL

Willesden: the old HQ

The two Willesden factories in the Park Royal Industrial Estate made up the original Lucas Rotax company. Until 1971 it was at Willesden that all the senior managers worked, and where the Rotax research and development centre was based. Willesden was also, in effect, the headquarters of trade-union activity in Rotax. The AUEW shop stewards' committee there was part of the North London District, a district well-known for its political and industrial militancy. Rotax was typical in having a strong Communist Party factory branch throughout the 1950s and early '60s. The toolroom was known as "Red Row", down which managers feared to tread. The trade unions made the most of Willesden's strategically central position within the Rotax group, and made it their business to get to know everything that Rotax management were planning. One shop steward remembers:

> We used to get all the documents meant for directors' eyes only. . . . We used to use the information in negotiations very effectively. Then management put the clampers down. Every document was numbered and shredded after use by the directors. But finding out their long-term plans has always been an important part of the job of trade unionists as we see it.

The trade-union organization which grew up in Willesden was in a strong position to obtain and to piece together information. It was based on a very skilled workforce. The production work was mainly skilled machining and fitting. The main product was small gas turbines for aircraft power-generating units. At the time of the first Combine meeting the workforce included a research and development centre of over 300. Another 400 worked on experimental production facilities to produce prototypes. There was a toolroom of 200, and a further 600 skilled engineering workers, some having served apprenticeships as long as seven years. A proud and committed workforce then, committed to both their trade unionism and to their skills; but by 1969 they were also a workforce for whom time was running out.

Ever since 1952, Rotax electrical work was done at a factory built by Rotax in the new town of Hemel Hempstead. At first it seemed that management was intending to maintain both factories, with Willesden concentrating on research, development and prototype work. But this was before Lucas's central management had drawn up their rationalization plans, in 1970, to concentrate production at four of the original thirteen Lucas Aerospace sites. Hemel was to be one of these sites. Willesden was to close and join the industrial graveyard that the Park Royal Estate was fast becoming as companies moved out of London to new towns where trade unionism was weak.

No doubt management hoped that by closing Willesden they would nip the Combine Committee in the bud. However, trade unionists from the one remaining factory at Willesden, both shop-floor and staff, continued to play a leading role in strengthening and extending the Combine. Jim Cooney, the Willesden AUEW convenor, was chairman of the combine for six years; Ernie Scarbrow, AUEW-TASS, was secretary for the Combine for ten years, and Mike Cooley, also of TASS, was editor of the Combine newspaper for a similarly long period. These three represented Willesden at the founding meeting of the Combine.

Hemel Hempstead: new-town trade unionism

The Hemel site was the other major southern site represented at the first meeting. The two main staff unions, TASS and APEX, and the two main shop-floor unions, the EETPU and the AUEW, all sent representatives. Ever since the Hemel factory had opened there had been regular contact with trade unionists at Willesden; there was considerable movement of work and personnel between the two sites which the shop stewards carefully monitored and controlled. But though the organizations at the two plants were in regular contact, they represented two very different approaches to trade unionism. The form of trade unionism which developed at Hemel was shaped by the circumstances facing workers moving to a rapidly expanding new town. The production process there required less of the engineering craft skills than at most other Lucas Aerospace factories. The machinery tended to be purpose-built and numerically controlled (i.e. partially automated). Many of the workers at Hemel had not served an apprenticeship but had come in from jobs outside of engineering. This too had an influence on the contrast — and the rivalry — between trade-union organization at Hemel and at Willesden. At Hemel there was an aggressive and confident trade unionism but at the same time it was a trade unionism whose objectives rarely reached beyond high earnings for Lucas workers there. "Plenty of overtime and good wages, that was the priority," commented Chick Hartman, a technical worker: "People had come from digs or a room in their mum's house in London and suddenly found themselves in a brand new two-bedroomed house with a garage, a garden shed and so on. Where were they going to get the money to buy all the beautiful furniture they needed? That was everybody's concern." As a result of this approach and the organization built up to meet these needs, Hemel soon became one of the best-paid sites in the company. Once they joined the Combine, and other sites got to know about their wages and conditions, Hemel was always being quoted in negotiations.

The peculiar conditions of a new industrial town did not, however, favour the growth of a more outward-going trade unionism with the traditions of solidarity typical of the North London engineers. This was partly because within Hemel itself there was little pressure for shop stewards' committees to give each other support or make direct contact. The labour market was so tight in new towns like Hemel, at any rate in the 1950s and '60s, that wages and conditions could be improved through plant action alone. During that period the habits of solidarity and of trade-union involvement beyond the plant never became really established among the shop-floor unions at Hemel.

As elsewhere, the aspirations and traditions of the site organization affected the nature of that site's commitment to the Combine. The involvement of the Hemel shop-floor stewards was always rather sporadic, some would say half-hearted. However, the involvement of individual staff members, such as Chick Hartman, Mick Young and Cyril Silverton — all members of TASS — deepened as the Combine progressed.

Though Hemel was one of the weaker sites as far as the national Combine was concerned, co-operation between staff and shop-floor workers had always been reasonable. This was partly because everyone faced the similar problems of making a new home, and reinforcing this was the fact that Hemel was a fairly close-knit town where people lived near each other and used the same social facilities as well as working in the same place. In this atmosphere the differences between manual workers and staff did not count for as much as they tend to in older and more sprawling industrial towns.

Morden: bought, sold and closed

In 1969 Hemel and Willesden were the two main Rotax factories. Three other small factories in the London area were taken over by Rotax as it mopped up its minor competitors in different aircraft component markets. Shop steward delegates from one of these, Vactric Controls at Morden, were at the first meeting. Initially they represented only a small minority of the full workforce of 400 skilled workers. In the first two years of the Combine the unionization of Vactric Controls and also Premier Precision was a top priority. The Willesden representatives took responsibility for this and organized a recruitment campaign which soon brought membership figures at both factories from about 20 per cent up to 90 per cent and over. However, the Vactric delegates had little chance to play a part in building the Combine. In 1971 Lucas management decided, three years after they had purchased Vactric Controls, that it was not profitable enough to meet their plans for a new streamlined Lucas Aerospace. The company, workers, machines and all, were sold off to Muirheads. Nine years later, Muirheads decided to close the Morden factory, making three hundred workers redundant, and integrating the other hundred into the main Muirhead factory at Berkhamsted.

Coventry: insecurity breeds parochialism

The largest site outside London represented at the first meeting was Coventry. The workers there, like those from Morden, had been bought, sold and exchanged, like a bag of old clothes. This caused a deep sense of insecurity; and it was this which brought them to Wortley Hall. First they were part of British Thompson Housman, then they were passed into the hands of AEI, which in turn was taken over by GEC, which finally closed down part of the Coventry site and sold off the rest to Rotax. In this final exchange 1,000 jobs were destroyed. Eddie Weaver, the AUEW convenor, feared that this was not all:

> We knew full well that the Hemel factory of Rotax made the same products as we did (actuators, starter motors, switch gear); we thought we'd be swallowed up by Hemel once Rotax management got to work. We thought that if we went to the meeting at Wortley Hall, at least we'd get information.

As it happened the Coventry plant survived, though most of the design and research work was moved to Hemel. But the plant never had its own product and as a result felt permanently under threat from the predatory ambitions of Hemel's management combined with central management's determination to reduce the number of sites. This deeply ingrained sense of insecurity tended to produce a rather parochial defensive trade unionism.

Bradford: solid commitment

The three or four shop stewards who came to Wortley Hall from the English Electric factory in Bradford represented the first northern site to join the Combine Committee. Like Coventry, Bradford was a site which Lucas management had taken over in 1969 and, it was feared, intended to close during the '70s. The Bradford shop stewards believed that in management's plans for rationalizing Lucas Aerospace down to "three or four sites", Burnley was to be the only northern site. Lucas took over the Bradford site and its 900 skilled and semi-skilled workers because they wanted the products, and generating equipment, and their good name. Their intention seems to have been to move the work to Hemel. The fear of the recurring pattern of a takeover and asset-stripping led the Bradford shop stewards, followed later by staff representatives, regularly to attend the Wortley Hall Combine meetings. Shop-floor and staff unions had not previously worked together. But the sudden and threatening changes brought about by the takeover flung them into working jointly to preserve their future. The Bradford site included a research and development centre at Shipley which employed fifty technical and scientific workers. Bradford is one of the two sites (the other is Birmingham) where women are employed on production work. Women, almost exclusively, do the semi-skilled work of winding the wires for electrical generators. There are fifteen of them, but they are represented on the shop stewards' committee by a male supervisor.

While trade unionists at Bradford, especially those from the shop floor, were quick to join up with their new colleagues in Lucas Aerospace, the top management, true perhaps to the independent spirit of Yorkshire businessmen, were constantly coming into conflict with the central management of Lucas Aerospace. For several years this gave the trade unions an advantage they were quick to exploit.

After the first meeting at Wortley Hall, each of the next four or five meetings welcomed at least one new site to the Combine.

G.E. Bradley's: kidney machines for sale

At the second meeting in January 1970 the first five sites were joined by representatives from G.E. Bradley's of Neasden. This was another of the small London factories — 300 workers — which Rotax had taken over, mainly because of the highly skilled workforce. Bradley's was an electronics company, taken over by Rotax in 1959, where since 1967 they made kidney machines as well as aircraft components. They became involved in kidney machines in order to keep the uniquely skilled workforce together, ready for the time when orders for military communication systems boomed again after the government cancellations. Before long Bradley's had a reputation for producing the best hospital-based kidney machine available in Britain: "the Rolls Royce of kidney machines", as Jim O'Neill the convenor, proudly if rather incongruously, put it.

Shop-floor and staff workers have always co-operated closely in the work process itself at Bradley's, and they have also worked together in trade-union matters. It has been shop-floor representatives, mainly Jim O'Neill, the convenor, who have travelled to Wortley Hall to represent the site.

At the autumn meeting of 1970 there were three new sites. One was the Luton aircraft factory of English Electric. The other was H.M. Hobson's of Wolverhampton, taken over by Rotax just a month before the Combine meeting. The third was Premier Precision of Bracknell, taken over by Lucas in September 1969.

Luton: starting from a weak base

Luton site is one of the smaller sites, 365 workers in all: 251 on the shop floor, 114 on the staff. It makes aeroplane windows and related components such as de-icers and ice-controlling equipment, as well as glass-fibre containers including containers for missiles. The Luton site had initially been owned by Napiers and then by English Electric before it was taken over by Lucas in 1969. Later, in 1977, Pilkington's were to try to take it over, with a view to using its techniques but closing the factory and sacking the majority of workers. The trade-union reaction, however, was so strong that Pilkington's withdrew.

In 1970, when the site first joined the Combine, trade-union organization was not very firmly established. In the mid-'50s nearly 100 per cent of the shop floor had been unionized, mainly by the AUEW, and a minority by the TGWU. However, this organization fell away when the AUEW convenor left in 1956. The AUEW district secretary, it is said, did little to remedy this; his attention was focused exclusively on the large Luton factories of Vauxhall and Skefco and weak organizations in the smaller factories did not get the back-up they needed. When the site joined the Combine Committee the organization was beginning to be built up again, partly because the original convenor, Dally Duncan, had returned. Staff members began to join TASS and APEX. Relations between the shop-floor unions and the staff unions were good. They joined the Combine together in response to a letter sent by the Combine to all sites that had not yet joined.

Wolverhampton: breaking with the Duffy tradition

Workers at H.M. Hobson's in the Fordhouses district of Wolverhampton were already having their first taste of Lucas's rationalization in November 1969, only days after the takeover documents had been signed. A condition for Lucas taking over this company was that one of the Fordhouses factories should be closed. In the process the number of jobs dropped by nearly a third. But at that time jobs for skilled engineers were easily available in the Midlands area; redundancy payments were made and the trade unions did not put up any sustained resistance. The main issue in the minds of the seven representatives who came to the first Combine — four shop-floor and three staff — was wages and conditions. As soon as the takeover had occurred the TASS members put in a claim for parity with other Lucas sites. It was through pressing for this that they first got to hear about the Combine Committee.

The shop floor were determined that being part of a big company would not take away from the long-established strength of their organization. It was important therefore that they keep informed about wages and conditions at other plants. And this is what brought them to Wortley Hall. The Combine Committee might be useful as a source of information, but the shop-floor representatives were sceptical about it being anything more than this. Hobson's had long been a well-organized plant: "We had management where we wanted them," was how one steward described their strength. Although wages were among the highest in the district, this shop-floor militancy went hand in hand with rather limited horizons as far as trade unionism beyond Hobson's was concerned. Terry Duffy, now president of the AUEW, started his trade-union career as shop steward and then deputy convenor at Hobson's. Although he had gone on to higher things by the time that Hobson's became part of Lucas, he had helped to build traditions that were hostile to multi-union multi-plant combine organization. Take for example his attitude to staff unions: when Brian Punter, who was to play a leading part in establishing a strong TASS organization on the site, told him about his plans to get the staff organized, Duffy just laughed and implied he wanted nothing to do with staff unions. At the time when Hobson's became involved in the Lucas Aerospace Combine Committee there was, according to both groups, "a complete split between TASS and the shop floor, which conditioned their attitudes to the Combine Committee". A TASS member describes how he felt: "My worry was the fact that this was the first time that manual workers and staff workers have pulled together union-wise. And I just wasn't sure how it could work".

An AUEW steward expressed even stronger doubts: "I was dead against the Combine in the first place, so were my members. Never believed the Combine would work." Another factor explaining these initial doubts about the Combine was the independence of Hobson's production from the rest of Lucas Aerospace. Hobson's have their own product, actuating systems for wing flaps, and their production is not tied into that of any other site. This, and also the size and history of the company, has tended to produce a feeling that they were "not really part of Lucas".

Premier Precision

Premier Precision was a small private company which had moved to the new town of Bracknell in the early 1960s before being bought by Lucas. It employed 230 skilled production workers, 12 labourers and 40 technical and clerical staff carrying out sub-contract work on parts of jet engines, mainly for Rolls Royce. Only about 20 per cent of the workers were in a union and no negotiations took place through the union. Soon after the factory was taken over by Lucas they received a visit from Ernie Scarbrow, secretary of the Combine Committee, who explained the importance of joining a union. Chris Haddon, an AUEW shop steward, takes up the story: "He explained the problems we'd face in a big multi-plant, multi-national like Lucas. . . . Soon after we had Mason, the Lucas personnel director, down telling us the demarcation boundaries for different unions. In no time we went up to a membership level of 80 to 90 per cent. And we started going to Wortley Hall. We felt in an inferior position initially. But the overall strength of the Combine pulled us up."

Birmingham

At the winter and spring meetings of 1971 and 1972 of the Combine Committee, shop-floor and staff representatives from the Birmingham factories came for the first time. They had been traumatized into involvement by the ruthless sackings made in the wake of the Rolls Royce crash in 1971. Before the crash, the three main aerospace factories in Birmingham employed over 4,000 workers. Afterwards the numbers were cut by a third. Several leading stewards, including Frank Wood, who had supported the idea of combine organization for many years, were among those sacked. The shattering experience of the Rolls Royce redundancies — which is still a reference point in discussions about resisting redundancies — shook leading staff and shop-floor representatives in Birmingham out of a complacent belief that being at the centre of the Lucas empire they were both secure and superior. The experience revealed the weaknesses of trade-union organization in Birmingham: in particular the lack of co-ordination across the Birmingham factories and across aerospace, and the lack of any strategy to resist redundancies. The Birmingham site consisted of four factories all involved in engine components. The Shaftmoor Lane BW5 factory was the largest, with 1,500 shop-floor workers and over a hundred staff workers. Then Marston Green with 500 shop-floor workers and about 50 staff workers; followed by Spring Road with 250 in total and Honily with 50. The Marston Green factory, with approximately 200 workers, was the other factory, along with Bradford, that employed women on the shop floor. Like Bradford the work was semi-skilled; in the case of Marston Green it was the wiring of electronic circuits.

One factor which had held back the Birmingham shop-floor unions from wholehearted involvement in the Combine was that in their wage negotiations they had always tended to liaise more with fellow Birmingham stewards on the car components side than with those elsewhere in aerospace. Until the mid-1960s the senior stewards in the Birmingham aerospace factories had been formally tied in with the senior stewards on the car side for wage negotiations. But they found that as a minority dominated not simply by the number of electrical (car components) workers but also by the two company-oriented senior electrical convenors, they had little control over the negotiations. In 1965 they broke away. But the electrical negotiations continued to be the major factor determining the company's final offer to aerospace.

As the Combine Committee became established and enabled sites with low wages to achieve parity with the highest paid sites, the Birmingham stewards developed a more national outlook. At the same time the Birmingham factories' involvement in the Combine Committee as a single site encouraged them to improve their local co-ordination. The Birmingham area has provided several leading activists in the Combine: in the early days, Frank Wood, Jack Gunter and Ernie Hunt, followed by Ernie Poland and Pat McSharry and on the staff side Ron Mills, Bob Dodd and a recent

secretary of the Combine, Brian Salisbury. The allegiance of Birmingham
stewards to the Combine has often had to weather the opposition of a
notoriously right-wing AUEW district leadership, as well as considerable
suspicion from the TASS officials.

Merseyside

The Birmingham affiliations to the Combine Committee were quickly
followed by the affiliations of the majority of unions at the two Lucas
Aerospace sites on Merseyside: the Victor Works in Liverpool and the ex-
English Electric plant at Netherton. The Victor Works, with 1,800 workers
(in July 1971, after the Rolls Royce redundancies), was and still is the
larger of the two. This factory was given to Lucas in 1951 by the
Ministry of Supply to enable Lucas to expand its gas turbine work for the
RAF. The Liverpool factory was therefore involved in the same work as
the main Birmingham factory at Shaftmoor Lane and subject to the same
fluctuations in orders, which meant that there was regular contact. At
times, though, it also meant rivalry and divisions between trade unionists at
the two plants.

Management destroyed six hundred jobs in Liverpool at the time of the
Rolls Royce crash and faced little resistance in doing so. This was not
because there were plenty of volunteers to sell their jobs, on the contrary.
Rather, the shop stewards were taken by surprise by the speed and ruthlessness with which the newly-appointed national management of Lucas
Aerospace carried out a centrally-planned rationalization that took little
account of local negotiating customs and procedures. The leading stewards
at Victor Works drew the obvious lesson: the different site-based trade-
union bodies needed to develop their own national organization and
strategy to counter this new ruthlessness on the part of central
management. From then on, until they both became local officials of their
unions, Dave Gough, the AUEW convenor, and Stan Kelly, the GMWU
convenor, played leading roles in building the organization and formulating
the strategy of the national Combine Committee.

Relations between the shop floor and the staff were co-operative from the
start but there was no joint organization. Compared to other Lucas
Aerospace sites the number of staff workers was small, because all the gas-
turbine research and design work was done in Birmingham. So it was the
strength and unity of the shop-floor committee which at Victor Works was
of vital importance for the Combine. And this unity needed constant care
and patience to maintain. There was a permanent source of tension in the
minority position of the GMWU representatives — representing 200
members — in a committee dominated by the AUEW representatives, who
represented over 1,000.

Before the Combine Committee was established, the shop stewards of
both the GMWU and the AUEW had tried to build an inter-factory
organization on a regional basis. The intention had been to bring together
all the five Lucas factories on Merseyside: the two Lucas Aerospace

factories, Lucas Girlings, Lucas CAV and Lucas Industrial products. But like the similar attempt in the south, issues around which to unite in a practical way were rarely found, and it proved difficult to maintain momentum as an organization. Informal contacts were always maintained though, and these served to mobilize support when necessary. It is a telling proof of the necessity of national combine committees that the only major sites now left — though depleted — on Merseyside are the Lucas Aerospace sites, the only part of Lucas where a national combine committee was sustained.

Burnley

The Burnley site was the most difficult to draw into the Combine Committee. There was no tradition — at least in the post-war years — of united resistance to management, though there were frequent strikes by individual craft groups. For example, the Sheet Metal Workers' Union had a particularly rich history of militant action. But there had been a history of inter-union sectarianism at Burnley especially between the Sheet Metal Workers' Union, protective of their autonomy and proud of their traditions, and the AUEW, who no doubt considered that the sheet metal workers should long ago have amalgamated with the AUEW. The staff unions were simply not taken seriously. One factor behind this slowness to take on management as a united group is that for a time Lucas's paternalism made it appear to some as a benevolent employer. The comparison in many Burnley people's minds was with the cotton employers who dominated the town until the war and with the small sweatshop engineering factories which grew up after the war. Lucas came to Burnley in the same way as it went to Liverpool: as a result of inducements from the Ministries of Supply and Aircraft Production. Four of the five Lucas Aerospace factories in Burnley were old cotton mills requisitioned for war production in the early 1940s. For a time wages compared well with others in the district, and the Burnley site had not been badly affected by the Rolls Royce crash. It was a priority site in management's plans and so gained some protection from fluctuations in demand.

In these conditions trade unionists whose horizons went beyond the hills surrounding Burnley were rare. There was, however, a group of AUEW members who in the 1950s and '60s were grouped around the Communist Party-influenced paper *Engineering Voice*. They worked closely together to build a more vigorous and outward-looking trade unionism in the district. One of these was Danny Conroy, who became the AUEW convenor at the Burnley site. He was involved in earlier attempts to establish a combine committee throughout Lucas Industries. When he was first contacted by the new Combine Committee in Aerospace he took immediate action: "I did what I've never done before or since, I paid the affiliation fee with my own money and then went to the shop stewards' committee for endorsement. Very undemocratic, I know. But I'm a great believer in combines." The shop stewards endorsed Danny's affiliation and, with considerable scepticism about what advantage joining with trade unionists from the south could bring, they sent a small delegation to Wortley Hall in January 1972. This was to be the start of a relationship which transformed the organization, the ideas and in some cases the whole lives of workers at Burnley, and at the same time injected a new strength and source of initiative into the national Combine. Roy Middleton, a TASS member from the works study department, and Danny Conroy became expert negotiators over pensions. Mick Cooney, AUEW convenor for several years, was chairman of the Combine Committee for five years, and Trevor Pilling, an AUEW shop steward, is now serving a term as treasurer. Terry Moran, an AUEW steward, and Phil Asquith, a TASS representative and now chairman of the site's joint staff and manual committee,* have both played leading parts in developing and spreading the ideas behind the Corporate Plan.

These then were the different trade-union organizations which met at Wortley Hall. By January 1973 all eleven sites, with in total seventeen factories, were affiliated. Attendance at that January 1973 meeting was well over sixty. At the first meeting there had been only fifteen. In many ways these shop stewards' committees were not, on the surface, a very likely lot to make up a cohesive national organization or to take initiatives which would place them in the vanguard of trade unionism. And indeed it was not the simple fact of these trade-union committees getting together which made the Lucas Aerospace Combine Committee an effective and creative organization. More important was the process by which this combination took place: a two-sided process which more often than not changed the site organization and enabled it, in turn, to make a stronger, more creative contribution to the Combine Committee.

One aspect of this was the way that the Combine brought out the talents of individual stewards that were not given enough scope by the factory committee. Moreover, combinations of a far wider range of capabilities and experiences took place through the Combine than was normally possible within local trade-union organizations. Another aspect was that the existence of the Combine meant that the strengths of some sites were spread. Initially the traditions of the Willesden site were most influential. Latterly it has been the Burnley and Birmingham sites which have given a lead.

The sites' organizations did have certain features in common, though, which are important for understanding the history of the Combine. First, they were dominated by skilled engineering workers. Secondly, with the exception of Bradford and Birmingham, no women worked on the shop floor; and only in ones and twos did women work in the design offices. In Bradford and Birmingham women worked in a separate, small and almost

---

* He has since left to work on new employment initiatives in the Employment Department of Sheffield City Council.

exclusively female section of the site. The position of women in Lucas Aerospace reflects the sexual division of labour throughout the engineering industry in Britain. In 1968–9 only 1.3 per cent of technical and scientific workers in engineering were women, 1.0 per cent of designers, and 0.1 per cent of craftsmen; while among workers in the least skilled category, "operators", 38.9 per cent were women. The only category in which there has been even a slight improvement in the last ten years is the technical scientific category, where the percentage of women has risen to 4 per cent.[1,2]

Another common feature of the site organizations was that when they joined the Combine no site had any formal joint organization between the shop-floor and staff unions, although relations were friendly and staff representatives would regularly pass on information to the shop stewards. For the staff and shop-floor workers who met together in December 1969, it was therefore the first time they had met to create a joint organization. How far they succeeded and how the site organizations we have just seen were transformed in the process will be the subject of the next two chapters.

5 A new organization in the making

1969–71: Modest beginnings

During the Combine Committee's first two years, its activities consisted of establishing regular communication with all the sites, exchanging information and co-ordinating campaigns about wages and conditions, monitoring and where necessary resisting managements' attempt to streamline its new empire. The initial organization of the Combine Committee was modest. The founding meeting decided that the new Combine Committee would meet for three weekends a year at Wortley Hall. If an emergency came up then delegates could meet for a day in Coventry. Four officers were elected for the year: the chairman Howard Hughes, from the ETU (as the EETPU then was) at Hemel Hempstead; the vice-chairman Jim Cooney, from the AUEW Willesden; the treasurer Ron Walker, from DATA (now AUEW-TASS) at Willesden, and secretary Ernie Scarbrow, also from DATA at Willesden. Thus two officers were from staff unions and two from shop-floor unions. This balance was an agreed principle later to be extended to an executive committee and formalized in a Combine constitution. For the first two years, however, there was no formal constitution. The committee operated on the basis of more informal understandings, which was not unusual among combine committees at that time. None of the GEC combine committees, for instance, had more than a statement of objectives.

The financial basis of the committee was elementary too, with each factory contributing £2-10s. per annum which from the first meeting gave the committee the grand total of £15. This was seen as a "first step towards placing the committee on a sound financial basis".*

The first job of the officers, particularly the secretary Ernie Scarbrow, was to piece together information which would enable the committee to anticipate the company's plans. For instance, each plant sent to the secretary details of their product ranges. Rationalization of product ranges was one of the first steps which a new management tended to take after a merger, so this information would give the Combine an idea of future closures and redundancies. Scarbrow collated a "Register of Information" which he then circulated back to the plants. The minutes of each shop stewards' committee were also circulated, via Ernie, to every other site.

This information exchange revealed wide variations in wages and conditions. For instance, workers at Bradford received relatively high, noncontributory, sick pay and death benefits compared to the original Lucas companies; on the other hand, shop-floor wages there were much lower. A vast range of similar differences emerged, the result of differences in shop-floor strength and trade-union tradition as well as company politics.

---

* Combine minutes, 13/14 December 1969.

Establishing common policies

All this information was used in negotiations by the different site committees to win a "levelling up" of wages and conditions, although the Combine Committee did not leave it at this. They were aware that management was also collecting this information and was preparing, behind the appearance of plant-based negotiations, to operate a central policy on wages and conditions. This meant that the company operated with a maximum wage limit which constrained the better-organized sites. Negotiators would find that, as Dally Duncan from the Luton site put it, "the highest offer seemed to be based on what Birmingham got; we had no option but to accept." On the other hand, the company set no minimum level; on the contrary, it had no hesitation in exploiting the weakness of the less militant sites. So the Combine tried to provide a means of co-ordinating different claims and advancing together against management's national policy. To achieve this, the Combine agreed on an important principle:

> that although ultimate responsibility for accepting or rejecting schemes lay with each shop stewards' committee, there would be repercussions throughout the group; therefore the Combine should have a chance to discuss each scheme before a site decision was taken. (Combine minutes, April 1970)

This was their first move towards developing a common policy on earnings while carefully avoiding any threat to the autonomy of site decision-making, and it led to a successful resistance of management's attempt in early 1970 to control the escalation of bonus schemes. This initial success was important in convincing the more sceptical sites of the Combine Committee's value. The ultimate objective in wages, however, was more ambitious: it was to co-ordinate the different sites' responses to the company's basic offer. The minutes of October 1970 indicated that this was not going to be easy:

> It had been hoped that all factories in the Combine would be able to accept or reject the offer as a group, but there are difficulties to be overcome before the committee reaches this happy position.

One difficulty was the difference between wage levels. For example in 1971 the average skilled wage at Burnley was £38 per week, whereas at Hemel Hempstead it was £45.

Another difficulty which to this day faces attempts by the Combine Committee to achieve a co-ordinated campaign on wage policy is that staff have completely different negotiating arrangements from the shop floor. In the early 1970s the staff unions, ASTMS, APEX and DATA, were negotiating the procedure agreement whereby all wage negotiations are carried on at a national level. The shop-floor unions, on the other hand, continued to negotiate at a plant level. As a result the Combine found it very difficult, if not impossible, to organize a united campaign on wages.

Equalizing conditions and building unity

A more favourable terrain for establishing the unity of the Combine was what are misleadingly called "fringe benefits", in particular sick pay and pensions. Until 1974 in the case of sick pay and 1975 in the case of pensions, these issues were not the subject of any national negotiations, even though the management had national policies. Consequently the Combine's campaigns on these issues were not cutting across official structures. On the contrary, they were filling a vacuum felt by staff workers and shop-floor workers alike.

Unequal provision for universal experiences such as sickness and old age are a major source of the resentment which entrenches divisions between shop-floor workers and staff workers. Differences in conditions such as over "clocking on", which symbolize differences in status, further reinforce these divisions. So equalizing conditions was not only important in itself but was vital to the unity of the Combine Committee. The fact that staff representatives were seen by the shop-floor stewards and their members to be genuinely attempting to challenge these inequalities, and indeed making this challenge a priority, was crucial in laying the foundations of trust.

The most important factor driving staff and shop-floor workers towards unity was the threat of redundancies. No single union had, or indeed could have on its own, any really effective national organization to resist redundancies. It was this vacuum which the Combine Committee was to fill most effectively. In the first two years it began to develop the necessary cohesion and discipline for this, which meant developing the ability to act as a unified force even when only one or two sites were at any one time under direct threat. From the start the Combine saw each closure or major redundancy as a threat to the whole workforce; this was the basis on which it campaigned. And indeed both management's public statements and internal memos made it clear that virtually every plant *could* be vulnerable. The Combine's response to the company's first moves to rationalize its new acquisitions illustrates the difficulties they faced.

At the third Combine meeting, in October 1970, delegates heard the grave news which many of them had been anticipating. As the minutes report:

> It had been apparent for a long time that rationalization of the group would be embarked upon by the company. . . . The problem is now with us. The closures of the Wolverhampton Integral factory has been announced.
>
> The company has also announced that the Willesden factory would either be closed or have a serious redundancy.
>
> Reports from the other factories all indicated that rationalization and redundancies would extend far beyond the announcements already made.

A sense of urgency led the Combine Committee to take immediate action and recommend a ban on all sub-contracting throughout the group. The

Integral factory could not be saved but it was not too late to save jobs elsewhere. The sub-contract ban was the first simultaneous action to be carried out in all the sites by the new Combine Committee. Site committees did not find it easy; in some cases order books were full and management was pressing hard. But the reports at the next Combine meeting indicate that the ban held throughout the affiliated sites which at that time — winter 1970–71 — were ten out of the full thirteen.

Between the October 1970 meeting and the January 1971 meeting, the situation had worsened. In January the company had announced that there would be a 25 per cent reduction in manning. On hearing this, Combine delegates argued that more needed to be done to stress to the members the seriousness of the latest redundancy threats. They decided unanimously that: "All factories in the group would hold mass meetings at 2 pm on Friday for day-shift workers and on Thursday night 28 January for night-shift workers to inform them of this serious development." This resolution indicated a remarkable degree of co-ordination for a combine committee which had been in existence for only two years. These mass meetings took place as planned, and Ernie Scarbrow, Combine secretary at the time, comments on their effectiveness:

> They reinforced the sub-contract ban and the blocking of any move-
> ment of work from threatened sites. For example some machinery was
> sent to Netherton from Willesden as part of the run-down of
> Willesden. The Netherton committee just refused to let them in.
> Thousands of pounds' worth of equipment were left to rust at the
> Netherton gates, until management brought them back to Willesden.

Then, a month after the January meeting, came the collapse of Rolls

Royce, and the threat of 2,000 redundancies. In the face of such a sudden escalation of the redundancy programme, brought about, so it was made to appear, by forces entirely out of Lucas management's control, the weak links in the Combine's grip on the movement of work began to break. Hemel Hempstead allowed work to come in from Willesden. And the six-month-long resistance at Willesden began to collapse. Management at Willesden started to wrench the machines out of their foundations. They flooded the main factory at Chandos Road and tore down the roof. However, a hard core of trade unionists managed to hold out and force management to reopen the smaller factory — for 350 workers — at Chase Road. They even won a "guarantee": "The Chase Road site will now operate with the same degree of permanency as is understood by other sites in Lucas Aerospace." But the very inconsistency in the idea of a "degree of permanency" summed up the precarious future of the workers who remained at Willesden.

Meanwhile, it was at Liverpool and Birmingham where the Rolls Royce crash was used to full advantage. However, the state of shock and the sense of powerlessness which the redundancies created was short-lived. The response of the stewards at Birmingham and Liverpool was to remedy the weaknesses which the defeat had revealed. By October 1971 both sites were affiliated to the Combine. At first they sent small delegations but the number grew from three to four from each of these two major sites to anything up to fourteen or fifteen.

The Birmingham and Liverpool delegates were impressed by the organization they found meeting at Wortley Hall. Some of the Liverpool delegates had been sceptical. They had already had experience of involvement in an organization across the sites on Merseyside, and some of them found that people used this to "dictate policies" to the affiliated sites. But the delegates at Wortley Hall seemed to have established a different kind of organization, as Tommy Quirk, another GMWU steward, notes: "Four people went from Victor Works. Two were for the Combine and two were dubious. We came back feeling that a combine of shop stewards for Lucas Aerospace was a very good thing. I found that with the Combine, people don't try to dictate. As a result things get off the ground far better. They are more of a co-ordination body. They don't take away the autonomy of any site committee." The Birmingham stewards too were impressed for similar reasons. "If it had been an authoritative body rather than a recommending one there'd have been problems. But as a recommending body it seemed to work," added Ernie Poland, the TGWU convenor at BW5, Shaftmoor Lane, the largest Aerospace factory in Birmingham; he was particularly protective of the autonomy of the factory's shop stewards' committee.

1971–3: Consolidating the organization

The newcomers to the Combine might have been reassured, even impressed, by the organization they came into. But the delegates already involved were

preparing to make major improvements in the Combine's internal organization. The involvement of three new major sites made this even more
necessary. (Burnley also affiliated in late 1971.)

Before these sites joined, the Combine was still a fairly informal
organization, run on a shoe-string and held together by a few very
committed individuals (in particular Ernie Scarbrow, Jim Cooney, and
Mike Cooley from Willesden, and Ernie Webber from Bradford). Yet its
potential power and influence was beginning to expand beyond what this
modest organization could harness and direct. At the same time Lucas
management had completed their own process of internal reorganization,
which had been going on parallel to the coming together of the Combine
Committee. The outcome of this was "Lucas Aerospace Ltd" with its own
centrally co-ordinated management structure, its own personnel department, and its own corporate plan. The completion of management's integration meant that Combine delegates lost the opportunities which the
trade union-management conferences connected with the company's
reorganization process provided for talking to each other between Combine
meetings. This, along with the pressure of increased work and responsibility, meant that the Combine executive needed to take on extra functions,
especially of communication. It also meant that the executive had to have
its own specially organized and financed meetings between Combine meetings, in order to follow up Combine decisions. At the April and
October 1971 meetings, three piecemeal moves were made in this direction.
First, a liaison officer was added to the initial four officers. Their job was to
relieve the secretary of some of the day-to-day communication work. Good
communications were central to the effective running of the organization:
communication about disputes and problems arising in between Combine
meetings; communication after the Combine meeting to receive and spread
reports back from the sites about how much support there was for
Combine recommendations; and sometimes, communication to prepare for
meetings with management.

As important as internal communications between site committees was
communication with the members. In 1971 Mike Cooley was appointed as
newsletter editor and work began to prepare a regular printed newsheet for
mass distribution throughout the group.

In April 1971 delegates decided after discussion in their site committees
to expand the executive to include an executive member from each site as
well as officers.

The problem of leadership
The creation of a full executive committee raised new problems: a combine
executive of this sort would have considerable power in determining the
development of the Combine's activities. How could the affiliated site
committees make sure it was fully accountable to them? How could it give
a lead without becoming a law unto itself? How could Combine delegates
ensure it was in practice representative of their views, rather than the

instrument of a sectional interest? How would it avoid the danger of being "bought off" by management or becoming out of touch with the needs of the membership? And what kind of power and resources would it need to be effective in carrying out Combine policies? Finally, how should the executives' meetings and expenses be financed?

The very effectiveness of the Combine in carrying out industrial sanctions meant that one issue in particular brought these problems to the fore: the issue of whether the Combine should aim to be the recognized vehicle for national negotiations with management. In the eyes of many trade unionists, the sign that a trade-union organization has "made it" is to take a formal, recognized part in negotiations with management. The reasons for this are obvious. In many ways negotiation, collective bargaining, is what trade unionism is essentially about. It is through collective bargaining that trade-union power is finally cashed. There is a tendency therefore for trade unionists to assume that a new trade-union organization, created to fill a serious gap in the established trade-union structures, will inevitably become, and should intend to become, a new formally recognized negotiating body. Combine delegates saw several problems with this, concerning the desirability of permanent, institutionalized national corporate bargaining.

Their fear was that corporate bargaining would lead to an over-centralized committee whose members would become out of touch with shop-floor feeling and therefore shop-floor power. They saw the danger of the autonomy and therefore the strength of site-level organizations being sapped by an overbearing national committee. Dick Skelland, a GMWU steward from Liverpool, explained the importance of this issue: "This question of the autonomy of the sites was the most controversial issue. . . . After all, shop stewards felt that the national union officials were already taking away a lot of their power. The last thing they wanted was a combine committee taking it away too."

On the other hand *management's* policies were nationally formulated and centrally orchestrated. So the question arose of how the Combine Committee could co-ordinate resistance to central management effectively on a national scale without destroying the site committees' autonomous decision-making. Could it meet with management as part of its campaigns of pressure without its relations with management becoming institutionalized and the committee itself becoming out of touch and drawn into management's way of thinking?

The problem of staff and shop-floor unity

A final problem concerned the need to consolidate some of the understandings and new (as far as British trade unionism is concerned) values established in the first two years of the Combine Committee's growth: in particular, the close relations between staff unions and shop-floor unions. These often depended on peculiar circumstances, for example the way all the unions in Bradford found themselves flung together by a common inexperience in dealing with a new management. Or they were the result of individual relations of trust built up over several years, as at Willesden.

In the early years of an organization, individual personalities and the values they symbolize can be very important. In the case of the ability of the Lucas Aerospace Combine Committee to win the allegiance of shop-floor as well as staff workers, the background of Ernie Scarbrow, the Combine secretary, was very significant, though he would be the last person to say this himself. His earlier experience as a skilled toolmaker and AUEW member and his present work as a product engineer and TASS member enabled him to be sensitive to both the real and the imagined conflicts of interest between the shop floor and the staff. Moreover as an ex-toolmaker he was respected by the shop floor for his skills. All this was important, because he was both the anchor man and the contact man at the centre of the Combine.

Unity based on these varying circumstances and personal characteristics was precarious, especially as it went so much against the grain of established trade-union institutions. How could a stimulus and encourage-ment towards joint organizations be built into the organization of the Combine?

Discussion of these problems, both in the formal meetings and in the bar afterwards, led Combine delegates to think that the answers that had been arrived at informally should be codified and written down in the form of a constitution. This would also help newcomers to understand what was going on, and it would enable everyone to get an overall view of the Combine's organization. Weak points could be identified, and any mis-understandings as to the status and objectives of the Combine could be clarified.

To meet these needs the Combine Committee embarked on a year-long discussion to produce a constitution. A first draft was sent to all the sites. Amendments were proposed, and these too were sent round the sites, often leading to further amendments. Nothing was left undiscussed, as the secretary Ernie Scarbrow witnesses:

> Every month I would get letters from sites occasionally with major amendments, but usually with little things, changing "woulds" to "shoulds". The more basic discussions went on in the sites before we prepared the first draft. And most of the basic principles had been established in practice as we confronted new problems.

At the January meeting, 1973, the end result of all these discussions was agreed upon. The final document is carefully and succinctly worded.

It provides a useful summary of the organizational principles underlying the new kind of trade unionism developed by the Combine Committee. It is worth reading closely before discussing the points of controversy and how it helped in practice to resolve the problems raised above.

CONSTITUTION OF THE LUCAS AEROSPACE AND DEFENCE SYSTEMS* COMBINE SHOP STEWARDS' COMMITTEE

Title
1. The Combine Committee shall be known as THE LUCAS AEROSPACE AND DEFENCE SYSTEMS COMBINE SHOP STEWARDS' COMMITTEE.

Composition
2. The Committee shall be comprised of representatives elected by the Shop Stewards' Committee at each Plant within the Lucas Aerospace Division.

Objectives
3. The objectives of the Combine Committee shall be in the first instance to support, co-ordinate and initiate such steps as may be necessary to improve the job security, wages and conditions of all Lucas Aerospace employees.

4. Further, it shall support the efforts of those elsewhere in the Lucas Organization and in its subsidiaries and associate companies abroad to establish parallel Combine Committees and to improve their job security, wages and conditions.

5. It shall work for vigorous democratic Trade Unionism, free from State or Employer interference, and 100% Trade Union Organization at each Plant.

6. Recognizing the Community of Interest of all working people everywhere, it shall support their efforts to improve wages and conditions.

Frequency of Meetings
7. In order that the objectives set out above (3 to 6 incl) can be energetically campaigned for, the Combine Committee shall meet at least three times annually to determine overall strategic policies. At these meetings the representatives shall reflect the views of their respective Shop Stewards' Committee. The minutes of these meetings to be circulated at the earliest opportunity.

---

* In 1973 management began to separate several of the small southern plants, Premier Precision, Bradleys and Horstmans, from Lucas Aerospace by calling them the "Defence Systems Division". The management structure remained the same. The Combine therefore incorporated the division into the combine to undermine management's attempt to split it.

Recommendations

8. The individual site representatives shall then recommend the Combine policies to each Shop Stewards' Committee and shall campaign for their acceptance. The outcome of the Shop Stewards Committee's deliberations shall be conveyed, in writing, to the Combine Committee Secretary within 14 days.

Combine Executive

9. In order that the policies of the Combine Committee can be properly progressed between meetings a Combine Executive shall be elected at the first meeting each year (the A.G.M.). It shall carry out the policies of the Combine Committee and report to and receive instructions from each Combine meeting.

10. The Combine Executive shall include the Combine Committee Chairman, Vice Chairman, Secretary, Liaison Officer, Treasurer and such other persons as the Combine Committee may deem suitable to serve on it to a maximum of eight Executive members in total.

Emergency Combine Meetings

11. An emergency meeting of the Combine Committee may be called by the Combine Executive or upon the request of a simple majority of the voting members (see 19 below) or upon the request of any Site in dispute.

Finances

12. The Combine Committee shall be financed by an affiliation fee of 10np per member per annum. This may be directly from Shop Stewards' funds or by way of a special levy.

13. The Treasurer shall be responsible for the funds and shall report on Income and Expenditure to each Combine meeting.

14. Cheques shall be signed by the Treasurer and either of two Trustees appointed by the Combine Committee.

15. Cheques for payments for approved purposes up to £10 may be authorized by the Treasurer. Those over £10 must be authorized by at least 2/3rd of the Combine Executive.

16. Executive members may claim expenses from the Combine Funds for attendance at Combine meetings or when acting on behalf of the Combine Committee. Details of the payment of such expenses must be included by the Treasurer in his report on Income and Expenditure to each Combine meeting. An audited statement of accounts to be available at the A.G.M.

Combine News

17. It is recognized that the success of the Combine Committee will depend upon the mass involvement of a well informed membership at each Site, To this end the Executive shall publish, on behalf of the Combine Committee, a newspaper which shall be called "COMBINE NEWS". This paper shall be published on a regular basis and shall campaign for Combine policies. No views other than these policies shall appear except as signed articles or letters from individuals or Shop Stewards' Committees.

Press Statements

18. No Press or Publicity Statements shall be made on behalf of the Combine Committee except by the Secretary or those whom the Secretary authorizes to do so on his behalf. All Press and Publicity Statements shall be in accord with the policies of the Combine Committee.

Voting

19. Each Shop Stewards' Committee may send as many representatives as they wish to each Combine meeting provided always that they meet their expenses. Voting shall however be limited to 1 vote per Site taken on a geographical group basis namely, Bath, Birmingham, Bracknell, Bradford, Burnley, Coventry, Hemel Hempstead, Liverpool, Luton, Neasden, Netherton, Willesden, Wolverhampton.

Combine Officials

20. The officials of the Combine shall be the Chairman, Vice Chairman, Secretary, Treasurer, Liaison Officer and 2 Trustees. They shall be elected at the first meeting each year (the A.G.M.) for a duration of 1 calendar year with the exception of the chairman *OR* Secretary, who, for the purpose of continuity, shall serve for a duration of 2 years. Each official shall be eligible to stand for re-election.

Alterations to the Construction

21. It is recognised that as the work of the Combine Committee grows and develops its Constitutional requirements may change in the light of actual experience. To facilitate such changes the Combine Committee, at its A.G.M., may alter the whole of the Constitution or the parts thereof provided that 2/3rds of the voting members (see 19 above) approve such alterations. Prior notice of proposed alterations must be circulated by the Secretary to each Site two weeks in advance of the A.G.M.

Quorum

22. All those entitled to attend Combine and Executive meetings shall be given proper notice of such meetings. Seven of the thirteen voting members of the Combine Committee as defined in 19 above shall cnstitute a quorum of that Committee.

   Five of the eight Executive members shall constitute a quorum of the Executive Committee

Majority Decisions

23. Majority decisions shall be binding and membership of the Combine Committee shall be conditional upon the acceptance of such majority decisions subject to the provisions of 8 above.

Did Combine Committee delegates have any models in mind when they began work on a draft of the constitution? "There were no models we could rely on. Most combine committees I knew of had come and gone," was Danny Conroy's reply. "We talked to people we respected in our own districts who'd had experience of combine committees and who had learned important lessons," said Mike Cooley from Willesden.

Tom Hill, an AUEW shop steward at one of the North London factories of Smith's Industries, was someone with whom they talked. There had been a combine committee at Smith's Industries (a producer of clocks and car components) since the end of the war. Hill expresses his doubts about its effectiveness:

> The combine committee was set up mainly to provide a national negotiating committee soon after the war. This emphasis on negotiations was partly a result of Communist Party policy at the time. It was also a result of the economic situation. The company was expanding rapidly. Management wanted industrial peace, so they were prepared to make concessions. They were prepared to recognize and negotiate with the combine committee.
>
> The negotiating committee was convenors really. It discussed policy and strategy at combine meetings but things never got back to the membership. The membership didn't learn about the negotiations until they got their pay packet. I thought we shoudn't get hooked on national negotiations. . . . Management was able to attack the combine at its weakest point, the gap between the combine and the membership. . . . The combine secretary was almost never in the factory. Management tried to sack him and got away with it. Later, when it suited them, management stopped recognizing and negotiating with the combine.

This kind of negative experience, along with the considerations mentioned earlier, underlie clause 8 of the constitution, which made the combine a recommending and campaigning organization rather than a negotiating one. Negotiations with management were not ruled out but they were to be pressed for as and when the Combine felt necessary, rather than being the main purpose of the Combine's existence. From 1971 onwards the Combine did succeed in pressing for meetings with management, at least twice a year, especially over redundancies.

How does this principle of recommendation work? The agenda of the thrice-yearly (later, quarterly) Combine meetings is discussed at each site, along with minutes of the executive meeting, a week or so before the site delegation goes to Wortley Hall for the Combine meeting. Delegations can be any size, as decided by the site committees. All delegates have the right to speak but the decisions taken at the Combine are on the basis of one site one vote. These decisions are not binding on the site committees. That would cut across the policy-making procedures of the different unions; and it would undermine the autonomy of the site committees. But decisions are binding on site delegates who are expected by the Combine Committee and by their own shop stewards to *campaign* on their site for these decisions. The result of their report back to the site organizations is communicated back to the Combine secretary who, with the executive, co-ordinates whatever action is required. This action might mean either pressing for a central meeting with management or co-ordinating negotiations through the different local negotiating procedures.

The principle of delegates campaigning for the Combine recommendations means that the dynamic of the Combine Committee is always *back* to the site committees and members. The principle of "one site, one vote" meant that the large sites did not outvote the small sites thereby permanently dominating the Combine and leading the small sites to feel they had no real voice through the Combine. The Combine was sensitive to the issue of how minority views could be expressed and this voting system seemed to be a solution. "One vote, one site" was also an affirmation of the united basis of the Combine. It was above all a combine of workers, not of members of a particular section or a particular union; though there was always the provision — later written into the constitution — for members with particular problems to form separate committees within the overall framework of the Combine Committee.

Principles in practice

Most site committees took the pre-meeting discussions seriously. Ernie Webber, the AUEW convenor for Bradford, stressed the financial incentive: "After all the committee are paying at least £100, usually much more, for delegates to come to the meeting. They want to make sure the committees' views are properly represented." Stan Kelly, a convenor at the Liverpool site in the early 1970s, stressed the importance of involving the members as well as the shop stewards in these pre-meeting discussions:

> We didn't always discuss the agenda with the membership; but if as a result of a decision the members could be involved in action I thought it was important to know their views before going to the Combine meeting. If we were going to have to confront an unpalatable decision at the Combine meeting I wanted to know what their feelings were.

Delegates who ignored the views of these site-based discussions were in for trouble when they returned; Tony Wyton, a TASS representative from Wolverhampton, told how: "The TASS reps were mandated on specific decisions. We then went and voted the opposite way. The membership went berserk, which shows how much they cared about what decisions the Combine Committee takes."

The principle of campaigning for Combine recommendations seemed to work in most sites. Ernie Scarbrow gives an overview:

> In general delegates did campaign for the Combine's recommend-ations. The major decisions were only taken after a lot of discussions with all minority views being heard and sometimes a new solution coming out of the discussion itself. After these discussions and the discussions on the sites preceding the meetings, delegates took the decisions seriously.

In discussions held at several sites in 1974 and taped for future use there was some disagreement, however, about the Combine's relation to the membership. In Birmingham one AUEW steward argued that the Combine was "too far ahead of the members". Another steward, Pat McSharry from the TGWU, agreed but felt the responsibility was on the delegates to keep the members involved:

> Probably you're right that the Combine Committee is a little bit advanced in front of the workers. But who is responsible for that? You can't put the onus logically on the Combine Committee. Because it is *our* responsibility to enlarge and fight for involvement in the Combine Committee, we've mentioned the use of better publicity, the use of talking to people. Have we done it?

As McSharry implies, weak spots in the Combine's support — and at that time Birmingham was one — can usually be traced to a break in the chain of communication between the union representatives on the site and the Combine meetings: a delegate who did not report back properly or a failure to discuss the Combine agenda at the shop stewards' committee and when necessary with the membership, before going to Wortley Hall.

The combine newspaper, *Combine News*, played an important role in repairing the chain of communication. It projected the Combine Committee as an organization that was close and and accessible to the members. Articles referred to "your Combine Committee". Its close connection with the familar plant shop stewards' committee was always stressed. They were linked together, for example, in an article on redundancies: "to protect your job, your shop stewards' committee and through them the Combine Committee will need your active support." The paper regularly gave details of the next Combine meeting and encouraged the members to: "discuss with your shop stewards any problems in your plant, any ways you can think of to make the Combine more effective, or other issues you wish to raise." In order to help members to identify with the problems of other sites, every issue of the paper reported on major developments at different sites. It also encouraged a sense of familiarity for the members of the Combine executive. Each issue contained a detailed personal and trade-union profile of an executive member. This was partly to prepare the ground for support, in case management tried to victimize one of them.

Combine News also acted as a means of implementing and co-ordinating decisions. Each Combine meeting's decisions were announced in the newspaper, with the arguments behind them spelt out. If a decision involved industrial sanctions, *Combine News* carried details of the work to be blacked. Later, in 1975 and '76, it also carried articles explaining the more general policies of the Combine, such as on workers' participation schemes or nationalization, and would ask for comments and debate.

By all accounts *Combine News* sold well at the sites. Nevertheless there were problems in getting news in from plants, which led to criticism. From Wolverhampton, for instance:

> There's not enough sent into *Combine News* by the rank and file. Liaison with the Combine executive isn't good enough. . . . We need more of a letters page. We should have more stories.

From Birmingham they had tried to overcome this lack of news coming from the sites: "We tried to develop news reporters from the site and to find people who can draw. But it takes time to build up that degree of commitment."

One site, one vote
The principle of "one site, one vote" might have been expected to be the most controversial part of the constitution. Certainly Ernie Scarbrow was surprised at the way the clause in the constitution was accepted:

> I expected this clause to be the one which caused the most argument with the bigger sites wanting more representation than the smaller sites. But it was the other way round, the bigger sites insisting on equal and united representation. It shows how important the idea of the Combine itself was to them at that time.

So long as there was no entrenched hostility between different unions at each site, the "one site, one vote" system acted as a stimulus for coming together to exchange views on the issues to be discussed at Wortley Hall. Usually votes would be taken at a meeting on each site of all the unions which were affiliated to the Combine. The site's delegates to the Combine meeting were expected to stick to this view as far as possible but they would not normally be mandated. Individual delegates were free to express dissenting views, though the majority view of the site would be reflected in the composition of the delegation. At the Wortley Hall meetings the delegates from each site sat together so they could consult on how to vote in the light of both the arguments at the Combine and the majority view of their own site.

This system broke down only when a deep and apparently unbridgable divison opened up between unions at a site level. This occurred at Liverpool in 1974 between the AUEW and the GMWU, and at Willesden in 1976 between the AUEW and TASS. When this happened the unions concerned would neither meet to agree on how the vote should be cast, nor would one side accept the legitimacy of the other side casting the vote. So in effect the vote of those sites were frequently cancelled out.

Difficulties such as these illustrate that, though constitutions consolidate principles and values, formal rules cannot in themselves generate commitment to principles. Combine delegates were to put these principles to the test almost at the same time as they were writing them into the constitution. It was these practical experiences which built up commitment to the Combine. 1972–3 was not only the year of the constitution, it was also the year in which the Combine achieved its first major success, from which others were to follow.

6　A new organization in action

Between 1972 and 1975 the Combine was involved in several campaigns through which it developed the organizational strength and the strategic thinking that, looking back, enabled it to embark on its alternative plan.

The Burnley strike

The Burnley strike, which lasted for thirteen weeks between July and September 1972, first gave the Combine Committee a full sense of its power to challenge Lucas's central management. For instance at Netherton the shop stewards, discussing the early years of the Combine, concluded that: "It was during the Burnley strike that the members became aware of a combine which would stand by them on the monetary side and if necessary on the physical side to attain what they believed was right." It helped to convince the more sceptical delegates, like some of the shop-floor committee at Liverpool, that it is possible to achieve united action across the different plants. Sid Fleming, a GMWU steward from Liverpool, said: "In spite of so many people with such different opinions, the Burnley experience united the Lucas Aerospace division and made us into one voice. It was the finest example anyone could wish to see of what the Combine could do."

Why was the Burnley parity strike so important? The few newspaper reports create an impression of a determined workforce which had support in other plants in the division. Nothing very unusual; newsworthy while it was going on, especially in Burnley, where Lucas is the largest employer, but once it was over its impact was of no interest. Yet behind the day-to-day "news" the experience of the strike was having a dramatic effect on the workers and management concerned, an impact which has lasted for years. Not only did it cause a dramatic shift in the balance of power but it also released energies and awakened a self-confidence, which led workers to take initiatives that previously would have been inconceivable.

There had not been a strike of anything like such proportions in Burnley since 1926 and it took management totally by surprise. The action began as part of the national CSEU claim for manual workers in engineering, in 1972. The CSEU had left it to local shop stewards' committees to fight out the claim with their local management. At first Lucas management were not even willing to negotiate. They found it hard to believe that "their workforce" whom, like children, they had taken on trips to Blackpool and provided with slap-up Christmas dinners, would take sustained united action against the company. This attitude explains why when management did eventually negotiate they offered just 50p when the full CSEU claim was £2.50 and the Burnley shop stewards had added a claim for parity with other Lucas Aerospace sites (they were about £4 below the average).

The workers were incensed at this paltry offer and imposed an immediate work-to-rule. Management responded a week later by switching off the power and in effect locked the workers out, seemingly thinking that this would cause enough panic and fear in the workforce to make them work normally, on management's terms. Evidence for this comes from office workers in the planning departments who reported to the shop stewards' committee that the company was making preparations for the night shift to return after the mass meeting on the response to the lock-out. But by this time "their" workforce had developed a will of its own. The mass meeting voted overwhelmingly to occupy the factory.

The purpose of the occupation was to show that the workers were available and willing to work, that it was management who were refusing to give them work. The shop stewards had some difficulty convincing their members to interpret this literally. As sections of the factory turned into bingo halls, and televisions were blaring out from every corner, the stewards had to go round persuading members to be more discreet in their leisure activities; they were after all supposed to be available for work! By mid-July 1972 the occupation had served its purpose, proving to everyone that management was determined to starve the workforce into submission. The action turned into a strike. Pickets were organized, a hardship fund set up, and the Combine Committee held an emergency meeting to organize support. The general manager, meanwhile, went around predicting the failure of the strike. "They don't have any money. It'll collapse within a week," he was reported as saying.

But as the weeks went by, the pickets and the weekly mass meetings grew, the local paper became more sympathetic, and, most important, the money came in. Wolverhampton, Hemel Hempstead, Bradford, Willesden and all the other Lucas Aerospace sites raised £12,000 for the strike. The general manager had not anticipated the difference a combine committee could make.

At the Combine's emergency meeting in July some people, in particular the Liverpool delegates, had argued for total strike action. Others, the Burnley delegates in particular, disagreed. They had a different approach to tactics. According to Trevor Pilling, an AUEW shop steward, total strike action would fail because there would not be the funds. The secret of any strike is having the finance, but if everyone is in the same boat nobody is able to raise money, was his argument. Moreover, the Burnley delegates were sceptical about how successful the other delegates would be in winning support from their members for industrial action. This debate on the best tactics for supporting Burnley illustrated a principle which continued to guide the Combine Committee in confrontations with management. It tried always to devise the action required to maximize trade-union strength according to the needs of the particular situation and the resources available. Total strike action did not necessarily meet these criteria. In retrospect, the Burnley delegates' assessment of the tactics required proved accurate. It was financial backing which, in this instance, made the vital difference.

The details of the organization of the hardship committee and the raising of its funds are worth telling because they illustrate much about the workings of the Combine and the ability of a shop stewards' committee to look after its members at a time when they had little else to rely on.

The strike was official but the highest strike pay was £4 a week; many strikers received only £2. The first stage of the fund raising, following the Combine's emergency meeting, involved mass meetings at every site to campaign for a levy. On 19 July Danny Conroy, who had recently recovered from a heart attack in March, went on the road to speak to all these meetings. Meanwhile back in Burnley the town's spacious AUEW offices were turned into the strike headquarters: "just as union offices should be," commented an AUEW shop steward. From here the Combine provided a twenty-four-hour service, raising and giving out funds. If, by the end of the day, hardship cases had come in faster than funds, a member of the hardship committee would ring the night-shift convenor at one of the larger sites, such as Wolverhampton and Hemel Hempstead, who would organize a levy that same night and send it through the post office as a money order for the hardship committee to pick up by 11 o'clock the next morning. The following list gives some indication of the extent of the Combine's support for Burnley towards the end of the strike.

LUCAS AEROSPACE BURNLEY
Received through the Combine:

	£
Hobson's	2,181.00
Bradleys	187.25
Willesden	785.50
Netherton	301.00

Premier Precision	156.00
Coventry	155.00
Hemel Hempstead	2,458.58
Hobson's TASS	370.00
Liverpool	1,204.68
Bradford	290.00
Birmingham	1,496.87½
Birmingham Eagle Works	317.50
CAV Acton	206.17
	£10,109.55½

The money was well looked after, as Danny Conroy describes:

> The principle was that people had to be honest about what their incomes were; and the hardship committee could not give money beyond the level of supplementary benefit. That was the basis on which we worked. But people came with all sorts of funny things which of course they felt were hardship. There was a member came saying that he was in real hardship and his daughter's wedding was coming up in three weeks. He had no money to pay for it. Could the hardship fund pay for the wedding? These are quite serious. Another man came saying he was in real hardship because his daughter was taking ballet lessons and he couldn't pay for them. So he made a formal claim. The committee turned them both down. In the first case their view was that you don't save for a wedding over the last few weeks, you save for a wedding over a period of time, it's your duty to your children. They did give him a loan, though! Over 50 per cent of the members never used the hardship fund. And 95 per cent of those who did use it never abused it.

As a result of this careful stewardship and sustained fund-raising the strike was still going strong in mid-August, by which time the CSEU leadership had come to an agreement with the Engineers Employers' Federation. They settled for a £1.50 increase. The EEF then organized negotiations with the co-operation of the national officers of the AUEW in companies which faced an intransigent workforce. As a result of national pressure, negotiations were organized at Burnley. By this time — mid-August — Lucas management had recognized that it was not going to be easy to get a favourable settlement, and the big guns had to be brought in. So Mr Marsh, the personnel director from Lucas Industries, came to the negotiations along with a national representative of the Engineers Employers' Federation. Mick Cooney, the AUEW convenor at the time, described the preliminaries to the negotiations:

> All of a sudden we were told we had to attend a meeting at the Lucas club (Burnley). . . . There was a massive buffet laid on — the best

meal we'd had since the strike began. As soon as we were in I got hold of Arthur Hearsay, the AUEW executive council member sitting there with his big cigar, you know, and said, "Well, Arthur, what's the score?" He said, "We've got to settle, the Employer's Federation has been on to us and got us to set up this meeting with Lucas management. That's why we're here." After hearing this we got Ken Abbott, the local CSEU official, to lead the negotiations on behalf of the unions. You could trust Abbott. You know local officials on a day-to-day basis. You can call them to account more easily.

The negotiations did not achieve an agreement but they did eventually hammer out a formula, based on an immediate cash offer, and as such it was quite a good offer. By this time, though, the strike had become more than one for more cash; after the national settlement had been made the principle of parity had come to the fore. There was disagreement, however, about how it should be achieved. Some stewards felt that the final push for parity could come later, others that they should carry the momentum already built up to its logical conclusion. There followed a long, hot meeting of the joint shop stewards' committee.

"There was much blood spilt at that meeting," commented one of those present. By a slim majority the stewards agreed to recommend acceptance of the offer to the mass meeting. The mass meeting, however, was split, as Trevor Pilling, recalls:

There was a fantastic turnout, in the field by Hargher Clough. The company had even bussed workers in from Clitheroe — Coop [the general manager] still thought the strike was just the result of a few left-wing nutters. Well, then Mick [Cooney, the deputy convenor] gave the stewards' recommendation. There was a hell of a bloody row.

People shouting, "Whoa," "You're not on.". . . The vote was 50–50. A lot of those that went in favour said they only did so because it was the stewards who'd recommended it. So the chairman declared the vote void. And from then on it was the people on the shop floor that won the strike.

By mid-September the members had led the strike to victory. Management conceded the principle of parity. Calculated in cash terms, this meant an average £4 a week increase.

The victory at Burnley was a victory for the Combine Committee too, and not only a victory against management but also a strengthening of the Combine's own organization. Perhaps the most important part of this was that the Burnley workers, the largest workforce in Lucas Aerospace, actively supported the Combine whereas before Burnley the connection had been tenuous. During the experience of the strike the Combine came to mean something to trade unionists at Burnley. It was not just a matter of the money. People from the different sites and from the Combine executive came to Burnley regularly while the strike was on, and there were representatives of the Combine speaking at every one of the weekly mass meetings. "These speakers from the Combine uplifted people's spirits," commented Jim Fleming, an AUEW steward. It also meant that people knew where the money was coming from; it was not just "the hardship fund", it was money from workers in Hemel Hempstead, in Wolverhampton, in Liverpool, in Willesden and so on. And the workers at Burnley heard from these speakers why workers living hundreds of miles away voted to give them a small part of their weekly earnings. They gained a sense of the interests they shared in common.

The first input that Burnley made to the Combine Committee was the remaining £2,000 from the hardship fund, which was put into a special Combine fund to provide support for future disputes. The delegates agreed that this was preferable to distributing the money back to the sites. After all, if management is prepared to lock out one plant, the others are also vulnerable. And there is no mechanism within the established trade-union structures by which immediate and sustained support from every plant could be organized.

"The company has too many people"

The Combine's next major campaign, the following year, was on a battle-ground on which few trade-union organizations, traditional or otherwise, had won victories: that of national and international company rationalizations. The Lucas Combine too had been defeated on this terrain in 1971, but by mid-1973 they were in a stronger position. In the *Combine News* of June 1973, they made the following confident threat against any future rationalization scheme: "The company have been warned. Our position is clear. Any attack on any plant will be resisted by the full force of the Combine Committee." This claim was soon to be put to the test. On 18 April Mr Clifton Mogg, the Lucas Aerospace production manager, announced that "the company still has too many people". The Combine insisted on an explanation and a delegation succeeded in arranging a meeting with several Lucas Aerospace directors. The directors, however, refused to give any details about whether, and how, Mr Mogg was intending to dispose of the "extra people". The Combine published the transcript of their interrogation of the directors in *Combine News* — as they did with most of their meetings with management. Here is an informative extract:

> *Combine question*: Given that the Coventry factory is now only used to take the overload of work from Hemel Hempstead, why is the empty floor at Coventry being rented to "Keelavite" instead of being equipped and staffed for more aircraft work?
>
> *Company answer*: No reply.
>
> *Question No. 2*: Given that there are some 26 sites, or work locations (i.e. seven Burnley, two Bradford, etc.), Willesden apart, do you see any vacant space during the next five years?
>
> *Answer*: Time required to reply.
>
> *Question No. 4*: What products will be located at each site?
>
> *Answer*: Not able to give a reply.
>
> *Question No. 20*: Where is the production of the Torpedo Motor (a contract worth £23m) going to be carried out, assuming we get the order?
>
> *Answer*: We have not thought that far ahead.
>
> *Question No. 9*: Is Shipley regarded as a permanent site?
>
> *Answer*: No reply.
>
> The management were reminded that question No. 2 remained unanswered and a short adjournment was agreed. Following the adjournment the management stated that too many of our questions were really local management questions and that question No. 2 was in this category. There would be no policy or pressure from the centre to close any site and it would be a local management decision.

This impression that local management take the decisions about closures contrasts sharply with the description given by Sir Bernard Scott of how such major decisions are taken in Lucas Industries:

> The managing director's job is to operate our corporate plan in a ruthless fashion. . . .
>
> Each manager has a commitment in terms of profit or cash. There is no quarter given or expected and the target isn't varied unless there is a real upset. The commitment is made in July and this stands for a year and nothing less than fulfilling that commitment is regarded as satisfactory. (Interview in the *Daily Telegraph*, July 1976.)

Not much sign of genuine local autonomy here! Neither was much discretion left to local management when in January 1974 central management announced 800 redundancies across the whole of the Aerospace company. The company told the Combine of these redundancies before making them public. Moreover they made a proposal to the Combine: that

it could have control over how the redundancies were implemented, that is, control over which workers are sacked. Management presumably calculated that the Combine would see this as an opportunity to gain recognition and legitimacy and that this was more important to the Combine than preserving jobs. In fact the Combine turned management's proposal on its head and used this across-the-board redundancy threat as an opportunity to launch their first effective national campaign against redundancies.

The redundancies threatened to hit virtually every factory and every union, so the campaign needed to be co-ordinated on a multi-union as well as multi-plant basis. It required a stronger unity than even the Burnley campaign; the Burnley strikers received funds from virtually every union on every site but that did not necessarily require strong multi-union *organization* on every site. And at Burnley itself the staff were not involved in organizing the strike although they contributed financially. The campaign against the redundancies, on the other hand, required day-to-day co-ordination between all unions and all sites.

The campaign plan was formulated at a Combine meeting in January 1974, ten days after Combine representatives had turned down management's offer of joint implementation. The meeting recommended to all shop stewards' committees and threatened that:

> If the Company attempts to enforce redundancy the following sanctions will apply:
> (a) Overtime ban
> (b) Withdrawal of key sections
> (c) Sub-contract ban
> (d) Work to rule
> (e) No recruitment.

How these proposals were implemented varied from site to site. It is interesting to see what happened at Wolverhampton and Birmingham, where before their affiliation to the Combine there had been little or no co-ordination between staff and shop-floor unions.

Staff–shop-floor co-operation at Wolverhampton

Wolverhampton, remember, was a site where many of the leading shop stewards had been very cool towards the staff unions, although the common participation in the Combine Committee had begun to break down these hostilities. The shop-floor stewards found that they could identify with the Combine. At first they had been sceptical, thinking that staff would dominate it, but they were reassured by the leading role played in Combine meetings by members of the AUEW and the TGWU.

TASS representatives at Wolverhampton, led by Geoff Tedstall and Brian Punter, were keen to take up any opportunity for joint action. The 1974 redundancy campaign provided just such an opportunity. Brian Punter describes how for the first time the unions came together at the Fordhouses site:

> The Combine meeting decided to fight the redundancies by taking out strategic groups, guerrilla strikes if you like. The idea was to levy everyone else to pay the wages of those who were out. . . . We set up a joint fund and a joint committee with representatives of all the unions. We met daily to monitor exactly what was going on and decide what to do. It was magic, the kind of co-operation we had. Management reacted to the growing resistance by naming people they intended to sack. The advantage of a joint organization of the staff was that the foremen who were members of ASTMS could be stopped from giving out redundancy notices. Eventually management went round giving them out themselves. The joint committee reacted quickly before people became resigned to redundancy and lost their morale.

The representatives of the different unions then decided on a series of strategic withdrawals. First the clerical workers — mainly women — in the dispatch department came out. There were only five or six of them but without them the company could get no cash for the products going out of the factory. Then the telephonists — all women — came out, so that the company's communications were crippled. This guerrilla tactic was not only very effective in its immediate impact on the company, it also gave to the workers involved a vivid sense of their own and each other's power. This had a much more lasting impact. It demonstrated the benefits of multi-union co-ordination especially in the face of redundancies. This must have remained in the memory of workers from different unions at Hobson's, for although relations between staff and shop floor later broke down over a wages campaign, nevertheless whenever redundancies have been threatened they have come together again.

The experience of the redundancy campaign did not lead to any permanent joint organization which would co-ordinate on wages and conditions as well as redundancies. One reason for this was that the two leading members of TASS at the time of the redundancy campaign, who had worked hard to establish co-operation with the shop floor, left the factory to work elsewhere. In theory perhaps an organization should not depend on individuals but in the creation of new organizations, against the inertia of established relationships, the networks of trust and understanding built up by individuals with a vision of the new possibilities are vital. These relationships are also precarious, so that if the committed individuals leave and no new institution has been established, the whole network which is a foundation of the new organization can virtually collapse. This was the case when Brian Punter and Geoff Tedstall left Hobson's in 1974.

Inter-factory co-ordination in Birmingham

In Birmingham, by contrast, the redundancy campaign was able to build on a staff and shop-floor organization which had already come together in autumn 1973. Ever since the Rolls Royce crash, trade-union activists had been working towards some joint organization across the five Lucas Acrospace factories in Birmingham. Their involvement in the national Combine Committee provided a model. And they proceeded to establish the Birmingham Lucas Aerospace Combine Liaison Committee, with a constitution very similar to that of the national Combine. Up to eighteen delegates attended the Liaison Committee meetings representing six unions (APEX, ASTMS, AUEW-Eng., AUEW-TASS, EETPU and TGWU) from five factories (Honily, Marston Green, Shaftmoor Lane and Spring Road). This Liaison Committee provided the ideal base for the campaign of guerrilla strikes in Birmingham. As a committee bringing together five factories they had a wide scope for guerrilla tactics. The most strategically important, yet smallest, groups were the dispatch and the transport workers. These were taken out in turn. A levy was organized among everybody else to cover the wages of these two groups while they were out.

In general this tactic worked well, as it did in Wolverhampton and most of the other sites, but not all unions responded with equal commitment. For example it took some time and patience before ASTMS would fully participate in the industrial sanctions and at times the Liaison Committee had to cool down a growing antagonism towards ASTMS, which was known as "the foremen's union". "Points to remember" were sent to every union representative and put on every notice-board at the beginning of the campaign. They included the following:

> That although ASTMS, at this time, are not applying sanctions, they are still considering. Don't let's get too emotional just because they're "bloody foremen". They were fully involved in yesterday's meeting taking part in the discussion, offering suggestions, and they could possibly have voted with us if we hadn't have had that unfortunate interruption.

We have come a *long way* in a *short time*, don't let prejudice stand in our way. Once we split we're "knackered" and the rest of Aerospace is as well.

That ASTMS stated at yesterday's meeting they would not provoke any of your members when you apply sanctions.

That ASTMS members are paying a levy.

The ASTMS members did finally give more active support to the campaign.

As the sanctions increasingly undermined management's ability to keep production going, the site personnel manager became increasingly frustrated. He tried to undermine the campaign. Ernie Poland, the TGWU convenor, described his tactics:

He'd burst into our meetings saying that they'd been able to get the redundancies which they'd asked for in other sites so we might as well give up our sanctions. We'd ring up Burnley and the others and find that management had been saying the same thing to them about us! So of course we kept the sanctions on.

This points to the importance of the mutual support built up through the national Combine Committee. The Combine Committee's role in the campaign was very important indeed. First, it co-ordinated the campaign on a day-to-day basis. Pat McSharry of the TGWU says: "We were on the phone daily to Ernie. What we did here went on at every other site. And Ernie would know what exactly was going on in the other sites, he knew which you could rely on and which were ropy." Secondly, the Combine kept the campaign together in a more strategic sense. Representatives from all the sites had agreed that this was an occasion where the Combine had to take on a negotiating role. If negotiations were to be allowed to take place on management's terms, in this instance at a site level, the campaign would be defeated. Sites would be easily divided. So whenever local management started pressing for local negotiations the site committees turned them down, insisting that sanctions would not be lifted until negotiations had been carried through with the national Combine Committee.

At Birmingham this commitment to national negotiations proved very important. By mid-February 1974, management tried again to have the sanctions lifted. They put out a statement that enough volunteers for redundancy had come forward and therefore normal work should take place. The Liaison Committee were able to show that in fact not even half the numbers that management wanted had volunteered. The Birmingham committee then insisted that: "Sanctions will remain until a mutually agreed negotiation has been conducted between the national Combine Shop Stewards' Committee and the Board of Directors." The insistence on national negotiations was sustained at every site. The industrial sanctions were working, and the levies for those on strike were still flowing in. By the end of February, management were looking for a face-saving solution. They agreed to meet the national Combine executive. At the meeting they agreed to withdraw all compulsory redundancy notices, on the grounds that they had found enough volunteers. The Combine Committee accepted the management's retreat and recommended to the site committees that they end the strikes. The bans on overtime and on sub-contracting outside of the company, however, were maintained. In the meantime the Combine did its own sums on the basis of information from the sites. On their calculations the number of volunteers came to three hundred, five hundred short of management's target.

For management this defeat over its redundancy plans was as serious, if not more so, than the Burnley strike, where the Combine had successfully challenged their right to put limits on wage increases. Now the Combine had successfully challenged management's more sacred right to determine how many people they would employ.

From that point on management began to seek new ways of defending its prerogatives. Up till then management had always been wary of the Combine, but management also saw it as an opportunity which they hoped they could use to establish a national consultative body. They were even heard to talk of a "Lucas Aerospace union". However, the Combine's refusal to participate in the latest redundancies and its success in blocking the majority of these redundancies led the personnel director and others to rethink their strategy. It was with the publication of the Combine's Corporate Plan that the company's tactics finally moved away from an attempt to live with the Combine, to an attempt to destroy it.

While management was licking the wounds of defeat, the Combine were not satisfied that they had found an adequate strategy to resist the destruction of jobs. The fact that they had stalled management's plans and in doing so developed a united organization were achievements to be proud of. But 300 jobs had gone, through volunteers and early retirement, and more would undoubtedly soon go in the same way. The problem was not lack of orders: order books had been full even as the redundancies were being announced. Reports from all the sites even indicated that the company was pressing for widespread overtime and was sub-contracting a large volume of work. The job loss was rather the consequence of management's restructuring of both its production process — towards longer production runs, more computer-controlled machines — and its investment in other European countries and the United States. The Combine discussed these tendencies. They believed they were confronting a new form of unemployment against which the traditional tactics of the trade-union movement had, in their own experience (the Willesden occupation and the recent campaign), proved to be inadequate. It was this kind of thinking which led a year or so later to their Corporate Plan.

7   Expertise and self-reliance

"We could see changes were going to come about so in order to be ready for them we began to equip ourselves." Danny Conroy was referring to the issue of pensions; but he could also have been talking about new technologies or about the recession. For the impact of the Combine Committee was not only a result of its capacity to support and co-ordinate industrial action. It was also a consequence of the Combine's ability to produce its own experts and to make use of outside experts, in order to educate and prepare itself well in advance of the need to take action. The Combine's work on pensions illustrates this ability.

It was the Crossman Pensions Bill of 1969 which first stimulated an interest in pensions among several Combine delegates. This Bill proposed for the first time an earnings-related state scheme instead of the basic subsistence-level flat rate which had been provided in the past. It also accepted the principle of private occupational pensions schemes, although it did not make detailed proposals about the conditions which employers would have to meet to contract-out of the state scheme. The Labour government was defeated before the Crossman Bill ever became an Act. But Combine members believed that legislation was bound to come in the near future which would, unintentionally perhaps, lead to trade unions becoming more involved with the problem of pensions. In the past trade unionists had seen pensions as primarily the responsibility of the Labour Party because it concerned state policy. But with the possible move of employers towards contracting out of the state scheme — encouraged further by the Joseph Act of 1973 — trade unions were going to have to make pensions a part of collective bargaining.

There were further reasons for the Combine's interest in pensions in the early 1970s. First there was the alarming rate at which the value of already inadequate pensions was being eroded by inflation. Secondly, the different companies which had been taken over to form Lucas Aerospace had a wide range of pension schemes. Shop stewards anticipated that Lucas management would want to develop a unified scheme. The Combine wanted to have their own proposals worked out and campaigned for well in advance.

Where could the Combine turn to for advice on this important matter? The national trade unions only really started to allocate research resources to the problem several years later, in 1975, with the passing of Barbara Castle's pension legislation. For instance, the first union to establish a pensions department (of three researchers and two secretaries) was the GMWU, and that was in 1975. The TUC did not start to produce literature and organize courses on the issue until 1976. So in 1972 the Combine had to look to its own resources. It looked not simply to its regular delegates but to other trade-unionists. Someone who had long been interested in pensions was Roy Middleton, a member of AUEW-TASS employed in the Works Study Department in Burnley. His interest arose as much from his Christian ethics and his activity in the local Presbyterian church as from his involvement in the union. "As part of my church duties I visited old people in the Lancashire area. I was shocked by the poverty that many of them lived in. Very few Lancashire industries had pensions for works people. I felt this was an issue I could do something about. You can't change the world but you can achieve things in the small area you know." Through Danny Conroy the Combine asked Roy Middleton to become their pension advisor, and to set up a Pension Advisory Committee whose first job would be to educate Combine delegates in the basic technical detail necessary for campaigning and negotiating.

The Combine Committee provided an ideal forum for this early preparatory stage of trade-union initiatives on pensions. Pensions are a national issue affecting all unions; a national multi-union organization is therefore the best context in which to develop policies. The Combine's direct relationship to factory committees was also an advantage, because the more directly the discussions on pensions fed back to the factory, the more power any negotiations would have behind them. The way the Combine conducted its meetings was important too: it could always set aside time at its quarterly Wortley Hall weekends, away from the immediate pressure of negotiations, to educate itself on the issue. The Combine pensions adviser made use of this and held a series of what were in effect "teach-ins" where, complete with a blackboard and hand-outs, he explained how pension funds were controlled, what actuaries did, and what were the interests and ploys of the company in running their own pensions scheme. A delegate commented on the importance of these educational sessions:

It helped us to negotiate with confidence. The trade-union side can be undermined when the company fetch in an actuary saying that he looks after pensions. You think he must be awfully clever, one of those special extraordinary people. In fact he's no more than a mathematician, working with a computer. When we started dealing with these sorts of people with the knowledge we'd got through the Combine, we found much to our surprise that they were lacking.

This self-education also provided the basis for drawing up a strategy and a set of targets. These involved both issues of structure, control and accountability of the pensions funds and issues concerning the pension itself, how the benefit was calculated, who was entitled to it, on what conditions and how much the employer should contribute.

The control of pensions quickly became a burning issue when people discovered the amount of money involved. In 1973 the works fund and the staff fund in Lucas Aerospace together came to £108 million, which was totally under the control of company-appointed trustees. The idea of trade-union trustees elected by and accountable to the workers was unthinkable. The company had only just in 1968 eliminated a clause in their trust deeds entitled "Forfeiture of pensions", which said among other things:

Rule 28 (i) The trustees may if in the exercise of their absolute discretion they shall think fit so to do forfeit and discontinue the pension payable to any pensioner who

(a) Discloses any secret or confidential information acquired by him while in the service of the companies

(b) Without the consent in writing of the company by whom such pensioner was employed enters any occupation or employment competing with the business

(c) Does any other act or thing which in the opinion of the trustees is inimical to the interest of any of the companies. . . .

(ii) In the event of the pension payable to any pensioner being forfeited and discontinued any pension payable under the provision of rule 11 to his widow if she survives him shall also be forfeited. . . .

For directors who had only recently abided by clauses such as these, the Combine's target of elected or trade-union nominated trustees accountable to a trade-union pension negotiating committee must have come as a nasty shock. It is no wonder that the company's most powerful pensions man, A.J. Nicol, stormed out of a meeting with trade-union representatives.

As far as the pension itself was concerned the targets set by the trade-union advisory committee were equally radical. There were two pension funds: one for "the works" and one for the staff. While the arrangements for staff were not good, they were better than the works scheme. The Combine's long-term target, as with sick pay, was to eliminate the inequalities between staff and shop-floor workers, which would involve eventually combining the two funds. In the meantime they decided to press for a scheme that would be based on the worker's final salary plus years of service. This was instead of a flat rate based on years of service. Equal pension rights for women was also an important target. The original scheme gave women less than half the male pension rate.

Staff pensions were already based on the final salary but on a very low proportion of this salary. The company's contribution to the scheme was also low, even compared with the schemes of other companies. The Combine set a negotiating target of at least two-thirds of the final salary, with employer contributions at least a 2:1 ratio to the contribution of employees.

The pensions campaign

With these and other detailed policies already worked out by mid-1973, the Lucas Aerospace shop stewards were in a strong position when later that year the company started moves toward a new unified pension scheme for the whole of Lucas Industries. The Lucas Aerospace Combine Committee could not directly negotiate on this issue. It had no wish to do so either, because it did not represent workers in other parts of Lucas. For the manual workers, a trade-union negotiating committee was elected of fifteen stewards from across Lucas Industries. On the staff side, a smaller group of three — one from each of the three main parts of Lucas — was elected to be the trade-union side of a Pensions Negotiating Committee. The

Combine's Pension Advisory Committee informally acted, as its name implies, as a "think tank" for the negotiators. But it and the Combine Committee as a whole also acted as a ginger group, making sure that the negotiators were backed up by a membership who understood the issues and would be prepared to take action if necessary. One way in which they got the issues over to the membership was through poster campaigns. Mona Cryer from APEX at Burnley recalls: "Posters were everywhere on noticeboards and walls. People were reading about pensions in the news-papers at this time [the time of Castle's legislation] so the two aspects connected. People really began to feel they could do something rather than just leave it to the supplementary benefit when they retire." The posters were so effective in fact that the company tried to pay the trade-union pension committees to remove them!

This combination of astute negotiating backed up by aggressive campaigning paid off. In 1975 *The Economist* was reporting that the outcome of pensions negotiations was going to have a substantial impact on Lucas's profits. The trade unions on the manual committee won their demands on the pension formula, on equal pensions for women and on the company's contribution. A measure of this success was that the new scheme would cost Lucas £3 million compared with the £1 million (1975 prices) of the old scheme. On the staff side too *The Economist* reported a development which would "make investment managers shift uneasily in their seats". The staff won the right to elect three of the seven trustees who have ultimate responsiblity for investing the £74 million in the fund. This fell short of equal representation between members and employers but, as *The Economist* puts it, "it is the thin edge of a very big wedge".

Soon after, the shop-floor negotiating committee drove the wedge in a bit further. They succeeded in getting trustees who were elected by, account-able to, and if possible part of, the fifteen-person trade-union negotiating team (which in turn was elected by the site shop stewards' committees). The "very big wedge" of course is the wedge that could open the door to workers' control or more widely social control over the investment institutions of which pension funds make up over 50 per cent.[1] It is a door which cannot be opened by groups of shop stewards alone; they will need political support. But shop stewards like those at Lucas can illustrate the possibilities and prepare the way for political action. Already they have amended the deeds of the staff pension fund to enable investments to be made which do not require an immediate return. And they have followed this up with discussions about investing in the West Midlands Enterprise Board to create jobs in an area where Lucas is fast destroying them.

The pensions campaign established a method of dealing with issues which became important later in the Corporate Plan. Jim Hulme, a TASS member for Wolverhampton, summed it up like this:

> Our work on pensions helped us approach things very deeply and very methodically. The one thing about pensions is that it couldn't be done

in a haphazard manner. There is a lot at stake. They involve masses of money. You've got to get your policies right in the first instance; you can't correct it the next year like you can with wages.

From pensions to technology

This emphasis on "approaching things deeply" led to the Combine setting up the Science and Technology Advisory Committee, created in 1974 to provide early warning and preparation for the problems arising from the introduction of a new technology or production process. Like the pensions advisory service it made use of the expertise of workers in Lucas Aerospace, among whom there was knowledge of advanced materials and production technologies. It also made use of members of the British Society for Social Responsibility in Science and the Socialist Medical Association, to which the Combine was affiliated.

The advisory committee acted as a resource for shop stewards at the different sites. If a problem came up concerning, as the minutes put it, "skill fragmentation, increased work tempo, job security, the dangers of shift working and possible hazards in the use of new processes and materials", the shop stewards concerned would contact Mike Cooley at Willesden, the convenor of the advisory committee, who would either deal with it himself or pass it on to other committee members. If it was a problem which needed more resources than were available to someone working full-time in the factory, then Cooley would contact a BSSRS member or other "socially responsible and sympathetic scientists and technologists" to use their academic resources to look into it. Information and suggestions would then be passed back to the site committee for use in negotiations.

Bargaining and legislation

The discussions about pensions and health and safety also contributed to the Combine's view of the relation between trade-union and government action, and led the Combine to emphasize the importance of *trade-union* action on social issues. Danny Conroy expressed the frustration many Combine members shared about the failure of the state to live up to the aspirations of many socialists, which the pensions issue brought to the fore:

> I've been working now since I was 20-odd for socialism to give me security in my old age. I am now rapidly approaching old age and there's no security there. The state is a massive machine which does not move if it doesn't want to. But over the company we have some bargaining power which we had to seize over pensions.

However, he did not think industrial bargaining power was enough. "We realized that the company would not bargain unless legislation forced it to. So Castle's legislation was helpful because it made the employers consult us, but we had to be ready to take it from there." The Combine carried over this idea of combining trade-union bargaining power and political support into their Plan for socially useful production.

III WORKERS PLAN TO MEET SOCIAL NEEDS

8 The origins of the alternative plan

By late 1974, Combine Committee delegates were in a self-confident mood. The October meeting included a discussion "to analyse the Combine's Achievements and Future Aims". The minutes of this discussion describe how delegates "felt that a really viable Combine structure now existed and that all sites had confidence in the Combine Committee on the one hand to formulate central policies and on the other hand to support them in the activities at each site without in any way undermining their authority". It was not that they felt they had all the answers to everything, just that they had the confidence now to move on to new ground in search of the answers.

The most difficult problem they faced was that of job loss. Although militant defensive campaigns had had some short-run successes, the number of workers still fell. Defensive strength was not enough. Management was able increasingly to slip out of the net of trade-union control by its international investment policies. The Combine Committee attempted to expand its organization in order to keep up with the new power and flexibility which management gained by these global options. For instance, the Combine established contacts with French and Spanish trade unionists. However, it became clear that the company would try to carry through further rationalization plans long before any effective industrial organization could be built at an international level. The Combine needed an additional strategy in the meantime.

At the march 1974 meeting, Combine delegates had unanimously agreed that "the necessity for a policy on redundancy" should be placed on the next agenda. At the same time, the Combine had heard about the proposals to nationalize the aircraft industry, drawn up by a working party of the Labour Party, the Confederation of Shipbuilding and Engineering Industry and the TUC. No shop-floor or office representatives from the industry were on this working party. Nevertheless, the existence of these proposals stimulated the Combine Committee to approach the problem of unemployment in a more political way than ever before. The Combine executive initiated a discussion of nationalization and of workers' control through the pages of *Combine News*.

Initially there was a strong reaction among shop stewards' committees against the Combine discussing political issues such as nationalization. Several shop stewards complained that *Combine News* was becoming more "like the *Daily Worker*" than a combine newspaper. In the course of a heated argument, Albert Hodson, a TGWU shop steward from the Spring Road Factory, Birmingham, gave his reply to this accusation (which was vociferously expressed at the Birmingham site):

> I would like to say here and now that you can't divorce politics from trade unionism. Look, you can't separate the political aspirations of a

company director from the company. We've just had an example of it
here. Sir Bernard Scott [chairman of Lucas Industries] made a public
statement about the Common Market which was a political statement.
And that's connected with his company strategy, isn't it?

We're in a new situation where politics is unavoidable. For instance,
the liquidity problem in the company is going to hit us hard. It will
mean political decisions from people like Tony Benn and whoever is in
power. You can't divide politics off . . . . We need to raise these
controversial issues which produce thought; from thought arises action.

The Combine Committee's thoughts on nationalization

The Labour Party's proposals concentrated on the airframe and aeroengine
sections of the industry, with little mention of the profitable companies
making components. It was clear that, left to its own devices, the Labour
government would not nationalize Lucas Aerospace or any other component company. Combine delegates, along with many other trade unionists throughout the aerospace industry, felt that the worst features of the
old approach to nationalization were all too present in the new proposals, in
spite of Labour politicians' declarations to the contrary. One of the fears
was expressed in the introduction to the Combine's alternative Plan:

> As trade unionists, we do not wish to see a relationship between the
> aerospace component firms and the nationalized sector of the industry
> which would be similar to the relationship of the equipment manu-
> facturers to the National Coal Board. Such a relationship would
> provide the opportunity for those who are hostile to nationalization to
> point out that the nationalized industries were economically
> unsuccessful whilst in practice they would cream off the research and
> development which was paid for by the tax-payer into component
> companies.

Another of the Combine's arguments was that in modern advanced
aircraft, the components and auxiliary systems often contributed to around
50 per cent of the total cost of an aircraft. Without nationalizing the
component companies, the government would be leaving out an
increasingly important part of the aerospace industry. Greater scope for
co-ordination and planning, a wider economic and technical base for
redeploying the skills and energies of aerospace workers in the event of a
fall in orders, and a better technical base for diversification into other
products would all be lost if Lucas Aerospace were not nationalized.

The argument which the Combine pressed most strongly was that the
company already received millions of pounds in government aid for which
management was not accountable to the tax-payer. In fact Lucas Aerospace, its profits and its dividends, would never have existed had it not
been for tax-payers' money. For instance, the development of Lucas's
capacity to make gas turbine engines was funded by the government.[1]
Nationalization would, Combine delegates believed, at least establish the
principle of public control over this money.

No Combine delegate believed that nationalization would solve the problems faced by workers in Lucas Aerospace, but they did believe it would provide more favourable conditions in which to fight for solutions. The battle lines would be clearer, the arguments for alternative work in place of redundancy would be stronger, and the possibility of appealing to the needs of the wider community would be greater. The Combine executive expressed its view in an article which initiated a debate about nationalization throughout the membership by arguing:

> Your Combine Committee is deeply aware of the problems National-ization would cause. We do believe that with the full involvement of all our members we could insist upon adequate safeguards against many of these. The advantages would be considerable, we would finally be working for our ultimate employers, and we could insist that they face directly the consequences of any cutbacks. (Now the employers chant, "It's not our fault — it's a government cutback.") We could insist that the skill talents of our members could be used on a whole range of ancillary products which the aircraft industry would be quite capable of handling. We could reduce the nagging insecurity which has overshadowed the industry for years, and start to give to the workforce in it a real sense of direction and purpose. We could begin to expand the product ranges the industry handles, to engage on socially useful products, such as monorails and hovercraft. We would be in a better position to create an industry where the skill and talent of our members used to the full, and in a much truer sense, is used in the interest of the nation as a whole. It would be at least a step in the right direction. [Combine News, September 1974.]

Thus the idea of socially useful work as an alternative to redundancy was already beginning to take shape.

These first discussions about nationalization in the spring and summer of 1974 led to a decison to present the case for nationalization of Lucas Aerospace to Tony Benn, Secretary of State for Industry. A meeting was arranged for November 1974. Every site was to send at least two repre-sentatives, one staff and one shop-floor. The two-and-a-half-hour meeting between the Combine delegation of thirty-four stewards and Tony Benn was unprecedented — and never to be repeated with the Lucas Aerospace Combine Committee. "There was great uneasiness in the office about my seeing them," commented Tony Benn. "My senior under-secretary in the Department hadn't even heard of the Confederation of Shipbuilding and Engineering Unions (CSEU), let alone shop stewards. The idea of talking to shop stewards then was anathema to most of the Civil Service. It was seen as a matter for the Department of Labour."[2] It was not only the Civil Service who was hostile to this direct contact between a minister and a shop stewards' combine committee, so too were some of the national trade-union leadership in engineering. Soon after this and other similar meetings, the CSEU executive passed a resolution stating that shop stewards must not make direct contact with government ministers. They must always go, via the district CSEU, through the national CSEU. The CSEU's insistence on controlling all contact between trade unionists in engineering and government ministers later proved to be a major difficulty for the Combine.

This first meeting managed to escape the normal web of red tape. The minister was impressed by the shop stewards' Combine:

> First of all they were very well organized. . . . secondly, what made it especially exciting was, here was a group who had done enough work to anticipate what was going to happen to them and wanted to see what could be done. Others, like shop stewards at Ferranti's and Alfred Herbert's, had come to me at the last minute saying their firm had gone bust and what could I do. But here was a group who had gone further and had some idea of what needed to be done.[2]

Benn replied to the Combine's case for nationalization by saying that the government's proposals for nationalization of the aircraft industry were not yet finalized. However, he told the delegation that he did not have the power to extend the proposals to cover Lucas Aerospace. Instead he suggested that the Combine Committee should, as their report of the meeting puts it, "be involved in drawing up a corporate strategy for Lucas Aerospace". The report of the meeting continues, "He (Benn) wondered if the Combine felt it would be desirable if he contacted the company to see if a tripartite meeting on this matter could be arranged". The delegates at the Whitehall meeting felt that the Combine was unlikely to want a tripartite discussion before a trade-union plan had been drawn up. However, the suggestion would be discussed at the sites and delegates would make their decision at the next Combine meeting.

The problem of management

When the delegation reported back to Combine members in 1975 at the January meeting, the discussion first focused on nationalization and what had gone wrong in the past. They concluded that a new approach was necessary and that they would have to embark on it, rather than wait for the politicians. This decision led them to face the problem of relations with management: would the process of drawing up a corporate plan undermine trade-union independence? The Combine's experience of dealings with the company in the past, over redundancies and over pensions, had produced a deeply rooted mistrust in Lucas Aerospace top management. Also the Combine's campaigns and advisory groups had built up a strong belief in self-reliance. An extensive information network had also been developed through the support the Combine received from people who worked in the accounts and planning offices, as well as those directly involved in production. The result was the impression to the outsider as well as to members, of a very professional workers' organization. In terms of organization and information there was little reason for the Combine to become dependent on management. However, the more complex problem of accepting, consciously or unconsciously, management's criteria of viability needed to be considered. Ron Mills, a TASS member from Birmingham, raised this:

> Management are now finding all kinds of ways to give us the impression that we are part of this crisis and that therefore we have to sit down with them and jointly solve the problem for them. You remember during the rationalization this time last year Mason said, "You want to look at the books, I'll show you our profits are very low." He then said that we could manage the redundancy, that's what he said, "You manage it." In other words, we should go round and if we see that old Bill's getting a bit slow in this great dynamic industry, we had better get rid of him. We have spent years fighting precisely that sort of brutality, and yet that's the position we would be put in.

Ron Mills was pointing to a problem that invariably faces trade-union attempts to have some positive effect on management's major decisions, on investment, technology, products and work organization: so long as the economy is predominantly in the hands of competing groups of managers and financiers, how can trade-union plans for production avoid succumbing to exactly the same pressures that lie behind management's decisions?

In this situation a workers' corporate plan would end up only marginally different from management's corporate plan. Mike Cooley suggested an idea which in a general way was expressed in the speeches of many delegates — the idea of drawing up a production plan to meet the needs of those nationally and internationally who suffer through lack of market power and inadequate social provisions:

> Now I think that the only way in which we could be involved in a corporate plan would be if we drew it up in a way which challenged the private profit motive of the company and instead talked in terms of social profit. Suppose we started to say we wouldn't allow the kidney machines to go. They are trying to get rid of them by selling off Bradley's. Or take the technology that is used to make the actuators on (aeroplane) flaps: those small mechanisms could be used to make artificial limbs for crippled people. If we proposed socially useful products, what would be said then? It is at this stage of the game that you see who really controls the industry. . . . I think it is an insult to our skill and intelligence that we can produce a Concorde, and not enough paraffin heaters for all the old-age pensioners who are dying in the cold. We have to look at these things now if we are going to do the Plan. In my view, the only way we could do it would be in a way that was completely independent of the company.

The minutes of the meeting record a sense of uncertainty about whether such a plan was possible: "There were deep reservations about getting involved in a corporate plan." A crucial factor in overcoming these doubts was the offer of practical support which had come from Tony Benn. Moreover they believed that if they did not follow up Benn's suggestion and draw up an alternative plan to put to the government, then the company would continue to pursue its own plans and make deals without regard for the interests of the workforce. The Combine realized that their members would, with some justice, feel they had been let down if they failed to develop their own plan.

To go through with an alternative plan based on fundamentally different economic criteria from those of Lucas's management would mean conflict. Recognizing this, delegates argued that the Plan would have to be put forward in negotiating framework. It would involve an extension of collective bargaining rather than joint decision-making or "participation". Stan Kelly from Liverpool put it starkly: "Certainly we would be in a situation of conflict. But in my view there will always be conflict with private enterprise and management on behalf of your members."

In one sense, the Plan was an extension of the accustomed work of a shop steward, but in this extension the Combine was about to embark on something new, with unknown consequences. Chick Hartman from Hemel Hempstead remarked: "I think we all recognize that we'll be walking a tightrope if we start this Corporate Plan. I don't see any other way, but we'll have to realize that we'll be learning all the time."

In view of the far-reaching importance of the Combine initiative it is worth standing back for a moment to consider the influences that led them to take it in spite of the risks and uncertainties.

Political influences

We have explained the broader context, in which structural unemployment was growing but traditional trade instruments had proved inadequate. Nevertheless there was still a mood of industrial self-confidence following the trade-union victories against the Heath government. This militancy had helped to power a Labour government on a manifesto that included cuts in defence expenditure and nationalization of the aerospace industry. What of the influences of Combine members on each other? John Elliott, an industrial journalist on the *Financial Times*, identifies one man, the "highly articulate far-left-wing trade-unionist Mike Cooley", as the crucial political influence: "a combination of Cooley's political fervour and the fear of redundancies led to the production of the plan."[3] The Combine Committee itself, as an association of thoughtful individuals with diverse political beliefs united by common problems and interests, does not figure in Elliott's analysis. Mike Cooley's political views, especially his sympathy for the Maoist tradition of self-activity and mass involvement, with its stress on socialists remaining at the base of the popular organizations rather than being absorbed into the superstructure, were indeed an important influence in the discussion. But so too were the views and experience of Jack Gunter, a long-time member of the Communist Party in Birmingham, with his ability to draw lessons from historical experience and his commitment to communist principles combined with an openness as to the forms through which they should be expressed. Danny Conroy, a supporter of the left of the Labour Party, shared a similar combination of stubbornness on matters of principle with an openness to new ideas about tactics and form. He was also a shrewd judge of the mood and the potential of his members. Mick Cooney from Burnley introduced a particularly confident, improvising and in some ways entrepreneurial approach into the discussion. His politics were totally intertwined with his trade unionism and he, like the majority of Combine delegates, did not belong to any political party, although he would support the Labour Party when it came to a choice. Thirty to forty individuals made important contributions to the politics of the Combine Committee in 1974 and 1975. Their contribution was not so visible to the public as that of Mike Cooley, but to ignore the genuinely collective way in which ideas were developed during those weekends at Wortley Hall, and at shop stewards' meetings, on the phone, in the car travelling to meetings, in the pub after meetings and at the Combine executive beforehand, is to grossly underestimate the Combine Committee. For the roots of the Combine's initiative lie in the history, continuity and political culture of the Combine Committee itself, in which the influences of many different individuals were at work.

Over the Combine's six-year history, delegates had developed many shared understandings and criteria by which to arrive at political decisions. Understandings about the workings of the state under the Labour and Tory governments (particularly from the IRC experience); understandings about the operations of financial institutions (from the campaigns over the Lucas pension fund); understandings about management's use of technology (from the initiatives of the technology and scientific advisory committee); understandings of the social uses of their own skills (from their discussions about problems in their local communities); and understandings about the purpose and strategies of management. Without amounting to an agreed politics as may be found in a political party, all this provided the basis for an independent and innovative response to industrial policies put forward by politicians. The proposals coming from the Labour Party, and in particular from Tony Benn, triggered off a process by which Combine members drew on these understandings to formulate an initiative with implications far beyond both their own trade-union organization and the political options available at the time.

Thus the idea of the Plan evolved pragmatically but on shared principles, with the Combine having, as one delegate had put it, "to learn as we go along". Following the January meeting in 1975, certainly, the executive had some quick learning to do if it was to carry out the Combine's mandate. There were no models to draw on, no trade-union handbooks on workers' plans.

9 Drawing up the Plan (January 1975 – January 1976)

After the Combine had decided to draw up an alternative Plan, the delegates went back to their shop stewards' committees to campaign for the recommendation. Terry Ford, an AUEW shop steward, described the initial response at Burnley:

> We came back to the sites and then we put to the joint shop stewards what we intended to do. We gave the outline of it. Don't forget we were on very strange ground, something that no shop stewards' committee had attempted before. As a general rule shop stewards at the first stage say, "Carry on with it, we'll review the situation as it goes along, and we'll see what emerges from it." Like the pensions campaign, it took some time in convincing people. The stewards' committee finally emerged and said, "We'll leave it to the executive to set the structure up." So the questionnaire and so on were designed by the executive. But the executive would not take one step without referring it to the sites.

Ernie Scarbrow gave an overall view based on the reports he received during the first three weeks after the Combine meeting.

> There was a hard core of stewards in just about every factory, in most cases staff and works, who knew what it was about and they did the explaining; and they found among their members that the idea of socially useful production was intuitively understandable. This period was the peak of the Combine Committee. Everybody did their best. They contributed differently, but they contributed their best.

There were only two sites where leading shop-floor stewards disagreed with the idea. One was Willesden, where the chairman of the Combine Committee, Jim Cooney, felt that the idea of an alternative corporate plan was far beyond the legitimate functions of a trade union. The other was Hemel Hempstead, where senior stewards also felt the initiative was too political. At these two sites formal discussion of the plan among shop-floor workers never went beyond the senior stewards; although at both sides the leading TASS members were enthusiastic and generated interest and support among a majority of the TASS members.

The Combine executive formed a "Corporate Plan sub-committee", consisting of Mike Cooley, Ernie Scarbrow, Danny Conroy, Phil Asquith and Jack Gunter, whose first move was to send out a questionnaire to all the shop stewards' and office committees. At first sight the questionnaire was straightforward enough, requesting information about the size of the factory, the number and type of machines, the details of the workforce and so on, and ending up with questions about alternative products and alternative ways of running the factory. In fact, though, the questionnaire led shop stewards to think in ways which were entirely new. Even the most mundane requests for information had this effect. Mick Cooney from Burnley described the significance of one of these questions:

They wanted to know what machine tools we had. It was quite amazing that no site knew what they had. The reason for this is that this information was for planning. Now planning production is a fundamental part of running a business. But management does the planning. Workers do the production. To do the alternative Corporate Plan we were having to think as if we were planning. It really made shop stewards sit up.

The questionnaire was in fact designed with a view to getting the stewards to sit up. The note accompanying it explained that "The planning process is as important as the plan itself because it involves questioning existing assumptions and generating alternative options." Some questions explicitly encouraged new lines of thought. These questions were very straightforward, almost naive. For example, "How could the plant be run by the workforce itself?" and "Could existing 'line' managers still be used?" The first of these two questions brought some confident replies. At the Shipley research centre the workers felt they could run the plant themselves "with ease". The problems, they said, would be non-union administrative staff and getting suitable contracts after present work was finished. From Burnley came the reply: "In our experience management is not a skill or craft. It is a command relationship, a habit picked up at public school, in the church or from the army. And we can well do without it." The final question asked, "Are there any socially useful products which your plant could design and manufacture?" to which some sites, for example Bradford and Birmingham, answered with a long list of suggestions and others, for example Burnley, concentrated on one or two.

At the majority of sites the shop stewards created a "Corporate Plan committee" which investigated the answers to questions of information and received ideas for alternative products. Notices were put up asking members for ideas. The overall idea of the Plan was explained at mass meetings, section meetings and in leaflets. It was not always easy for the Corporate Plan committee to meet during company time since its work did not count as "official union business". And involvement would have been restricted if they had held the meetings in the evenings. Consequently meeting time had to be snatched during lunch hours. At Burnley the committee used to hold its sessions, which were open to any member of any union who was interested, in the canteen on a Friday lunchtime and afternoon. It was an informal affair and sometimes none too sober; but over the six months during which the Plan was drawn up these Friday afternoon discussions led to a common commitment on the part of shop floor and staff to the ideas of the Plan. The personal closeness of the Burnley shop-floor and office stewards, in particular the fact that they knew each other's families and drank together, is one reason why the Burnley site has been the strongest base for the Corporate Plan among both shop-floor workers and staff.

But what were these discussions in the Burnley canteen, in the union room in Bradford and Birmingham, in Ernie Scarbrow's office at Willesden, the canteen in Liverpool, and the AUEW convenor's office in Luton actually about? On what basis did they answer the question about the social uses to which the machinery and skills at their plant could be put? To start with, what kind of machinery and skills were they working with?

Technology at Lucas Aerospace

Lucas Aerospace, as a modern high-technology-based company, is involved with a very wide range of technologies, spanning almost the whole of the engineering field. For example, it manufactures mechanical and electrical control equipment for aircraft flight controls (flaps and ailerons), aircraft electrical generating systems and associated electrical switch gear, jet engine ignition and fuel control systems, jet engine thrust-reversing systems (for braking), de-icing equipment and cockpit instrument lighting and display equipment.

The range of technical expertise required to produce these products is extensive: aerodynamics; stress and structural analysis; engineering design; mechanical, electrical and electronic engineering associated with hydraulic systems, servo-mechanisms and actuators for aircraft control systems and fluid control and combustion science for fuel management. The emphasis in aerospace is thus on technical flexibility and also on relatively short runs or batches rather than on mass production. Prototype projects are common.

In some cases it was fairly clear how some of the aerospace technologies could be utilized for other purposes. For example, the recirculating ballscrew (manufactured at Lucas-Rotax) is a device used for the precision control of aircraft flight controls (e.g. flaps) — but it can be, and is also used in industrial machine-tool control systems. Servo mechanisms generally can be used for remote control devices where remote precision control over the position and movement of some component or tool is required: for example, in undersea oil rig maintenance, mining or fire-fighting using robotic devices. Since the emphasis in aerospace is always on minimizing weight and size, some aerospace "remote control" expertise might also be expected to be relevant to the problems faced in the design of improved artificial limb controls.

Some other potential applications of aerospace technology are more obvious. For example, the Combine's Plan included proposals for developing windmill technology using aerospace aerodynamics and aerofoil design expertise as well as basic electrical and mechanical skills. Windmill production is an area in which aerospace firms in the UK and more notably in the USA have subsequently begun to be increasingly interested.[1] The more general mechanical, electrical and electronic skills of the Lucas work-force could have myriad other applications, many of which were suggested by the shop stewards. For example the Combine proposed to use their fluid-control expertise for the development of pumps and a control system for use with domestic solar-heat collecting units. Combine members also felt that much of their expertise in hydraulic systems could be used to provide power take-off for the rotor blade speed control in some types of windmill. Small "ducted fans" wind turbine systems are used in some aircraft to provide auxiliary power — essentially a small windmill tapping energy from the slipstream. These provided another potential area for development, that is ducted fan windmills (see technical glossary).

Lucas's experience with various types of small conventional power packs (used in aircraft) and fuel cells (used in spacecraft) could be put to a wide range of uses. So too could its knowledge of heat-pump technology. The Combine also felt that some of the expertise associated with aircraft blind-landing systems might prove relevant to the provision of sight substitution aids for the blind.

Salvaged from management's waste

Management itself had at one time made use of the varied potential of aerospace technology to diversify into non-aerospace products. In con ditions of boom and labour scarcity in the 1950s, management needed to ensure that it maintained a good team of technical workers in spite of periodic military cancellations. One way of doing this was to allow the design teams to develop civilian products until the defence orders picked up. Within Lucas, a heat pump, a guidance system for a road-rail vehicle, a total valve system for the gas or oil industry, and brake retarders for coaches and trains had all been developed in prototype, in one form or another, but they had never been given the resources to go into sustained production. One of the questions in the Combine's questionnaire was intended to gather information on these past products at each site, asking workers to assess the relevance of these products, both socially and technically, for the Combine's Corporate Plan.

Some of these past products, in modified form, were chosen as part of the Corporate Plan. In many cases they had originated as ideas by individual designers responding to a social need they believed they could meet. For example, one of the earlier diversification projects was an improved railway level-crossing barrier, the idea of a designer at Willesden. He had noticed the primitive and unsafe barriers used in many areas and decided that some of the aerospace technologies with which he worked could improve their safety. It was exactly this kind of experience and stimulus, spurred on by a collective determination to resist redundancy, which lay behind the ideas of the Combine's Corporate Plan. The difference, however, was that in the past the designers with ideas that could help to solve social problems were entirely dependent on management's goodwill for seeing the project through. They had no power with which to fight for resources for a socially important project once the "private" objectives of the company had squeezed it out. The same would be true of any proposal which a shop-floor worker put into the company's suggestion box. More often than not such a proposal would be stimulated by social concern, a concern about safety or a concern to reduce wastage. However, whether or not and how it was taken up would depend on the company's view of how its own best interests were to be met. Without the power of a workers' organization these private criteria could never be challenged. Workers seemed to realize this difference. At the Bradford site, for example, the suggestion box in the corner of the workers' entrance to the factory is gathering dust. Yet workers there proposed around fifty different ideas to the Corporate Plan committee set up by the shop stewards at Bradford.

The contradictions of armaments technology

In addition to these ideas from past experiences, the Combine was also able to draw on and give constructive vent to a more general frustration among designers and skilled workers with the limits on innovation in the arms industry. There are periods when the arms industry is the source of major technological advances and consequently a dynamic force within the economy. It could be argued that this was the case in the United States and Britain in the 1940s and '50s. But the conservatism of government defence departments and the armed forces on the demand side and the intense competition between a small number of prime contractors on the supply side produced an approach to technological change which holds back radical innovation. This combination of competing suppliers for a mono-polistic and traditionalist customer has for the last decade or so led to "trend innovation" rather than the more fundamental "product or process innovation". The race between the prime contractors is often a race to elaborate on the weapon systems first designed in the 1940s and '50s. Several writers on the arms industry have called this "baroque" technology. Mary Kaldor describes this as consisting "largely of improvements to a given set of performance characteristics. Submarines are faster, quieter, bigger, and have longer ranges. Aircraft have greater speed, more powerful thrust and bigger pay loads. . . ."[3] Morris Janowitze describes the routinization of innovation in the military establishment, which lies behind "baroque" technology in the armaments industry, as "a form, though a modified one, of technological conservatism. Whether the problem is missiles or manpower, planning towards the future tends to be a perfection of trends rather than an imaginative emphasis on revolutionary develop-ment."[4]

Lucas Aerospace, as a prime supplier of components to the prime con-tractors, is even more rigidly locked within this traditional thinking because it has to meet the technical requirements set by the prime contractors. It has even less scope to determine the direction of technical change. The result for any imaginative engineer who works for Lucas Aerospace is frustration. Their frustration is experienced in two ways: first, in having innovative projects turned down by higher management. Secondly, as the projects become more elaborate, the contribution of the individual engineer becomes more restricted, more fragmented and less satisfying.

Such experiences were and still are common to engineers in both the relatively routine research laboratories such as at Burnley and in the more high-level New Product Group which existed in Bradford in the early 1970s. This kind of frustration on the part of engineers did not provide the initial impetus behind the Plan. However, once the Combine, for trade-union and political reasons, set in motion an unofficial design process outside the constraints of the aerospace industry, some of the ideas behind this frustration were released. And even where engineers, especially more senior engineers, felt unable to contribute directly to the Plan, they looked upon it benignly and often provided indirect help — even if only by not being obstructive.

Cyril Silverton, an assistant principal engineer at Hemel Hempstead, is an example of a fairly senior engineer who became committed enough to the social objectives of the Plan to make a direct contribution. The idea of an alternative corporate plan based on social criteria struck a chord with his own thinking about the future of industry:

> Hearing my sons and their friends talk about industry worried me. Industry in its present state was clearly not going to attract good scientists and engineers. Young people see industry as authoritarian and wasteful; lacking in social purpose. I thought the Combine Committee's Corporate Plan would help to overcome that image, and I made several proposals.

Hemel Hempstead was a site where there was little activity around the Corporate Plan. As a result, Cyril Silverton made direct contact with the central Corporate Planning Committee — the sub-committee of the Combine executive — suggesting the idea of heat pumps using natural gas and an internal combustion engine. The original Lucas heat pumps made in Burnley were electrically powered, which would have made them very expensive to run. Gas-powered heat pumps would provide an ideal way of providing cheap heating. Silverton also suggested that Lucas could make small portable kidney dialysis machines. There were several other engineers like Silverton whose ideas had been inhibited by the rigidity of the company's priorities. In many instances they gave to the Corporate Plan ideas which the company not only had rejected, but had refused to make available to others on the grounds of commercial secrecy. Several of them were deeply angry about the wastage of funds, human skills and ideas which could have been of practical and social use, but which never saw the light of day simply because they did not conform with Lucas's priorities. In the past this was a grievance which they would not look to the trade unions to take up. But the Combine Committee's Corporate Plan enabled some of them to contribute to trade-union policy on the wider social and techno-logical concerns which before they had only talked about in worthy but powerless discussion societies.

Connections outside the factory

The process of drawing up the Corporate Plan involved the social interests and commitments of apprentices and shop-floor workers as well as design engineers. In fact at several sites, Burnley, Bradford and Luton, most of the initial ideas came from the shop floor; technical workers would often follow up these ideas by looking through technical journals for background information. In two cases local connections between the workforce and a local hospital or home for disabled people was an important stimulus. For instance, at the Wolverhampton site there had been a long connection between a nearby handicapped children's centre and a charity club based in the factory. In 1966 one of the apprentices in the factory designed a vehicle which could be used by children at the centre suffering from spina bifida. He was able to mould the back of the cast to suit the shape of the child's back. The "Hobcart", as it was called, could have made a huge difference to the lives of these children had it been developed and manufactured on a large scale. Lucas would not consider it, even though the Australian Spina Bifida Association placed a large order. The apprentice, Mike Parry-Evans, did not at the time consider it was worthwhile to press the project on Lucas.

In the end the cart was made, with meagre resources and without the further development needed, at a borstal. This was just the kind of product which could be pressed for through the Combine's Corporate Plan. So although Mike Parry-Evans was in the United States his colleagues suggested that the Hobcart should be one of the proposals for the Plan.

At Bradford, too, there has been a robust tradition of charitable activities in support of a school for handicapped children: sponsored pub crawls, sponsored walks across the Pennines and so on. The connection between these and support for the Corporate Plan was not as direct as at Wolverhampton, but some of the individuals involved saw them as related. It seems that the Plan tapped some of the same social concern which led people to support the charities. Danny Broomhead, an AUEW steward, for instance, has been active in both. He explains:

> In my mind they went together when I first heard of the Corporate Plan. But I've shifted my involvement more towards the Corporate Plan and the Combine Committee. Charities are well and good, but they often feel like a drop in the ocean. With trade-union power behind some of their ideas I think you've got a greater chance of getting something done.

This is just one example of the way the drawing up of the Corporate Plan generated enthusiasm among workers for whom trade-union activity had never been a priority, who sometimes thought of trade unions as rather narrow in their horizons. The Plan often ended up drawing such people more deeply into the trade-union movement than they would ever have envisaged.

What about the experts?

The first sections of this chapter have sketched the background to the contribution of different groups of Lucas Aerospace workers to the alternative Plan. Before these contributions were complete the Combine executive requested practical suggestions from scientists and technologists outside Lucas Aerospace. Jack Gunter explains: "It seemed the obvious thing to do because these academics had been writing books for donkey's years telling everyone else what the solution to their problems were. We wanted solutions to our problems, so all of us thought it was right to contact these academics." Ernie Scarbrow sent a letter to around 180 organizations and individuals well known for their interest and expertise in alternative technologies, and in the use of technology in a socially responsible way. The letter set out the objective of the Combine's Corporate Plan, described the skills and equipment at Lucas Aerospace and concluded with a request:

> If you know of alternative technologies on which a workforce of this kind could become engaged, in particular if these technologies would be socially useful, we will be very pleased to discuss the matter with you further. We are particularly keen to see that the very considerable skill and ability of our members is used to solve the wide range of human problems we see about us.
> . . . We will greatly appreciate your advice and suggestions, and would, of course, treat your reply in confidence if you so wished. . . .

Out of the 180 to whom letters were sent, only three responded. Two of these, David Elliott, who was based in the Technology Faculty of the Open University, and Richard Fletcher of North-East London Polytechnic, had had previous informal contact with the Combine Committee through the Science and Technology Advisory Committee. The third was Professor Thring, who was working on remote-control devices at Queen Mary

College. Thring is a well-known advocate of humane engineering; he had developed ideas for robot mining systems as well as various innovative types of power packs for use in the Third World.[5] The inability of any other academic experts to respond to a practical request from a group outside their usual circles made the Combine cynical about talkers who lack practical involvement with what they talk about. Ernie Scarbrow wrote:

> . . . one of the things that disappointed us most was that in spite of years of talk about alternative technology only from three sources did we get anything positive or useful. The Corporate Plan . . . is therefore largely our own work and of course there is nothing wrong in that kind of self-sufficiency.

Nonetheless the Combine made considerable use of the three people who did respond.

At that time the idea of close relationships between academics and workers was unusual, though now this direct involvement of researchers with shop-floor and local trade-union groups has become more common. Each of the three people who responded provided details of alternative technologies they considered to be relevant. David Elliott outlined possible options as far as alternative energy was concerned, which were sent out to all the site committees for discussion in May 1975. Ernie Scarbrow's covering note gives an indication of the Combine's use of outside help:

> This particular section deals in the main with "Alternative Energy Sources" and is therefore quite technical and complex in parts. However, I am sure you will not be intimidated by this — certainly I always feel "common sense" is just as important in these matters as "technical expertise". We shall be selecting a number of potential alternative products from this section and would welcome your advice. . . . Please advise us as soon as possible which products could be designed, developed or manufactured on your site.

Richard Fletcher's proposals for a road-rail vehicle and Professor Thring's for telechiric devices were discussed and incorporated into the Plan on a similar basis. Thring's ideas on hybrid electric engines were also used, and subsequently the Lucas stewards informally provided technical help on the development of a test unit at Queen Mary College. The proposals from these sympathetic individuals were not, however, incorporated without modification. The Combine's response to some of the alternative energy options, which Elliott drew from "alternative technology" movement literature, was critical. The Combine felt that some of these would be relevant only to small "self-sufficient" experimental groups; they did not want to produce what one of them described as "gimmicks for individual architect-built houses" or "playthings for the middle class". In the next chapter we will see what alternative energy systems they believed would have a more widespread appeal.

The problem of time off and the dangers of victimization

Co-ordinating the input of these outside researchers, liaising between the sites and dealing with the growing press interest, all put a tremendous burden on Ernie Scarbow, the Combine secretary, and on other members of the executive. Few of them had separate offices or special facilities of their own, and they were not full-time trade-union officials. The company was ambiguous about the provision of facilities. Scarbrow had initially been allowed time off; but as the direction of the Plan became clearer, management became more restrictive. This meant that Scarbrow and others on the central Corporate Plan committee had to take whatever facilities they could. It also involved the risk that management would victimize leading members of the Combine, so the issue was discussed at length at the Combine meeting of March 1975. The discussion ended with the agreement that: "The secretary and those whom he delegated to help him should take facilities (room, telephone, duplicator, typewriter etc.) on the Willesden site and the rest of the Combine Committee would be prepared to support them if there were any consequences" (Combine Minutes). As we shall see later, this commitment was frequently put to the test.

The alternative Corporate Plan is proposed

By the time of their next meeting in October the Combine executive, in spite of the lack of adequate facilities, were ready to present the Corporate Plan. They had worked fast because the need for an alternative to redundancy was growing more urgent with each month's unemployment figures. By October, unemployment was as high as 9 or 10 per cent in the north of England; and in the Midlands, the centre of the post-war boom, unemployment had reached 7 per cent.

10 "A positive alternative to recession and redundancies"

An orthodox corporate planner would not recognize the Combine Committee's alternative Corporate Plan as a corporate plan. It is a "corporate plan" in the sense that just as management's corporate plan sets out the objectives and strategy of the company over, say, a five-year period, and on this basis makes its month-to-month operational decisions, so the Combine's Plan sets out the foreseeable needs, objectives and strategy for the workforce which then provides the basis for particular bargaining and campaigning positions. The Combine's Plan, however, has a different starting point and different objectives from those of a traditional corporate plan. Unlike management's corporate plan it does not start from an overriding commitment to increasing the dividends and the value of the shares of Lucas Industries. On the contrary, in the long run most Combine delegates would prefer to see Lucas Aerospace under some form of social ownership and democratic control. In the short and medium term the Combine's objectives are to fight for secure, useful and dignified jobs for all those who work at Lucas Aerospace; to create such jobs for those whose skills and energies are at present wasted; to establish training facilities for such jobs for youth and women who at present have limited access to skilled jobs; and to make products which help to solve rather than to exacerbate human problems.

The Combine Plan is more than a propaganda initiative: the specific proposals are negotiable, and its analysis lays the basis of the Combine's strategy.

Summary of the Plan

For the purpose of summarizing the Plan, it can be divided into four parts, although in actual fact these parts are interwoven throughout the Plan They are:

(i)   a documentation of the productive resources of Lucas Aerospace;
(ii)   an analysis of the problems and needs facing workers at Lucas Aerospace as a result of changes in the aerospace industry and the world economy;
(iii) an assessment of the social needs which the available resources could meet;
(iv)   detailed proposals about the products, the production process and the employment development programme which could contribute to meeting these different needs.

The Plan starts with a summary of the skills of the workforce, the numbers and type of machine tools and the research and development facilities at Lucas Aerospace. Full details were provided in the detailed appendices which backed up the main argument and proposals. The latter were presented at the Combine Committee in a fifty-page document. In what follows, we have drawn on the version of the Plan released to the press and the company in January 1976 which included a detailed section on alternative energy. A shorter version (without the energy section) was released to the public at the same time, and this, with a few omissions, was eventually published by the Institute for Workers' Control.[1]

Among the problems and needs facing workers at Lucas Aerospace at the time of the Corporate Plan, redundancy and recession loomed largest. These were seen partly as a consequence of problems specific to the aerospace industry: the effects of possible cuts in defence expenditure and of the "energy crisis" on the industry. The Combine Committee viewed the cuts in defence expenditure as both inevitable and desirable. Consequently a new strategy was required, otherwise, the Combine argued, workers in defence industries would be placed in the position of being made redundant or pressing for higher levels of defence expenditure.

As well as these internal problems in the aerospace industry there was the more general problem of industry tending to become capital-intensive rather than labour-intensive, leading to structural unemployment. The Combine documented the growing number of people facing the possibility of permanent unemployment in the United States and West Germany. It showed how the structural problems producing these figures are likely to be further compounded by the rationalization of the European Aerospace Industry within the Common Market. Moreover the Combine anticipated that Lucas Aerospace would attempt a rationalization programme with its associated companies in Europe.

Fear of losing their jobs was one problem facing Lucas Aerospace workers; the other problem which the Plan identified was the declining skill content and interest of the jobs which remained. The introduction to the Plan argues that the past seventy years had seen systematic efforts to fragment jobs into small, narrow functions and to perform them at an increased tempo. The introduction continues:

> This process which oddly is known as "Scientific Management", attempts to reduce the worker to a blind unthinking appendage to the machine or process in which he or she is working. . . .

The Combine identified with the resistance of workers whose work had long ago tied them to the pace and requirements of the machine. The Plan gives examples of the ways in which these workers are refusing to be treated as sub-human. In Volvo in Sweden, for instance, the labour turnover in 1969 was 52 per cent and absentee rate reached 30 per cent in some plants. In the United States the reaction has been even more dramatic; in General Motors' Lordstown plant, workers have directly sabotaged the computer-controlled production line.

As the Combine's Plan points out, these problems are not confined to the shop floor. The past ten years have seen the extension of various forms of

"Taylorism"* into the fields of white-collar and mental work. Already in the early 1970s it had become clear, the Combine argued, that management's attempts to replace human intelligence with machine intelligence by, for example, emphasizing the universal importance of computer-controlled machine tools as against human skill, have had disastrous results. One purpose of the Corporate Plan was to campaign for radical job re-design which would protect Combine members from this deskilling process and enable them to extend their skills.

The Plan then goes on to document social needs in the wider community, which Lucas has the technology to meet. It argues that "the aerospace industry is a particularly glaring example of the gap which exists between that which technology could provide and that which it actually does provide to meet the wide range of human problems with which Combine members were familiar from their own experience". The Plan then lists some of the ways the gap could be closed. These are divided into six major areas:
1. Medical equipment
2. Alternative energy sources
3. Transport systems
4. Braking systems
5. Oceanics
6. Telechiric — remote control — equipment.
The proposals within these areas are drawn from the 150 or so ideas which Combine delegates gathered together in response to the questionnaire.

---

* Frederick Winslow Taylor is the founder of "Scientific Management". He tells us "the workman is told minutely just what he is to do and how he is to do it and any improvement he makes upon the orders given to him is fatal to success". Taylor was not unaware of the implications of what he was doing and once said "that the requirements of a man for a manual job is that he shall be so stupid and so phlegmatic that he more nearly resembles in his mental make-up the ox than any other type".

1. Medical equipment

We propose that Lucas Aerospace should:

(i) increase production of kidney machines at G.E. Bradley's by approximately 40%, and look into the development of a portable kidney machine.* We regard it as scandalous that people could be dying for the want of a kidney machine when those who could be producing them and working them are facing the prospect of redundancy.

(ii) in conjunction with the Ministry of Health build up a "design for the disabled" unit to look into, among other things:

a) artificial limb control systems, which could use Lucas Aerospace control engineering expertise.

b) sight substituting aids for the blind, drawing on the radar technology involved in blind landing systems.

c) developing the "Hobcart"; the vehicle designed in the early 1960s by an apprentice at Lucas Aerospace at Wolverhampton to give mobility to children suffering from Spina Bifida, which Lucas had refused to develop on the grounds that it was incompatible with their product range.

(iii) manufacture an improved life-support system for ambulances. An ex-Lucas Aerospace engineer turned doctor has offered to help design and build a prototype of this, using a simple heat exchanger and pumping system.

2. Alternative energy technologies

One of the basic problems facing society is the scarcity of *energy resources*. The recent energy crisis has brought home to many people the political and economic insecurity of our advanced technological society, resting as it does on fossil fuel energy supplies, access to which is limited. And beyond this there are absolute and finite limits to the resources that are available, and to the capacity of the ecosystem to absorb pollutants and environmental degradation without undergoing irreversible changes.

Consequently there is a need to find not only new *sources* of energy but also new forms of energy use. New, renewable, sources and more efficient methods of conversion must be developed.

Solutions to the problem based on nuclear power give rise to new problems of health, safety and even survival. Instead R & D should focus on new sources of energy and new types of energy conversion transmission and storage. Such long-term investment in technological development would, in addition to its intrinsic benefits, help to reflate the economy; and the development of alternative energy systems would relieve the balance of payments problem by reducing oil imports and

---

* In 1975 the Combine had worked with the unions and the local trades council and local hospital workers to prevent the company selling off its kidney machine division to a large international monopoly.

perhaps also enlarging exports of these systems.

The following are some proposals for energy-related products which could be produced or partially produced with the resources available at Lucas Aerospace.

(i) Development and production of *heat pump* units. Heat pumps are potentially a very efficient and economical form of heating. They operate like a refrigerator in reverse. Instead of pumping out the heat from the air in an insulated cabinet, they absorb heat from a thermal mass (whether air, water or soil) and provide heat for warming air or water in an insulated space (e.g. a house). Heat pumps do not *generate* energy, only convert it: they require fuel in order to pump heat from "cold" to "hot". But they can deliver up to three times more heat than would be produced if the fuel was

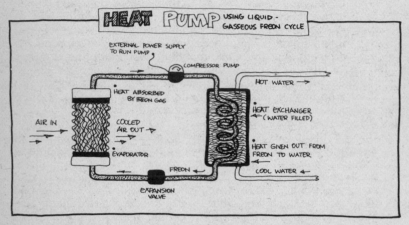

burnt conventionally. Local authorities would be interested in heat pumps to provide cheaper heating for council tenants. Lucas used to produce electric heat pumps itself, but this product line was not developed.

(ii) Development of existing solar-cell technology (Lucas Marine are marketing solar cells for use in boats and caravans) and flat-plate solar collectors to provide for low-energy housing. Lucas workers' main contribution would be likely to be in the associated electrical and mechanical control equipment; for example, switching circuits and fluid control systems.

(iii) Development of *windmills* both for electricity generation and direct (friction) heating, using Lucas Aerospace's expertise in aerodynamics. We suggest ducted-fan windmills and pneumatic power transmission systems as possibilities, together with rotor speed regulation systems.

(iv) Development of *fuel cell* technology. Fuel cells, widely used in spacecraft, work like electrolysis in reverse: hydrogen or natural gas is fed into a chemical cell that produces electricity. Units for domestic use had already been developed in the USA.

(v) A flexible power pack which could provide power for a wide range of purposes, e.g. generating electricity, pumping water, lifting equipment, and providing compressed air for pneumatic tools. It has a basic prime mover which could run on a wide range of fuels including naturally available materials, methane gas and so on. It also has a specially designed variable-speed gearbox so that it is possible to vary the output speed over a very wide range. This power pack would be especially appropriate for people in many Third World countries. At present there is no such flexible pack available. Instead people have to buy different packs complete with different prime movers for each purpose. The Combine Committee sees the present situation in relation to power packs as an example of the neo-colonialist nature of our trade with Third World countries.

3. Transport technologies
(i) Road-rail vehicle

We propose the development and production of a complete wheel and axle unit for a lightweight coach which would run on road and rail, combining two important innovations. By using a small guidewheel running on the rail, with servo-mechanism feedback to the running wheels, the wheel can be steered along the track while pneumatic tyres run on the rails. As a result there is not the same problem of shock absorption as there is for traditional trains running on metal rims. And therefore it is no longer necessary to have the heavy, costly, rigid superstructure which has always been necessary to absorb shock. Not only does this lightweight vehicle make it easier to follow the natural terrain of a country in laying down tracks, it also makes these tracks cheaper *and* makes it possible to go easily from the rail to the road. This lays the basis for integrated transport systems and better transport facilities for remote areas. We propose that Lucas make contact with Richard Fletcher of North East London Polytechnic who has been working on these ideas.

(ii) A new hybrid power pack for motor vehicles

The Combine sees pollution and toxic emissions from cars as a major ecological problem. It is also concerned at the expense and scarcity of fuel as further disadvantages of the traditional wasteful ways in which cars use fuel. Battery-powered vehicles are often seen as a substitute, but they have their own problems as far as normal car use is concerned. It is necessary to recharge the battery at least every hundred miles. Furthermore it is necessary to carry a considerable weight of batteries. We propose a solution, drawn from the experience of the Ground Support Equipment Group of Lucas Aerospace. This group has had considerable experience in the packaging of coupled prime movers and generators. It has also developed considerable expertise in the silencing of units of this kind without greatly impairing the efficiency of the engine. On the basis of this kind of experience we propose that a hybrid system be evolved utilizing the internal-combustion engine connected to a generator which would charge the battery which in turn supplies the power to the electric motor driving the vehicle. Initial calculations suggest a 50 per cent fuel saving in such a hybrid. Such a system would greatly reduce atmospheric pollution — the toxic emissions would be reduced by some 70 to 80 per cent — and noise pollution would be reduced likewise. Such a power pack could last for 15 years or so. Maintenance services would have to be developed to repair and maintain them, thus requiring the creation of more skilled jobs. This is completely contrary to the whole ethos of existing automotive design which assumes the desirability of a virtually non-repairable throwaway product with all the terrible waste of energy and materials which that implies.

(iii) Airships

In Western Europe the pressure of urbanization and the density of population will mean that transport systems, other than rail and road, will increasingly be sought. There is a growing and understandable public hostility to conventional air traffic systems with the problems of air and noise pollution in the immediate vicinities of airports. These considerations and ones of economy are likely to give rise to a growing interest in airships, especially for cargo. Explosion hazards associated with hydrogen are likely to continue to make that an unsuitable lifting source, and helium is extremely expensive. Docking, loading and unloading problems are considerable. To release a load of 250 tons would require a release of nearly 9 million cubic feet of helium and cost something in the order of £100,000.

In addition there is growing concern as to the availability of helium in the future. The present rate of consumption of the resources of crude helium can only be expected to last for a few more decades. Given these problems the Plan suggests using a modified version of the vertical and horizontal vectoring power unit used in the Harrier jump-jet to control the loading and unloading position of the airship. This would avoid the costly

need to vent some of the helium in the ship before unloading. We suggest that Lucas could make a major contribution to this. It is proposed that direct contact should be made with Dr Edwin Mowforth and his team at Surrey University who are working on the problem of a viable airship.

4. Braking systems

In Britain public attention has been dramatically focused on the weaknesses of existing braking systems by the Yorkshire Coach disaster which claimed 32 lives in May of this year. The *Sunday Times* of 1 June stated: "Last week's crash might have been avoided if the coach had been equipped with an extra braking device such as an electro-magnetic retarder which is being fitted to an increasing number of coaches in this country." In fact it would appear that only 10 per cent of Britain's 75,000 buses and coaches actually have retarders fitted to them. There is, therefore, clearly a vast market available to Lucas if it adopts an imaginative approach to this problem. It is not suggested that Lucas should simply produce dynamometers, rather what is proposed is that they should analyse the whole nature of braking systems through a wide range of vehicles, including buses, coaches, articulated lorries, underground and overhead trains as used by British Rail. It is proposed that a braking system analysis and development team should be set up to take an overview of this problem.

We propose a combined electro-magnetic eddy current braking system — based on experience gained with dynamometers — coupled directly to a traditional mechanical brake based on a Lucas Girling disc. This could be fitted as a fail-safe auxiliary unit to heavy vehicles, trains, etc. This electro-braking system overcomes the fundamental weakness of normal mechanical brakes which is that when subjected to long braking periods they overheat and as a result the brake linings tend to temporarily lose their gripping qualities. Such systems also make it possible to store energy which would otherwise be lost during braking, for example in electric powered vehicles.

5. Oceanics

We suggest three main purposes for which the ocean bed is likely to be exploited on an increasing scale: the exploration and extraction of oil and natural gas; the collection of mineral-bearing nodules; and submarine agriculture. Lucas Aerospace workers could contribute to these different activities in the following ways:

(i)   with the use of existing Lucas Aerospace valve technology and ballscrew manufacturing facilities, to provide a complete valve operating and controlling system for North Sea oil work.

(ii) The generating and actuating systems for the submersible vehicles needed for all three kinds of underwater work. This would require Lucas Aerospace to enter working agreements with submersible manufacturers such as Vickers Oceanics.

(iii) Telechiric machines

Telechiric means "hands at distance", which would enable workers to carry out underwater operations by remote control. This is preferable to a robotic device which eliminates human improvization completely. The repair work involved in oil rigs clearly requires the kind of intuitive and flexible diagnostic skills to recognize and deal for instance with a barnacle on a vital nut, for which no computer can ever be adequately programmed! Telechiric devices have a wide range of applications for example in mining, and any other work in unsafe or unpleasant conditions.

Our support for such systems is based not only on a concern for safety but also on a desire to develop systems which enhance rather than eliminat human skill. From this point of view the importance of telechiric devices is that they are capable of mimicking in real time the actions of a skilled worker so that when the worker stops the system stops, and the worker is in control all the time. Thus the system does not "absorb" or "objectivize" human knowledge. It merely responds to it. It is therefore possible to link advanced technology with human skill to provide for human-centred equipment rather than equipment deskills, controls or even displaces the human being.

Given adequate research and development backing, human-centred systems could be designed for many fields of work. In the case of skilled machining such as turning, it would be possible to design analogic equipment which would enable the worker to "programme by doing". As with the telechiric device, the tacit knowledge — the sense of feel for the job — would be retained.

Socially useful production

At first the meaning given to the term "socially useful production" tended to be intuitive and implicit. As with many aspects of the Plan, the definitions and theories emerged from discussion of the practice and experience rather than the other way round. As the discussion developed Combine Committee delegates spelt out one approximate definition of a socially useful product.

— The product must not waste energy and raw materials, neither in its manufacture nor in its use.

— The product must be capable of being produced in a labour intensive manner so as not to give rise to structural unemployment.

— The product must lend itself to organizational forms within production which are non-alienating, and without authoritarian giving of orders. Instead, the work should be organized so as to link practical and theoretical tasks and allow for human creativity and enthusiasm.

The way that the shop stewards applied these criteria and identified social needs was inevitably somewhat *ad hoc*. The institutions for the kind of popularly based planning which they were initiating simply do not exist. The Lucas stewards would readily admit that they were improvising as best they could with the means available, that each of their proposals needed further research and, where possible, further direct discussion with the people for whose use the products were intended. The Combine Committee were not trying to lay down the law as to what was socially useful and what was not. However, the implication was that the basis on which choices are made at present about products and resources is no less arbitrary. The Lucas stewards illustrated that the present way in which product choices are made and market power is distributed leads to social needs going unmet, even when there are the resources to meet them. Options are closed off which are both technologically feasible and socially desirable. Consider for example the Combine's proposal for a hybrid vehicle. The technology for it has been known for decades. The need for it has existed for even longer. People would very likely have been buying it, had they had the option. The problem is they would not have been buying it in sufficient numbers for it to be profitable for the mass-production giant car firms to make the extra investment required. And the car industry is such that the giant mass-production firms determine the options which we face on the market. Until the energy crisis possibly makes the hybrid vehicle profitable for the major corporations, this option of a non-polluting town car is not available on the "free" market. The implication of this and many similar examples highlighted by the Lucas stewards is that products are not only things; their existence and their design are the consequence of social purposes and social values, however hidden and implicit these values often are.

The Lucas stewards are not the first to have challenged the social values behind product decisions. The disarmament movement challenges the production of the bomb; feminists have identified and challenged the degrading assumptions made about women in the decision to make, for instance, vaginal deodorants and in the marketing of many other cosmetics; and the anti-nuclear movement regards decisions about energy production as politically and morally loaded. The newness of the Lucas workers' initiative is that they are challenging these values *as producers* as well as as citizens, users and consumers. It is for this reason that their notion of socially useful production refers not only to products but also to the production process itself; which leads us to the final aspect of their Corporate Plan.

Employee development

At least one quarter of the Plan's proposals insist on an "employee development programme". In particular the Combine called for the creation of working organizations "in which the skill and ability of our manual and staff workers is continually used in closely integrated production teams, where all the experience and common sense of the shop-floor workers would be directly linked to the scientific knowledge of the technical staff" (Combine press release, January 1976). They also made proposals for retraining schemes for both blue- and white-collar workers, including women and young people, to help break down divisions and develop skills. In relation to retraining, the Plan argues that it is essential to develop "the capabilities of our people to meet the technological and sociological challenges which will come during the next few years". It proposes that "in the event of work shortage occurring before the alternative products have been introduced, the potential redundancy could be transformed into a positive breathing space during which re-education could act as a form of enlightened work-sharing".

On employee development, the Combine points out that there is no indication that the company is working on an adequate programme of apprenticeships and the intake of young people. It adds: "the company is making no attempt to employ women in technical jobs and, apart from the recruitment of these from outside, there are very many women doing routine jobs well below their existing capabilities. Quite apart from the desirability of countering these discriminating practices, the employment of women in the male-dominated areas would have an important 'humanizing' effect on science and technology." It concludes: "it is our view that the entire workforce, including semi-skilled and skilled workers are capable of retraining for jobs which would greatly extend the range of work they could undertake."

The Plan is agreed

These were the far-reaching proposals which the Combine executive brought together out of the different sites' contributions and presented for discussion at the Combine meeting in October 1975. Not surprisingly, given the scope of these proposals, several delegates expressed caution about immediately launching it publicly or presenting it to the company.

Delegates from Burnley and from Wolverhampton stressed that a lot more educational work needed to be done on the sites before their members would be in a position fully to support the Plan. So the final unanimous decision by the fifty-three delegates was that: "This Combine Shop Stewards' Committee accepts the concept of the Corporate Plan and will take it back to their sites and fight for its acceptance" (Minutes of October 1975). By the next Combine meeting in January 1976 the large majority of sites had expressed a commitment to the Plan and the Combine executive had worked out proposals for campaigning around it. The shop-floor committees at Hemel Hempstead, Coventry and Willesden opposed the Plan, although Hemel Hempstead and Coventry withdrew their opposition before the final vote. The Willesden shop stewards led by Jim Cooney, then chairman of the Combine, abstained in the vote and later Cooney wrote to dissociate himself and his seven shop stewards from the Corporate Plan, though he participated in public presentations of the Plan. (Only one Willesden AUEW shop steward has actively supported the Corporate Plan.)

Cooney's argument against the final Corporate Plan was that it represented a fundamental challenge to the assumptions both of Lucas Aerospace management and of our society as a whole. "It will change society," he is said to have exclaimed at the January Combine meeting. And he did not believe the Combine could or should go down such a path. Jack Gunter answered him with all the urgency that came from facing an immediate threat to jobs in his own site (the threat of closure was hanging over the Marston Green Lucas electronics factory in Birmingham):

> The problems of the way the Lucas Aerospace and the rest of industry is run is now with us. We cannot hold back hoping that someone else will solve it. It's not a theoretical question, an abstract debate about the proper and improper role of trade unions. Workers now have no alternative but to look for radical solutions. There is 7 per cent unemployment in the Midlands area. That's unprecedented in my memory.

This argument represented the first major division within the Combine Committee. It also heralded the parting of the ways between the old trade unionism and the new. The vast majority of the delegates were prepared to contribute towards the new. They did so with an air of confidence. In the introduction to the Plan they state:

> Trade unionists at the point of production through their contact with the real world of manufacturing and making things are conscious of the great economic power which workers have. This growing sense of confidence by working people to cope with the technological and social problems we see about us is in glaring contrast to the confusion and disarray of management, particularly in the highest echelons of industry.

Even more strikingly the Combine commented that "perhaps the most significant feature of the Corporate Plan is that trade unionists are attempt-

ing to transcend the narrow economism which has characterized trade-
union activity in the past and extend our demands to the extent of questioning the products on which we work and the way in which we work
upon them."

A transitional strategy

Although the Combine in this way was setting ambitious objectives which,
as it turned out, challenged some of the most powerful vested interests in
Britain, it had in mind a practical transitional strategy.

> It is not suggested in this report that Lucas Aerospace is going to cease
> to be deeply involved in the aerospace industry. We recognize,
> whether we like it or not, that the aerospace industry is going to
> remain a major part of the economic and technological activity of the
> so-called "technologically advanced nations". The intention is rather
> to suggest that alternative products should be introduced in a phased
> manner such that the tendency of the industry to contract would firstly
> be halted, and then gradually reversed as Lucas Aerospace diversified
> into these new fields.

The Combine's tactics were to negotiate for this diversification on the basis
of offering the company products that would be profitable along with
products which would meet urgent social needs without being profitable.
At the same time they would press the government to purchase these
socially useful products as alternatives to defence orders. To start these
negotiations delegates asked the executive to arrange a meeting with the
company at which representatives from all sites would present the broad
outline of the Plan within a negotiating framework. The executive was also
asked to arrange a meeting with the Secretary of State for Industry.

The Combine delegates who drafted the Plan (the executive's Corporate
Plan Committee) recognized the limits of these tactics so long as the
Combine Committee in Lucas Aerospace was working in isolation: "It is
certainly not the assumption of this Corporate Plan that Lucas Aerospace
can be transformed into a trail-blazer to transform this situation in
isolation. There can be no islands of responsibility and concern in the sea of
irresponsibility and depravity." At the January meeting the Combine
mapped a campaign to win the support of other trade unionists and to have
an influence on public opinion. It was agreed that the best approach to the
trade unions was through the district or divisional committees of each
union and through the TUC. In additional site committees agreed to
contact their MPs. Finally the Combine planned a press conference for the
end of January to launch the Plan publicly.

"I evolved with the Corporate Plan"

Before considering the consequences of all these decisions it is worth going
back to Chick Hartman's comment — "We're going to have to learn as we
go along". One of the most important lessons concerned the constraints
and obstacles which the Combine faced as it tried to implement the
Corporate Plan. There was also the self-confidence that Combine delegates

learnt in their own abilities and those of their members. What did delegates think during the first stages of the Plan, especially about how it would be implemented? Brian Salisbury, a Combine delegate from Birmingham for whom the learning process was especially important, said: "I evolved with the Corporate Plan. At the beginning I was just on the margins." His view of how the Plan would be implemented reflected a common assumption — that it would be like any other collective-bargaining process: "I imagined we'd draw it up and then present it to management, perhaps like a wage claim. I thought that as a result of the negotiations we would go back to the government together for funds for a negotiated plan."

Terry Moran, an AUEW steward from Burnley involved with the Combine since the first discussion of the Corporate Plan, has also been changed by the experience: "I must be a completely different person from the person I was six years ago. I used to think everything was Burnley. The Corporate Plan has broadened my horizons unbelievably." How did he feel then, six years ago, when the Plan was first discussed?

> Quite honestly, I thought the company would have welcomed it. I'd worked with the company almost all my working life. The people who represented the company in Burnley were people I know in the town. I'd been at school with them. I'd been to church with them. The parity strike had begun to make me aware that these were not really the people who ran the company. But, still, I did think the company would see the Corporate Plan as constructive trade unionism. I thought it would just happen.

Not everyone in the Combine thought it would be as easy as this. The Plan itself comments: "We recognize that (the Plan) is a fundamental challenge to many economic and ideological assumptions in our society . . . . no matter how many sections of workers in other industries take up these demands, progress can only be minimal so long as our society is based on the assumption that profits come first and people come last. Thus the question is a political one, whether we like it or not."

11 A question of power

On 9 January, in the conference room of the Lucas Aerospace Shaftmoor Lane factory, seven members of Lucas Aerospace top management received a delegation unlike any it had received before. Representatives of staff workers and shop-floor workers from every site, thirty-seven shop stewards in all, had come to present to management a plan for the long-term job security of their employees. In the two-hour meeting which followed, the shop stewards presented a summary of the Plan. They held back the technical details for each group of products until — as they hoped — negotiations had got underway.* This technical work, especially the work on those products which were likely to be profitable as well as socially useful, was one of the Combine's negotiating weapons. Unless the Combine kept it under their control, management would pick and choose from the Plan on its own terms, gaining a free consultancy service out of the Combine's work.

Another negotiating weapon, or so it was hoped, was support and even funding from the government. Combine delegates ended their presentation to the company with an offer of a joint approach to the government on the basis of proposals from the Corporate Plan:

> Now we have had meetings with the Department of Industry as you know, with Gerald Kaufman (this was over redundancies in Birmingham in December 1975). He asked us to come back to him again with the Corporate Plan in its completed form. The Department of Energy, Benn and others, want to meet us first as a department and then to meet some of their technical people, and the Department of Employment want us to meet to talk about a whole employee development programme. It seems to us that we have got to face the fact that there is going to be more government intervention, whether you like it or not. We think if handled properly it could be in the interests of all of us, because there are large sums of money about.
>
> The price for our co-operation is that we must see this as leading to long-term job security for our members, and a real involvement in saying how the future of our members should be structured. . . .

The personnel manager's reply was non-committal beyond accepting a copy of the Plan with a promise to consider it and come to a second meeting with a detailed reply. One or two of the technical management expressed genuine interest in the product proposals. However, in the following months it became clear that something other than the product proposals was on the minds of the managers with the power. The decisive factor for

---

* The proposals on energy were given because the company had already had access to a copy through a somewhat naive member of the alternative technology movement who had leaked it, evidently in the belief that this would bring the two sides together.

them was where the product proposals had come from. Bill Williams, a technical manager for Lucas Aerospace in Birmingham, summed up what was really at stake: "I'm quite sure personally that the issue was not the viability of the products from an engineering point of view: the real issue at stake was who manages Lucas."

Who manages Lucas was and still is a non-negotiable issue. And so too, as far as management was concerned, was the Corporate Plan. Management would not even meet the Combine to present their reply. The promised second meeting, initially arranged for 27 April, was cancelled. Moreover the reply was sent not to the Combine Committee exeucitve but to individual convenors, presumably to avoid de facto recognition of the Combine's Committee. Even Ernie Scarbrow, the secretary, did not officially receive a copy. The reply argued that the only way to secure jobs was to continue with the existing product range. It stated that the Combine's product proposals were not compatible with the company's product lines, since the company emphasized short runs of high added value products, whereas the Combine's ideas — as the company depicted them — implied a move to mass production of less sophisticated low added value products.*

Only the summary section — reproduced here — of the company's reply was made public, in May 1976; the rest was deemed "commercially sensitive". This latter part contained a brief review of the results of an earlier assessment of the potential for diversification made by the company, during which they claimed they had looked at many of the products in the Combine's Plan and rejected them. The summary section concluded by offering to consult on the issues raised in the reply through "local consultative machinery", ignoring completely the Combine's arguments for national negotiations.

COMPANY STATEMENT AND SUMMARY

The Combine Shop Stewards' committee presented a report entitled "The Corporate Plan" to the Company in January of this year. In its reply to that report the Company explains that it intends to concentrate on its traditional business which involves the development of aircraft systems and components for the aerospace and Defence industries.

The authors of the report suggest that there would be a contraction in the aerospace components industry as a result of successive Defence cuts, a trend which they regard as desirable. On this premise they believe that the Company should be protecting the jobs of its employees by diversifying into socially acceptable/useful products such as those indicated in the report.

---

* In fact this was truc only of a few of the products, such as the heat pump. This was proposed for a plant like Burnley which already made products with a lower value added.

The Company points out that the oil crisis had depressed the aircraft industry in common with many other industries, but that recent Defence cuts had not affected Lucas Aerospace to any great extent. The Company is actively engaged in widening its international markets. This activity, together with work-sharing projects with overseas companies, is generating more work for the factories within the United Kingdom. It cannot accept that aircraft, military and civil, do not have a social utility. Civil aircraft are needed for business and pleasure activities and it is necessary to maintain military aircraft for Defence.

The Company reminds the report's authors that it has a long-standing capability and reputation for producing a wide range of aerospace systems and components, and believes that the only way to secure jobs in the market economy is to manufacture the products which the Company is best at producing efficiently and profitably.

The Company strategy is to concentrate on work applicable to high technology aerospace and Defence industries, but it constantly reviews opportunities in non-aerospace fields where there is a related equivalent level of technology.

The Company proposes to widen the debate regarding some of the ideas in the report by referring these matters to the local consultative machinery, where elected plant representatives and local management can periodically review the order book and market trends at the point where the opportunities and difficulties can be properly identified.

Subsequently the company refuted "any suggestion that the whole plan had been turned down", referring to this consultation offer.

But it was not only the Combine which interpreted it as a rejection. For example, *The Engineer* (13 May 1976) commented: "with the total rejection of the Corporate Plan prepared by shop stewards at Lucas Aerospace factories, the firm's management may have scuttled potentially profitable ideas as well as a peaceful future".

The company's tactics shift

The company's emphasis on "local consultations" as opposed to national negotiations, and its subsequent refusal to meet the Combine to discuss the Plan, represented a considerable shift in tactics. From December 1971 until the presentation of the Corporate Plan the Combine had been able to arrange meetings with top management relatively easily. Four or five senior managers, including several directors, usually attended. The largest and most acrimonious meetings concerned workload, job security and the company's rationalization plans. The company tried to avoid meeting on any issue which concerned Lucas Industries as a whole, notably wages, fringe benefits and pensions. However, on several occasions campaigns on these issues forced management to meet the Combine. The meetings with management were often reported verbatim in *Combine News*. The Combine had wanted to tape-record them and play them back at the sites (rather as the Polish Union Solidarity had a principle of broadcasting or tape-recording its negotiations with the Polish government), but management prevented this. The Combine's questioning was aggressive and, judging from the verbatim reports, management appeared in a bad light. Moreover the Combine would consistently caricature management in order to ensure that they could not intimidate workers. A senior manager called Coop was nicknamed "Chicken Coop" after one occasion when, it is said, he was so scared by a group of workers who had taken action against a lock-out that he let his pipe fall from his mouth!

Nevertheless management continued to meet the Combine. Two factors must have entered into management's calculations about this approach. First, they needed a channel of communication with the unions across all the parts which made up the Lucas Aerospace. In other parts of Lucas Industries such channels had been built up over decades, to management's general satisfaction — despite a minority of plants who would not co-operate with the joint consultative bodies. Lucas Aerospace, on the other hand, was a new company. No such channels of communication existed. Yet, faced with the problems of integrating six different companies into one, management needed such channels. The Combine had established itself as a credible, representative body, before management could put down the roots of a Lucas-type national joint consultative system. Official union arrangements for meetings with central management were still haphazard. So at first management had little option but to meet with the Combine Committee. Moreover, traditionally Lucas preferred to deal with its own shop stewards rather than outside officials. In the other divisions Lucas had succeeded in creating a layer of senior shop stewards who co-operated with the company's consultative arrangements. If they persisted, management must have reasoned, could they not achieve the same with the Combine Committee in Lucas Aerospace? Sometimes their tactics for achieving this were none too subtle. Ernie Scarbrow tells what he found when he and Mike Cooley arrived early at the Combine's first meeting with management in 1971:

> We found that all the chairs were arranged in a circle. We wanted to make it clear that we were seeing management as part of a conflict. We weren't interested in cosy chats. So we proceeded to rearrange the chairs in opposite rows; to show the reality of the situation.

And in 1974 there was the company's offer to allow the Combine Committee to "manage" the redundancies; a tactic of building up the Combine's sense of its own importance, but making that importance

dependent on good relations with management. Had the offer been accepted, the company would, Ernie Scarbrow believes, have provided the Combine with facilities such as paid time off to meet during working hours. Even though the Combine did not co-operate, management continued to allow Scarbrow and Cooney, the secretary and chairman, facilities and time off far beyond what they needed for their local trade-union duties.

The signs of a shift in management's personnel tactics were apparent from 1975 onwards. For instance there would be many more obstacles in the way of meeting management as a Combine. The personnel manager put up all kinds of procedural difficulties which in the past had never existed, or had been bypassed. From the Combine Committee's point of view these began to look increasingly like attempts to divide the Combine. The first tactic was to try and establish different negotiations for the South and the North. The next was to refuse to allow staff to participate in certain meetings, even though the outcome concerned staff members. Another tactic was to argue that the factories covered by the new Defence Systems group, Premier Precision, G.E. Bradley's and Horstmann's, must be excluded from meetings between the Combine and management, even though the new group was not a manufacturing group, only a marketing group. Jim O'Neill, the convenor of the Joint Shop Steward's Committee at G.E. Bradley's, summed up the way things were going in a letter to *Combine News*: "It is time that both Aerospace and the Defence Systems sites faced up to the situation that the company is playing ducks and drakes with us, and is carving us up one at a time."

Other changes in management tactics were more subtle. It is only in retrospect that their significance has become clear. They include seemingly trivial things like the fact that the central personnel manager was always busy when Ernie Scarbrow called, and he never called him back in response to messages and so on. Yet at the same time the manager was always available to Jim Cooney, the Combine chairman, who during 1974 and 1975 seemed to distance himself from the Combine. Cooney was later, in 1977, to instigate a split from the Combine Committee. There is a lot of mystery surrounding Cooney's personal change of mind.* Although he opposed the Corporate Plan, his change in attitude pre-dated it. Those on the office committee at Willesden and the one or two manual stewards at Willesden who have remained committed to the Combine believe that management put some kind of pressure on him while he was convalescing from a heart attack in a company home at the company's expense in 1974.

The other shift in management's tactics was towards playing off national officials against the Combine Committee. Sometimes this was simply a matter of using the "official channels" as an excuse for not talking to the Combine Committee. For example this was given as the main reason why the company could not negotiate over the Corporate Plan: "We are anxious not to work through bodies which are not part of the recognized consultative machinery . . . this would damage official relations with the trade unions through the National and District Committees" (Company press release, 1977) — all this despite the fact that the company had regularly met with Combine representatives in the previous five years.

These shifts in tactics coincided with important changes in top management personnel. In 1974 Mr Coop, who had been the general manager at Burnley during the strike, became Manufacturing Director of Lucas Aerospace. He brought with him into top management Alan Whitney, the personnel manager at Burnley during the strike, who replaced Mason as group personnel manager in 1975. Coop had reason to feel particularly threatened by the Combine Committee. At Burnley he had been determined to see the strike out to the bitter end rather than concede. He had been overruled by central management. No doubt he never forgot this, and once he and Whitney were in positions of power, they followed a very much harder line towards the Combine Committee.

With this change in personnel came a change in the style of industrial relations in Lucas Aerospace. According to Combine delegates, Brian Mason had been "honest and fairly independent in his approach". "We had our disagreements," Scarbrow recalled, "but at least he was honest. We always knew where we were with him; whereas Whitney was a wheeler and dealer. In my opinion Mason would never, however informally, make deals with full-time officials in the way that I believe Whitney does." Such assessments can never, by the nature of the secrecy of large corporations, be "proved", but Scarbrow's view reflects that of many trade-union representatives in Lucas Aerospace. This change of personnel certainly contributed to the particularly defensive and short-sighted way in which management responded to the Corporate Plan.

The style of dealing with the Combine Committee might well have been

---

* He has refused to be interviewed and has no contact whatsoever with Combine delegates.

different if Brian Mason were still the personnel manager at Lucas Aerospace, but it is unlikely that the final, negative, outcome would have been different. One indication of this latter point is the support given to Whitney and Coop by the policy committee of Lucas Industries and by the chairman Sir Bernard Scott. When Bernard Scott was interviewed by the *Sunday Telegraph* two months after the company had given the Combine its reply, he allowed no room for negotiations: "The managing directors' job is to operate our corporate plan in a ruthless fashion. The plan is sacrosanct." (*Sunday Telegraph*, 19 July 1976). One reason why Sir Bernard Scott could be so confident, and why the hardliners in Aerospace had no difficulty in receiving his support, was because of changes that had taken place in the Labour government. The industrial policies talked about during the first year of the Labour government had caused some anxiety in the boardrooms of companies like Lucas, especially when the talking was being done by Tony Benn. Benn's talk was of compulsory planning agreements with trade-union involvement. The precise meaning of this may not have been clear but it would certainly have obliged Lucas to consider the Combine Committee's plan more seriously, if only to be sure of future government subsidies. By the beginning of 1975, however, Harold Wilson had allayed their fears. He had set up a cabinet committee under his own chairmanship to take charge of the direction of industrial policy. His main purpose in doing so was to restore business confidence. Planning agreements became voluntary and the trade-union role in them became an optional extra. In July 1975 Wilson moved the remaining obstacle: Tony Benn himself. So by 1976 when the shop stewards' plan, itself encouraged by the Labour Party's policies, was ready, management was under no pressure whatsoever to give it serious consideration. As a result the Combine had lost one of its most powerful negotiating levers.

Weaknesses in the Combine

How strong at this time (mid-1976) was the Combine's other major negotiating weapon, its industrial strength? Was the Combine Committee in a position to force the company to the negotiating table over proposals based on the Corporate Plan? Could the Combine organize an effective national campaign of industrial action around the proposals in the Plan as it had around the more defensive objectives of the 1974 redundancy campaign?

During 1975, management's hardline tactics, their closer liaison with certain full-time union officials and their attempts to exacerbate any source of division within the Combine had begun to have an effect. The fate of the Combine's campaign for index-linked wages in 1975 illustrates that management had learnt how to out-manoeuvre and make use of divisions between the Combine Committee and sections of the trade-union leadership.

The Indexing Campaign

The idea of a claim for monthly indexing came up at the Combine meeting of January 1975, during a discussion about the tactics to be used in the annual wages campaign. The effect of wage restraints and a rate of inflation of over 20 per cent meant that an increase of £15 across the board would be needed for workers simply to maintain their living standards. All delegates agreed that their members would not be prepared to take action for a claim of such a size. The need for a large claim would not be understood. However, if the claim took the form of monthly indexing related to the Retail Price Index, the logic of a high claim, given the rate of inflation, would be immediately apparent. Moreover, such a claim would be consistent at least with the letter of the Social Contract,* though no one expected that this would melt the company's opposition to the claim.

An advisory committee led by Tom Layko, an AUEW member in Burnley, was given the job of preparing both the case to management and the campaigning material for the membership. At the same time TASS shop stewards agreed to put the claim to the company at a regular meeting of their negotiating committee. A joint staff and shop-floor meeting with management was arranged but to no useful effect. Management turned down the proposal to negotiate over indexing without even giving a reason.

The Combine decided to organize a campaign of industrial sanctions to force management to negotiate over monthly indexing. By this time management had, as Tom Layko put it, "wakened up to the strength of the Combine and decided to break it". Management combined tough tactics with soft, very effectively.

The first seeds of division

After one month, when the industrial sanctions were beginning to hurt, management locked out the shop-floor workers at Wolverhampton — probably the weakest large site in the Combine. At the same time Alan Whitney was intimating that management was considering the possibility of central negotiations on wages with manual workers. He had already, with the agreement of Jim Cooney, insisted on the exclusion of the two staff members of the Combine executive from a meeting on wages. For several manual worker convenors, this offer of separate central negotiations was an attractive carrot. Others, in particular at Burnley and Bradford, considered this to be a diversion from the indexing campaign which would benefit staff and shop floor alike. And a diversion it proved to be. For although morale and commitment at Wolverhampton were high, the Combine found it very difficult to organize support from manual shop stewards' committees in some of the other sites. There was a lively poster and leaflet campaign, but convenors in Liverpool and at Willesden believed that separate central meetings with management on wages, without the staff, were more important than winning the indexation claim.

Whitney's informal offer to leading shop-floor convenors was one factor undermining a united campaign; the other factor came from the staff side.

---

* An agreement made in 1974 between the trade unions and Labour Party leadership under which unions would restrain wage claims in return (in theory) for a programme of social legislation.

The TASS members at Wolverhampton joined the shop-floor workers' occupation, expecting support on other sites. The indexing claim had been agreed by the conference of TASS representatives in Lucas Industries, so the Wolverhampton members were expecting the TASS national executive committee to give support to those taking action in line with an agreed policy. Instead, four days after the lock-out had begun, TASS representatives in Lucas Aerospace heard that the TASS national officer for Lucas had recommended to the TASS executive that "any TASS members responding to a strike call *not involving the TASS-EC in decision-taking* [emphasis added] will *not* be financially supported in any way."

This statement indicates a remarkably centralized and restrictive view of trade-union action. It rules out the idea of trade unions expressing immediate solidarity with the decisions and actions of others. It is no wonder that, as we shall see later, there was a continuing clash between AUEW-TASS and the united Combine Committee with its emphasis on initiatives from the base of the unions. In the case of the indexing campaign the implication was that because it was the Combine Committee which had originally recommended strike action in support of the Wolverhampton workers the TASS-EC should not support and implement the call. The Combine was not strong enough to lead an unofficial strike of TASS members, so in the absence of official TASS support the Wolverhampton workers were isolated and defeated. This defeat rebounded seriously on the unity of the Combine and caused shop-floor resentment towards the staff members on the Combine.

The minutes of the Combine's appraisal of the indexing campaign sum up the implications of this defeat:

> The company had succeeded in dividing the Combine into four, i.e. a works combine, a staff combine, the combine that meets in Wortley Hall, and the combine which the company is prepared to meet when it suits them.

As an organization able to co-ordinate sustained industrial action, the Combine Committee had thus been severely weakened by the company's attempt to woo leading manual convenors and by the hostile attitude of the leadership of AUEW-TASS. On wages the Combine has been unable to overcome these problems. On redundancies, however, the Combine Committee was able on the basis of its Corporate Plan to give a lead which for the time being neutralized both management's attempts to divide manual workers from staff and the hostility of the TASS leadership, though the Combine never re-established the industrial strength and confidence which it had reached at the time when it began to draw up the Corporate Plan.

12   Local victories: the Plan in action

The Combine wanted national rather than local negotiations on the Plan. This was because many of the proposed products required the integrated work of several plants. Indeed, this had been one criterion in the selection process, so as to make the best use of resources. Secondly, local negotiations would always be constrained by the major investment and strategic decisions at a national level. Thirdly, it was feared that local negotiations could be used to divide the Combine and hive off the "money-spinners" in the Plan. However, the Combine had to be flexible about the local use of the Plan. Two major localized redundancies took place in autumn 1975, before the Plan was finally launched. It was felt that these redundancies could not be allowed to pass simply because the Plan was not complete or because the company might refuse national negotiations. In the event, "mini-corporate plans" were central to the two redundancy campaigns at Birmingham and at Hemel Hempstead, and both campaigns were successful in preventing the redundancies. Moreover, they generated a longer-term commitment to the alternative Plan as part of a practical strategy for resisting redundancies. This credibility proved vital when a national campaign became necessary in 1978–9.

Birmingham: the first contingency

The Combine Committee sub-titled their Corporate Plan: "A contingency strategy as a positive alternative to regression and redundancies". The first contingency was at the Marston Green Electronics factory in Birmingham. On 23 September 1975 Rolls Royce terminated a contract with Lucas for electronic engine control units known as the Main Engine Control Unit (MECU) for the Multi-Role Combat Aircraft. The consequences of the cancellation were potentially disastrous not only for the 160 men and women working on the contract (and 500 new electronic jobs in the pipe-line) but also for workers throughout the company's Engine Management Group (EMG) based in Birmingham.

At that time, Lucas management's commitment to electronics was shaky. Some sections of management argued that there was no hurry for Lucas to get seriously involved in electronics; others believed that electronics was the control method of the future, and that it was vital for Lucas Aerospace rapidly to build up an electronics capacity. With these differences within Lucas Aerospace's top management, the termination of the Rolls Royce contract could have tipped the balance against electronics and this, in the shop stewards' view, could mean a further loss of over two thousand jobs in the rest of the Engine Management Group. Shop stewards' committees in all the Birmingham factories believed that the future of the hydro-mechanical work of the EMG depended on the company being able to sell a package of electronic controls and hydro-mechanical devices. A senior technical manager who used to work at Marston Green and still works for Lucas in Birmingham gives us an indication of one of the problems behind the precarious position of electronics:

> My personal view, from contact with Lucas senior managers and members of the board, is that there is always a large area of conservatism which does not like to see the old ways being changed. Electronics represents a threat to those people because they can see the old traditional processes they understand disappearing and a product range which to them is totally incomprehensible appearing in its place.

Workers in the Electronics Department at Marston Green had already suffered from Lucas's half-hearted approach to electronics. The Department was formed in 1969 and from the beginning had been short-staffed and under-financed. Such conditions were partly to blame for Rolls Royce's dissatisfaction with Lucas's handling of the MECU/MRCA contract. Moreover several commercial contracts which would have widened the base and thereby secured and created jobs had been turned down, including a particularly large contract with the GPO.

Workers at Birmingham's Lucas Aerospace factories felt strongly that they were going to suffer as a result of management's incompetence. Unemployment at around 7 per cent was unusually high in Birmingham. Already that year, 9,000 jobs had been lost at British Leyland, 3,000 at Lucas Electrical and 1,500 at Norton Villiers.

A strong shop stewards' Liaison Committee had emerged from the 1974 redundancy campaign, bringing together representatives from the unions in all four Lucas Aerospace factories in Birmingham. On 29 September 1975 this Liaison Committee launched a three-pronged campaign to save the jobs at Marston Green. First, with the backing of mass meetings and of the national Combine Committee, the Liaison Committee told management that there would be industrial action if they went ahead with redundancies. Secondly, the stewards then brought in local MPs to help put pressure on Rolls Royce, either to renew the original contract, or to give Lucas the contract for the RB208 — a contract broadly similar though less advanced than the original MECU contract. This would not provide long-term job security but it would be a holding operation while a more diversified product strategy was prepared. Furthermore, the Liaison Committee put forward a detailed programme of alternative products, referred to as a "mini Corporate Plan". This was based on the capabilities of the workers and plant in the Electronics Department, and it drew from both the general approach and some of the specific proposals of the national alternative Corporate Plan.

The "mini Corporate Plan"

The main short-term proposal in the mini Corporate Plan was to move into hybrid circuitry on a larger scale for use in medicine, communications and industry, as well as in aerospace. A second short-term proposal was for power units which used automatic sensing and starting systems for the computer industry. A third proposal was for control systems for flexible power packs for the Third World, as suggested in the main Corporate Plan. These short-term proposals, particularly the proposals for expansion of hybrid circuitry, were argued for on fairly orthodox commercial lines. The costing and the market research for the hybrid circuitry was based on work which Lucas had commissioned but had then rejected as a result of the low priority accorded to electronics. The scheme was viable in commercial terms for the Electronics Department itself. The argument was over the relative priority of electronics in the company's overall plans. As it has turned out, electronics have become increasingly important within aerospace and within industry generally. Three years after Lucas Aerospace came near to running down its main electronics factory, the new managing director, James Blyth, was to say that "electronics is the technology of the future". In the case of their short-term proposal, then, the stewards' urgent need to defend jobs, combined with their awareness of new markets, led them simply to challenge the commercial conservatism and inertia of Lucas Aerospace management.

However, the mini Plan's medium- and long-term proposals involved a more fundamental challenge to the company's corporate strategy. Perhaps having seen the incompetence of management on its own terms, the stewards felt their own criteria had as much claim to legitimacy as those of management. The medium-term proposals suggested extending existing capacities within the remote-control field to develop telechiric devices for fire-fighting, underwater activities and mining. The long-term proposals carried this idea further to suggest looking into the feasibility of complete systems for submersibles. They suggested working with other companies on the devices required for marine agriculture and for the collection of metal-bearing nodules from the ocean bed. Another area covered by the medium-term proposals was medical electronics. Electronics workers met with doctors, nurses and hospital administrators associated with the Birmingham branch of the Socialist Medical Association, and jointly they drew up a list of medical products for the Plan. It included humidifiers for bronchitis sufferers; an electronic device for measuring blood pressure; various diagnostic systems; defibrilators (at one of the meetings a doctor described how a child had died in a Birmingham hospital because a suitable defibrilator had not been available to restart the heart); electronic thermometers; and electronic control systems for artificial limbs. Other long-term proposals were in the fields of musical equipment, telecommunications and microprocessors.

The Birmingham mini Corporate Plan was a detailed document, fifty or so pages long. But was it any practical use in the campaign to save the Marston Green jobs? Anne Caudwell, a shop steward for the predominantly women assembly workers at Marston Green, and the only woman on the Liaison Committee, points to its importance: "It brought the staff and the shop floor together as a team. A fine team we were then. We had something

to fight for. Management had put all their eggs into one basket; we were saying we needn't be in that situation. Yes, the Plan was important. What else did we have?" The stewards for the assembly workers supported the Plan enthusiastically; it helped to create a sense of common purpose with the staff. But the "fine teamwork" of the campaign was not the approach to drawing up the Plan. Anne Caudwell and her members had not been involved in drawing up the Plan. "The design staff drew up the Plan. It was really their baby. We supported it. You see, I use my hands, not my brain — though I do sometimes use my brain. But a lot of design stuff is above me," said Anne.

At Birmingham the staff members of the Combine put together the Plan in about one month. There was not the time for the long discussions which went into, for example, Burnley's contribution to the national Plan. Moreover the design staff in Birmingham had not formed the close relations with the unskilled women workers which the Burnley staff had developed with craftsmen at Burnley. Nevertheless the mini Plan served its immediate purpose, of providing a positive focus for the campaign. A focus to fight for and hope for was especially important because the workforce had no work for nearly nine months from the end of September 1975 until May 1976 when Lucas eventually got the RB208 contract. Under such conditions workers often tend to take voluntary redundancy, especially when the company offers good terms.

Lucas offered attractive redundancy terms halfway through the campaign in January 1976. Bob Dodd, a TASS representative at Marston Green, describes how the Plan helped to keep up the momentum of the campaign:

Once we'd drawn up the mini Corporate Plan, people knew there was an alternative. They felt it was worth hanging on. At a mass meeting in January they rejected the company's voluntary redundancy scheme. We'd been able to convince them that there was a good chance of winning electronics. . . . About ten individuals did negotiate voluntary redundancy, but two of them were nearing retirement age and nine of them were pregnant. In general we held out.

In the end they did more than "hold out" for the existing hundred or so jobs. Once the RB208 contract was won, they successfully pressed the company later in 1976 to create more jobs and move into a new factory at York Road. By that time (December 1976) Lucas Aerospace management had fully realized the advantages of expanding their electronics capacity. But if the shop stewards' Liaison Committee had not built such a strong campaign around detailed job-creating alternatives, the company might not have had the initial capacity on which to expand. This was certainly the impression of the local MP, Syd Tierney, who had several discussions with senior management and helped the Liaison Committee to lobby government ministers: "It was my impression that the Electronics Department would have been considerably run down if it had not been for the trade-union campaign." The final jobs were jobs on a military aerospace contract. Paradoxically, then, although the shop stewards' alternative Plan had an offensive, positive intention its main importance was as the motivating force behind a mainly defensive victory.

Diversification discussions called off

Why did this successful defence of jobs not lead to negotiations directly about the alternative products? At the a meeting in November 1975 where alternative products were mentioned, senior management in Birmingham were frivolous and scornful of the shop stewards' suggestions. Mr Rivett, a Lucas Aerospace director, ridiculed the idea with mocking remarks about "electronic chicken coops". When pressed by the MPs present at the meeting he simply said that "the company is capable of all the forward planning that is necessary" (thank you very much!).

A month later, on 10 December 1975, Birmingham shop stewards, along with Ernie Scarbrow, openly present as secretary of the full Combine Committee,* had presented the mini Corporate Plan to Gerald Kaufman, Minister of State for Industry. The civil servants' report of the meeting describes Kaufman as having "welcomed the Combine's approach". The trade-union report of the meeting records that Kaufman thought "the proposals that had been made were a refreshing change and might well be of interest to the NEB which must not be allowed to become a responsi-

---

* Later on, Kaufman and other government ministers refused to meet Combine representatives, arguing the Combine was not representative of the workers.

bility for dying industries". The minister concluded by saying he would "like to meet the delegation again at any time".

The stewards took Kaufman literally. Ron Mills, the Liaision Officer for the Birmingham shop stewards, described the meeting in enthusiastic terms in his weekly report to the Combine Committee executive: "The talks went very well and all the stewards who attended were very impressed and satisfied."

This initial government response to the mini Corporate Plan had a considerable influence on the discussions at the Combine the following January, when the details of the campaign for the main Plan were finalized. The experience of the Birmingham stewards certainly raised the expectations of Combine delegates that the Corporate Plan would get support from the government. However, the Birmingham stewards soon discovered that, when it came to the crunch, far from the government helping what Kaufman described as a "constructive group of trade unionists" to put pressure on the company, the government, in fact Kaufman himself, merely sent the stewards back to talk to the company on their own.

At the end of January, when management were trying to persuade the workforce to accept voluntary redundancies, the shop stewards' Liaison Committee, having taken Kaufman at his word, tried with Syd Tierney to arrange an urgent meeting with Kaufman and possibly the NEB. The reply came back that the minister did "not think a meeting with the NEB or himself would be useful at this time". Instead, the minister would like the trade unions "to pursue diversification initially with the company to decide on some definite joint proposals". Ron Mills drew the lesson of this experience in his report to the Combine executive that week (20 February 1976): "It looks as though we will have to push even harder for our Corporate Plan."

Nevertheless they did as Kaufman requested and approached the company for a discussion about a joint proposal.

Several months later, during which time the main plan had been presented to management, Mr Brassington, the personnel manager at the Birmingham site, agreed to a series of local meetings about diversification with representatives of the shop stewards' Liaison Committee. In February, the first — and, as it turned out, last — diversification meeting took place. Bob Dodd describes what happened:

> Brassington must have thought it would get nowhere, that our ideas would be pie in the sky, and we'd have no technical expertise to back them up. But once we'd explained our proposals, the two technical managers there could see what we were getting at. They got into detailed discussions and seemed really interested. Brassington must have got worried because he intervened and poured cold water on the whole thing. He never fixed up another meeting after that.

Bill Williams was one of the technical managers who had taken the product proposals seriously though not uncritically:

> George Orloff [the other technical manager] and myself had discussed the products as engineers. I don't think that was what was wanted. My expectation was therefore that if they're not able to push the meeting in the way they want, they won't have another one. It was said at the end of the meeting that there would be a second one. I knew it would not take place.

Nine months after this meeting, Mr Brassington put his argument against the Corporate Plan in black and white in answer to some written questions from the shop stewards' Liaison Committee. No comment is needed:

> Our fundamental objective is always to provide work in the short term for the people we currently employ. Anything which diminishes this effort is, in our view, counter-productive and not in the best interests of Lucas employees. Many of the projects in the Corporate Plan need a fairly massive investment before initial work can be started on a production basis, and it is our considered opinion that the government will not be interested, at this stage, in this form of diversification.

Lucas management clearly knew more about the Labour governments real intentions than did the shop stewards. And that, as far as diversification was concerned, was the end of the matter at Birmingham.

Hemel Hempstead: fighting for a product

At Hemel too the company's corporate plan was sacrosanct, and if the local trade unions at Hemel had accepted this then a valuable export business providing 167 skilled jobs would have been sacrificed on its altar. The history of the industrial ballscrew division at Hemel illustrates both the range of applications of the aerospace technology and the obstacles facing any trade-union pressure to retain a non-aerospace application.

Lucas Rotax had had a long and distinguished history as a manufacturer of ballscrews for aircraft actuating systems. In the late 1950s, changes in the machine-tool industry created a demand for industrial ballscrews, based on similar principles to the aircraft ballscrews. The industrial ballscrew consists essentially of a steel shaft and nut and provides a means of transmitting power and motion at unprecedented levels of efficiency. It became increasingly important with the expansion of the field of numerical-control machine tools.* In 1961, the Lucas board decided to create a separate and therefore more flexible framework for the manufacture of industrial ballscrews.

Rotax Precision Products was set up for the design, manufacture and marketing of ballscrews. Sales rapidly increased from £100,000 in 1961 to £1,425,000 in 1969–70. 70 per cent of the business was in exports so it avoided the cyclical effects of the machine-tool industry in Britain. In 1970 Rotax opened a purpose-built extension to their Hemel Hempstead factory. It cost £2½ million. Newspaper reports heralded it as likely to "hold the key to a revolution in the British machine tool industry" (the local *Evening Echo*, 8 February 1970). The paper went on to quote one of the directors describing the factory as "the most modern ballscrew factory in Europe, if not the world". At that time Rotax Precision Products forecast sales going up: (1973–4 £1.7 million; 1974–5 £2.3 million; 1975–6 £2.8 million; 1976–7 £3.2 million). In practice, however, the sales moved down or remained static, rather than going up. (In 1970–71 the sales were £1.2 million; in 1971–3 they were £850,000; 1972–3 £775,000, and in 1973–4 £850,000.) In July 1975 it was decided that the business was no longer viable.

Trade unions in the industrial ballscrews section suspected that these disastrous results were due to mismanagement, rather than market processes outside management's control. They also suspected that it had a lot to do with the integration of Rotax Precision Products into Lucas Aerospace, and therefore its subordination to the priorities of aircraft production. At the time, the immediate job loss was not the main concern of the unions at Hemel: "We were concerned about saving the product for job security in the future. As an industrial product with a large export market it meant we were not totally dependent on the ups and downs of aerospace," commented Mick Young, a TASS member at Hemel who became deeply involved in the campaign (and, as a result, in the Combine Committee and the Corporate Plan). It was on this

---

* The steel shaft has a semi-circular helical groove machined along the length of its operating distances. The nut is formed by machining an internal corresponding semi-circular helical groove through which steel balls run in the track formed. A transfer "crossover" provides the recirculating path for the steel balls when the ballscrew is in operation.

basis that the industrial ballscrew staff and production workers decided to fight to save the product.

Initially it was treated as an issue for the industrial ballscrew division alone, and management did their best to keep it that way. The workers in that division, however, found that they had no power on their own so they organized wider support, which led to the formation, for the first time at Hemel, of a combined union committee, involving every union, staff and shop-floor. Bans on overtime and on sub-contracting were imposed throughout the site. And the committee organized a 50 pence levy on every worker on the site in preparation for further industrial action. However it was not just extra muscle which a combined organization provided. The other benefit was information — from which the committee was able to piece together a picture which confirmed their worst suspicions:

* The rigid aerospace procedures had resulted in a vast quantity of unnecessary paper work, a slow-down of production and a considerable number of cancellations due to late delivery dates.
* With the top-heavy accountancy procedures of Lucas Aerospace there had been a dramatic escalation of costs.
* The marketing procedures of Lucas Aerospace led to a breakdown of liaison between the marketing office and the factory, with the result that orders were very slow to be acknowledged and customers sometimes consequently cancelled their orders. The company declined to tender for a whole range of orders.

These accusations were based on photocopies of letters, telexes and memos passed on to the campaign committee by union members in the commercial departments.

This campaign to save the industrial ballscrews section was building up at a time when the Combine Committee nationally was finalizing its Corporate Plan. The Hemel union representatives, especially those of the shop-floor unions, were not very involved in the Combine Committee. One consequence was that workers at Hemel knew little about the Corporate Plan. The shop-floor delegates rarely distributed *Combine News* on a wide scale, and there had been no detailed discussion of the Plan at the shop stewards' committee. Among the TASS representatives there was, however, slightly more interest. They could see the connection between the Plan and the criticisms which they were making of management. Chick Hartman, a TASS representative:

Basically we were both attacking the company's narrow view of what they should produce. We were both bearing in mind the best uses to which the skills of our people could be put. It's not a long jump from commitment to saving one product, because of the social benefits of producing it, to suggesting further products for the same reasons.

It was this kind of thinking which led the senior TASS representative at the time, Phil Tate, to make contact with Ernie Scarbrow and Mike Cooley. These two then worked with the combined union committee at Hemel to produce a "mini Corporate Plan" for industrial ballscrews. This consisted mainly of a collation of all the information gathered by the different unions, into an analysis of management's failings. It went on to suggest other uses of industrial ballscrews in addition to the machine-tool industry. This indictment of management, combined with a clear demonstration of the importance of the product and the work of those producing it, strengthened the confidence of the workers in the industrial ballscrew division. There were few signs of anyone wanting to take voluntary redundancy. The mini Corporate Plan also acted as a basis for gaining government support. A meeting was held between the Hemel joint trade-union committee, Lord Beswick, a minister at the Department of Industry and Lucas management. Beswick was impressed at a group of stewards so concerned about preserving a product in an area where jobs were at that time not an immediate problem. Almost uniquely, in the experience of the Combine Committee, this minister followed up his commitment. He made it clear to management that the government would not look favourably on Lucas in other respects if they continued with their plan to close the ballscrew division. Negotiations then began between management and the unions. The unions' bargaining position was backed by industrial sanctions and the threat of a refusal to work on the aerospace ballscrews which the company wanted to keep. By the end of September 1976 the Industrial Ballscrew division was saved, for the time being.

Burnley: the first and only extension of collective bargaining
In Hemel Hempstead and in Birmingham the focus was on a local plan rather than the national Corporate Plan, out of necessity, as a defensive measure against a local redundancy. The national Combine Committee generalized from these experiences and the September 1976 issue of *Combine News* announced:

> The Combine's Corporate Planning Committee is now in a position to draw up a mini Corporate Plan for each site. It has collected a wealth of information about product ranges which could be introduced at each site in the event of further structural unemployment. This can be done at very short notice with the co-operation of the shop stewards' committee at the site involved.

The next step would be to push for negotiations on the Plan's proposals at a local level *in advance* of redundancies. At Burnley the joint shop stewards' committee felt that since there was no immediate prospect of getting management to negotiate on the proposals of the Corporate Plan centrally, then strong site committees should, with the support and advice of the national Combine, immediately start pressing for local negotiations. Moreover, Burnley stewards argued, success at one site, exploiting differences within management, would increase the credibility of the Plan among workers at other sites and thereby strengthen the pressure for central negotiations.

Burnley was a good site at which to experiment with this tactic. Ever since the Combine Committee's outstanding support for Burnley's parity strike in 1972, the Burnley shop stewards were staunchly loyal to the Combine Committee and very enthusiastic about the Corporate Plan. The membership, too, identified with the Combine Committee. *Combine News* usually sold at least 500 copies among the 2,000 workforce, and most of these would be shared. The idea of the Corporate Plan was widely known in Burnley through the newspaper, leaflets and posters and a very successful meeting in the town hall in July 1976. The town hall meeting was a follow-up to a mass meeting held in the factory on 6 February 1976 when shop stewards explained the redundancy threat and the Combine's alternative strategy. The Burnley shop stewards' Corporate Plan Committee then worked with Burnley Trades Council to organize one of the largest and most enthusiastic meetings that Padiham Town Hall has ever witnessed. Over three hundred people from Lucas, from other engineering factories in the town, from public-sector unions and from the Labour Party heard speakers from the Combine and from the Burnley shop stewards' committee explain the ideas proposed in the Plan. The speakers also presented a slide show to convey the ideas vividly. And certainly the ideas seemed to connect with the hopes and needs of people in the audience.

Even some of the local Lucas managers, a few of whom had also attended the meeting, were caught up in the enthusiasm; as one put it, "Eventually I think we will give it our blessing and I hope that the central management will also accept the Plan when they see how enthusiastic our employees are about it".[1] The success of this meeting illustrated another advantage about Burnley: the close contact between the Lucas stewards and other trade-union and political organizations in the town. The Lucas Aerospace shop stewards' committee is one of the largest in Burnley, a medium-sized town, and between them the Lucas Aerospace stewards are involved in just about every socialist or radical organization in the town. This connection between people's involvement in factory-based organizations and in local and community-based ones meant that in Burnley the connections implicit in the Corporate Plan between producers and consumers, and between industrial workers and public-sector workers, came easily. They were also made later, arising out of the possibility of making kidney machines in Burnley and a proposal to produce the hybrid power-pack and a road-rail mechanism for a local authority bus.

After the success of the town hall meeting, the Corporate Plan Committee wanted to get down to negotiations. In the words of Alf Deane, an APEX representative: "We felt that after the big splash of publicity and interest with all the alternative products, something needed to be done towards getting work started on a product. If we did not, we feared that management would announce redundancies and call our bluff. We had to start turning theory into practice." The Combine Committee supported Burnley in this experiment and kept closely in touch, providing advice and information when necessary.

Negotiations versus consultation

In summer 1976 the Burnley Corporate Plan Committee started to press management for a meeting to open up negotiations. The committee was confident that they could turn these discussions with management into genuine negotiations which had practical results. Earlier that year the AUEW, the majority shop-floor union, with the support of the joint shop stewards' committee, had made it clear, by withdrawing from the Joint Works Council, that consultation was not good enough. Consultation schemes, the AUEW argued, however they were dressed up, gave workers no control whatsoever over management's decisions. In effect, consultation simply enabled management to find out trade-union responses. Management are under no obligation to take account of those responses. Against this background, management could not satisfy the Corporate Plan Committee with mere consultation.

By October of 1976 management had agreed to discussions on new products. In a way they had no option but to agree to some kind of local discussion because national management had, in the reply to the Corporate Plan, committed management to local discussions. The Burnley stewards called central management's bluff and pushed the local discussion on the Combine Committee's terms. The trade-union Corporate Plan Committee made up the trade-union side of the discussions. Their committee, made up of four AUEW members, two TASS members and one APEX member, was accountable and reported back monthly to the joint shop stewards' committee. This fifty-strong shop stewards' committee saw to it that the discussions on new products were kept on a negotiating basis.

At first management did not present serious obstacles to this. Some of the local Burnley management probably had a certain interest at that stage in discussions about new products. G.F. Williams, the general manager of the site, admitted to the trade-union representatives that the Burnley factories were too dependent on Rolls Royce and the ups and downs of the aerospace industry.[2] Such a "local" problem would often be of little concern to the typical site manager in a multi-plant organization, on his (rarely her) way up the corporate ladder, but Williams was Burnley "born and bred", with some commitment to the future of the town and with no interest in promotion within Lucas Aerospace (he is at retirement age). He was also from an engineering background with an interest in production, rather than just in the balance sheet. Certainly the discussions at Burnley got off to a better start than those in Birmingham a few months earlier. Another factor in this is that the site personnel manager was never present at the Burnley discussions. It seems from both the Birmingham and the national experience that the personnel department, as the custodian of management prerogatives, was the most hostile to the Corporate Plan.

The first meeting of the New Products Committee, as the discussions were called, took place on 20 October 1976. From then until January 1978 meetings occurred on average every six weeks. Management tried to lay down terms of reference which would have restricted negotiations to take place within "the overall economic and company guidelines which may exist from time to time". The trade-union representatives managed to set this aside indefinitely and get on with negotiations over products. These negotiations gained a special urgency when, at the end of October, management announced that 300 workers were "surplus to requirements". Management had spread it about that voluntary redundancies would be welcome and terms would be favourable. However, a mass meeting of all 2,500 members on 27 October passed overwhelmingly a resolution rejecting voluntary redundancies and calling for the implementation of proposals from the Corporate Plan.

At this meeting the existence of detailed work on alternative products was a strong argument in the hands of the stewards. With this argument they built up sufficient support from the members to force management to withdraw the threat of 300 redundancies. As Pete Flynn from the AUEW put it: "We had specific proposals for other work, yet the company seemed hell-bent on more sackings. It showed the hypocrisy of their recent statements that they intend building up their UK base. In this way, the Corporate Plan was a real confidence-builder at the meeting."

The heat pump

With this kind of support behind them the trade-union representatives on the New Products Committee were able to press for development of one specific product — the heat pump. They were helped by contact with the Energy Research Group at the Open University in Milton Keynes. ERG was interested in heat pumps driven by a conventional engine, fuelled by natural gas, as a particularly efficient form of heating in overall energy terms.* ERG also had good contacts with the Department of Energy who seemed likely to provide some funds. Moreover, one of its members worked as a part-time consultant for the Milton Keynes Development Corporation (MKDC) and there was a possibility that he could negotiate for the MKDC to test the finished heat pump in one of its council house units. The initial idea, as relayed by the stewards to the New Products Committee meeting on 6 January 1977, was to produce two small prototype pumps (one air-to-air machine and one air-to-water unit). In principle, the plant managers at Burnley had power to allocate limited funds at their discretion for site-based projects like this. Although there might have been pressure from company headquarters to resist yielding to the stewards, local management were protective of their autonomy. These conflicts within management were one factor behind the breakthrough over the heat pump, in addition to the strength of the union organization on the site. By January 1977 all seemed set for the project to get under way — with at least the

---

* Typically the useful energy delivered by a gas-fuelled heat pump of this sort is 1.3 times the energy that would be produced if the fuel was burnt direct. Electric heat pumps are themselves more efficient (delivering perhaps two or three times the input energy) but that ignores the 70 per cent primary energy losses associated with generating electricity from fuels, which reduces the advantage considerably. In total energy terms an electric heat-pump based system might have an overall energy efficiency at 0.9 compared to a gas engine pump system at 1.3.

tacit support of local management. Indeed some of the technical members of the New Products Committee were evidently very keen on the project.

However, as detailed discussions progressed on the project, management began to make things difficult. One event in particular, on 18 January 1977, gave the stewards the impression that at least some parts of management were deliberately undermining the project. Management had agreed, under pressure, to a visit by members of the ERG to discuss details. When the visitors arrived the managers concerned refused to see them, saying they were busy. Unknown to the visitors a small group of stewards, led by Mick Cooney, virtually had to occupy the manager's office before the meeting could take place. As Cooney later remarked in a *New Scientist* interview (16 February 1978), "We had a hell of a struggle to get them to meet the OU scientists."

This kind of obstructive behaviour from at least some of management was not the only problem. The Department of Energy also presented obstacles, in their apparent reluctance to put money into the project. This could partly have been a reaction to what they perceived as lack of management enthusiasm for the project, as well as normal bureaucratic inertia. For example, the original application by ERG for funds from the Department of Energy's Energy Technology Support Unit (ETSU) at Harwell was made in May 1977, and after several delays a negative decision emerged eighteen months later in October 1978.[4]

The stewards approached Tony Benn, then Minister for Energy, to see if he could help. Benn, however, evidently was not able to speed up the process or enable the project to be given priority: the wheels of Civil Service bureaucracy turn slowly. . . . Mick Cooney commented later, "We may as well not have met him." The delay nearly undermined the whole project — and many of the stewards believed that the delay played into the hands of management. The development of one pump (the air-to-water configuration) went ahead nevertheless. The ERG produced a design specification for Lucas, and further design and assembly work got underway at Burnley from August 1977 onwards.

Eventually the Energy Technology Support Unit provided a retrospective grant to pay for the subsequent development and testing work at the ERG — £10,000 for the salary of a full-time research engineer, £5000 for instrumentation and running costs, plus £10,000 towards Lucas's costs. Lucas themselves had put in an initial £5000 for materials and provided a development engineer who liaised with ERG, together with a machinist and a fitter to build the unit. The total Lucas contribution was about £26,000, matching that obtained by ERG for development work from the Department of Energy. In the end, the company's willingness to provide even this relatively meagre contribution came more as a face-saver than any wholehearted commitment to the project. Certain well publicized incidents during the negotiations had put them in special need of a facesaver.

For instance, in April 1977 they had been through a very embarrassing experience over market survey for heat pumps carried out by Frost and Sullivan. Copies were handed out to the trade-union representatives as part of the back-up material for the New Products Committee. Management made no comments on it. Nevertheless they had signed it, implying they had read it. Danny Conroy, a trade-union representative on the committee, took it home to read:

> It was a big thick document, but if you bothered to read it as I did, it predicted a (European) market for heat pumps of £1000M by 1985 at 1975 prices. I took it into work the next day and when we challenged management — who were always saying they didn't see a future for heat pumps — you could see by their faces they hadn't read the document. And they didn't expect us to read it.

The Burnley stewards made a lot of this incident. It illustrated to them an important point about the Corporate Plan. Terry Moran explains:

> It vindicated our proposal to create jobs by making the heat pump. It showed there was a massive demand for heat pumps. In this way it also showed that advance thinking comes best from the people on the shop floor who are concerned about their jobs and about their country, rather than about how to get the easiest profits. There would probably not have been a profit in the short term with the heat pump. But they would have provided jobs and exports and in the long run it would have been commercially viable.

The shop stewards at Burnley certainly won the propaganda war over the heat pump. Meanwhile the prototype was being built at Burnley based on the specifications produced by ERG. The machinist and fitter evidently became very involved in the project* and the practical interaction among the members of the Burnley team was very much along the lines encouraged in the Corporate Plan, i.e. an "integrated project team" of blue- and white-collar workers.

In May 1978 the disassembled prototype was moved to the Open University at Milton Keynes for the ERG team to test and develop it. The tests and development work went well, if slowly. There were, as is usual, many technical bugs to eliminate.[5] By the end of 1979 the prototype was operating reasonably successfully — although by this time other researchers working in the field had in some ways been able to overtake the ERG team.[6] The real problem besides Lucas's halfhearted approach was that the relatively low level of funding, and the difficulties experienced by ERG in obtaining funds, slowed progress.

With the basic technical concept proved viable, the stewards were keen

---

*Such was the enthusiasm generated that one of the team, Ronnie Bell, the fitter, and an ardent Plan supporter, subsequently signed up for a night school course on energy technology.

to take related ideas further. The prototype had, after all, always been seen as just a one-off demonstration project — using an engine (an 18kw 5HP marine engine) which in many ways was not ideal.* It would be more sensible, as the stewards recognized, to use a larger, cheaper mass-produced car engine for a unit suited to providing heat for a *group* of houses. ETSU had already expressed interest in such systems and ERG was keen to develop the idea — perhaps in conjunction with British Gas.

Burnley stewards and the Combine Committee had hoped that even if Lucas did not produce such units, they could at least obtain work on design and component controls. And this would only be a start. As *Combine News* said in January 1977: "These small units are in keeping with Lucas Plants traditional skills." This idea was subsequently taken up elsewhere — outside of Lucas.**

Lucas management, however, remained unmoved — showing no interest in following up the turbine concept or even the gas-engine pumps*** — and there the matter rested, mainly because the action of the stewards' committee was drawn away from Burnley, where jobs were for the time being secure, to the national problem. In March 1978 the company had announced redundancies of over 2,000, including two factory closures: at Liverpool and Bradford. The Burnley stewards became heavily involved in a long struggle to save these jobs. One of them has commented: "as soon as we were diverted into the rationalization issue, we lost the dynamic of pushing them [Lucas] into the commercial-sized heat pump". However, the heat pump *idea* was used during the campaign to resist the 2,000 redundancies nationally.

The Burnley stewards saw the overall exercise of having successfully forced the company at least to develop a prototype as an important

---

* The marine engine was the smallest suitable power unit available, but the heat pump was still too powerful and bulky for a single house. This was one reason why it was not in the event tested by the Milton Keynes Development Corporation — the other reason being a delay in the availability of a suitable house.

** For example the Department of Energy is currently supporting work by the Glynwed Group on a turbo-compressor system, in conjunction with the EEC. Other projects included a 10Kw single house gas engine compressor pump (Task Power and Control Ltd) and a 6–8Kw absorption cycle system. See the DoE's *Energy Management*, July 1981, and *IEE News*, 1 June 1981.
Overseas gas heat pumps technology developed even more rapidly, particularly in West Germany.

*** The stewards had also been pushing other products ideas for Burnley on the New Products Committee — including the equipment for remotely piloted aircraft (e.g. crop spraying helicopters), an idea which evidently has since been developed by Lucas. Kidney machine production was also suggested by the Combine — but not followed up by the company. By 1978 the Burnley New Products Committee had ceased to function.

precedent. Subsequently, each time the company talked about shortage of
work — as in the 1978 rationalization threat — the stewards were able to
say, "Why not develop the heat pump?" The Combine in fact suggested
that heat-pump production would be ideal for creating work for the
Liverpool workforce following the 1978 redundancy threat; a detailed plan
for a new production unit was even developed. Later the heat pump idea
re-surfaced when Sheffield City Council began to consider introducing
units for house heating. Overall then, the heat pump — like the road-rail
vehicle developed at CAITS/NELP, which we will be discussing later —
provided a concrete example of the idea of "socially useful products".

Equally important were the confidence and political understanding
which the Burnley workers had developed in the course of extending
collective bargaining on a local level. This meant that Burnley stewards
made a major contribution to the national campaign. By that time (1978)
the future of the Corporate Plan, the Combine Committee and jobs in
Lucas Aerospace was no longer the outcome only of a struggle between the
Combine Committee and the company. By then the political support for
the Plan had grown to such a degree that both from the management's
point of view and, for different reasons, the Combine's point of view, it was
necessary to look towards government intervention.

IV BEYOND THE COMPANY

13 The Lucas Combine provides an example

While shop stewards in Birmingham, Hemel and Burnley were testing the practical value of the Plan for saving jobs in Lucas, many trade unionists, socialists, environmentalists and peace campaigners throughout Britain and eventually throughout the world were contacting the Combine Committee in the hope that the Plan could open up new possibilities for their own campaigns. At the end of January 1976 the Combine had presented their proposals to a crowded press conference in the upstairs room of a Fleet Street pub. During the following two years the Combine's proposals for jobs and for human-centred technologies were the subject of literally hundreds of articles, radio and television programmes. Two plays and an opera have been written about it. (One play, *The Participation Waltz* by the Broadside Theatre group, was written in close collaboration with the Combine Committee and was in effect part of the Combine's campaign.)

Press coverage

Most of the press gave enthusiastic accounts of the Lucas stewards' initiative. "The plan is one of the most advanced yet prepared in the UK by a group of shop stewards. One of the most radical alternative plans ever drawn up by workers for their company," commented the *Financial Times*.[1] The *Guardian*[2] described it as: "thinking and experience which should stimulate similar exercises elsewhere". The *Engineer* went so far as to call it "a twentieth-century version of the industrial revolution".[3] And the *New Scientist* welcomed it as "a unique alternative".[4] Not all these papers supported the Combine Committee but they did recognize its importance. On the other hand the "popular" newspapers such as the *Daily Mail*, the *Daily Express* and the *Sun*, who persistently berate trade unionists for being selfish and destructive, were completely silent about these constructive trade-union proposals. The *Daily Mirror*, although it claims to provide a more balanced coverage of the trade unions, only whispered a mention of the Lucas Plan with a report that barely covered two inches of the paper. There were no loud headlines slamming the irresponsibility of Lucas management for rejecting workers' positive proposals for job creation.

The case of local newspapers is more complex. The *Liverpool Evening Echo*, the *Birmingham Mail* and the *Bradford Telegraph* are no less anti-union on many occasions than the *Sun* and the *Daily Express* but sometimes the local loyalties and interests of their readership require them to report local action against unemployment, more sympathetically. For example, the *Bradford Telegraph and Argus* carried two sympathetic feature articles on the Plan and its implications for Bradford, including one by a TASS representative at the Lucas Aerospace factory. It also carried a leading article on Lucas Aerospace entitled "Jobs in Jeopardy" which mildly criticized Lucas management for rejecting the stewards' proposals while being unable themselves to provide Bradfordians with the opportunity to "learn and retain skilled jobs". Similarly, in Burnley, where Lucas Aerospace was the main employer, it was the shop stewards' commitment to local interests, to saving jobs for the town, which made the campaign around the Combine's Plan a regular story for the two local papers, the *Evening Star* and the *Burnley Express*. Steve Entwhistle, a reporter on the *Star*, explains why the *Star* gave the Lucas stewards a lot of coverage: "The Plan was launched against the background of considerable cutbacks in Aerospace, so a positive plan to save jobs there was seen as important for the whole town. Also, the local management foist you off to Birmingham, while the stewards do a very good PR job locally."

The campaign around the Plan has, in the eyes of the local press in Burnley, given leading stewards the authority to make public comments on national economic developments. For instance, after Geoffrey Howe's first budget, as well as the usual comment by a local businessman, there was a half-page column devoted to a call for "the abandonment of all the government's monetarist policies", from a Lucas Aerospace shop steward.

This media coverage and the Combine's own campaign aroused an extraordinarily widespread interest in the Combine Committee and its alternative Plan — not so much because of the intrinsic quality and originality of the Plan but rather because of the way that it gave vivid expression to ideas and hopes which people already held in a vaguer form. For this reason there is a danger of over-emphasizing the Lucas Plan's importance by focusing on the way that different movements took it up as an illustration or development of something they were already thinking. In most instances the Plan was only one of several sources of inspiration and a new questioning about trade-union and socialist strategies at the time. This qualification should be borne in mind in looking at the way in which trade unionists, both in industry and in the public services, responded to the Combine Committee and the alternative Plan.

From the Combine's point of view, the most encouraging response was from shop stewards' committees facing the same problems of rationalization which they faced at Lucas Aerospace. The technical and shop-floor workers' representatives from Ernest Scragg Ltd in Altringham were one of the first such groups of workers to make contact with the Combine Committee. Their company had just been taken over by Stone Platt Industries Ltd and, as they feared, Platt's management had decided to close the Altringham factory. The Scragg stewards believed that further closures would follow and they wanted to share experiences about the problems of building multi-union combine committees and fighting redundancies. They had talked to several academics and businessmen about alternative proposals to those of management, before AUEW colleagues put them in touch with the Lucas Aerospace stewards. Brian Horrocks, AUEW convenor of Scraggs, describes the importance of the contact:

It gave us a lot of confidence to talk to workers who had been far-seeing enough to work out alternatives. Back at the factory it gave the lads and lasses a straw to hold on to. But we couldn't get Stone and Platt to back our ideas. Maybe if we had prepared ourselves earlier we might have been stronger.

For similar reasons workers facing closures and redundancies — including those at Britten-Norman, a company making small aircraft in the Isle of Wight; at a Tri-ang factory at Merthyr Tydfil; at Hawker Siddely in Hull and near Harlow; at BAC Preston; at another Stone and Platt plant in Accrington — all made contact with the Lucas stewards during 1976 and 1977. This interest was not simply in the Plan as an idea, but in the fact that it was a plan produced by a strong trade-union organization able to back up its ideas with action. For many shop stewards this confirmed their own belief that there could be and should be alternatives to redundancies and that they had the capacity to develop them. In effect, the experience of the Lucas stewards gave them more confidence in themselves.

Another kind of contact came from groups of workers who had already begun to establish joint staff and shop-floor committees and to consider positive alternatives to management's strategies.

Thinking along the same lines

Early in 1976, for instance, a joint committee of shop-floor and staff representatives from Chrysler, Coventry, made a devastating attack on the asset-stripping operation which Chrysler had carried out on Rootes and which now put the future of the jobs at Chrysler UK in jeopardy. Like the Lucas Aerospace stewards, the Chrysler committee proposed both short-term solutions, based on existing and related products, and longer-term alternatives based on more socially efficient and ecologically sound forms of transport.* They concluded by saying:

> The widespread ecological and environmental criticism of the private petrol-driven car as a socially irresponsible form of transport suggests to us that we must explore the feasibility of new kinds of products of a socially useful kind to harness the skills of the existing plant and machinery, and to direct it away from a commodity whose profitability and usefulness is rapidly declining.[5]

In this way the Chrysler stewards came to question the very basis of the present car industry, after starting from a more limited concern simply to protect their jobs against the ravages of the giant car companies competing for a diminishing market. Like the Lucas stewards, the Chrysler stewards found that their criticism of management gave them the confidence to put forward proposals based on their own needs and objectives.

---

* For further details of the Chrysler stewards' case see "State Intervention in Industry; a Workers' Inquiry" by Coventry, Liverpool, Newcastle and North Tyneside Trades Councils.

Meanwhile in Manchester, the TASS committee at the huge GEC Old Trafford site were also learning lessons from the Lucas Aerospace initiative. Behind their interest in an alternative plan for the power-plant industry was a fear that the future of the Old Trafford site was no longer secure. This led several TASS representatives to work for six months or so with the Energy Group of the Conference of Socialist Economists to produce detailed proposals for the industry.* In the course of this work the Lucas Aerospace example provided a source both of confidence and of practical ideas. Ron Murphy, a member of the TASS negotiating committee for the site, describes how he saw the connection between this work and the Lucas Plan:

> At first I was only hazily aware of the Lucas Plan. Others in the group knew more about it. Gradually I saw our initiative as part of the same approach. At one point we went to Burnley and met several of the Lucas Aerospace stewards in a pub. I learnt a lot from that. I realized that the idea of workers drawing up alternatives need not be just something done by a few individuals but really had a wide appeal. I had not expected the trade unions in Burnley to be so involved.

Another group of workers who from 1975 onwards were in close contact with the Lucas Aerospace stewards was the combine committee at Vickers, which had been formed in 1974 partly, as at Lucas Aerospace, to overcome the powerlessness of isolated plant committees in the face of management's centrally directed rationalizations.[6]

The Vickers combine committee was almost entirely shop-floor based. Delegates tried to involve staff representatives but both management and union officials made this difficult. Moreover the numbers of technical and design staff at each factory was small. Consequently there was not the strong trade-union commitment among staff which grows more easily in the large design offices and research laboratories of a research-intensive company like Lucas Aerospace. This lack of staff involvement affected the kind of alternative plan that the Vickers combine committee later produced: "We could never develop our proposals to the level of detail which is in the Lucas Plan, because we just couldn't get the TASS members involved. There were one or two exceptions, but the key one got squeezed out of his job by management who did not like the way he was getting involved," commented Jim Murray, the Combine Committee secretary. The involvement of the Vickers shop stewards in drawing up an alternative plan arose out of a request in 1975 from the Defence sub-committee of the Labour Party NEC to work with them on alternatives to the Chieftain tank. In response to this suggestion the stewards in the armaments division of Vickers, based at Elswick in Newcastle upon Tyne,

---

* These included proposals for tidal, wind and wave, geothermal and solar power; for energy storage technology; for the structure of the industry, covering nationalization and industrial democracy.

discussed several alternatives with members of the Defence sub-committee, including recycling plant, oil spillage pumps, small brewing machinery, wave. power systems and agricultural equipment for the Third World.[7] Although at first these proposals were intended mainly to back up the Labour Party argument for defence cuts, they were also used as part of the Combine's campaign against closures and redundancies. In this respect the Lucas example was an important stimulus. "It helped us to generalize our proposals and to think of workers' plans as part of a wider strategy against company rationalizations," says Jim Murray. These are some of the more well-known examples of trade-union initiatives developed at the same time and with similar ideas as the Lucas Plan. We will see later how contact between these and other shop stewards' committees in manufacturing industry developed into a more organized network.

Although the most developed workers' plans came initially from industrial workers, based mainly in engineering, there was also a much wider labour movement response to the Lucas plan, among public-service unions, trades councils, constituency Labour parties and other socialist organizations. This reflected a recognition that a new, more political, trade unionism was necessary at a time when unemployment was growing while social needs were becoming more desperate. The Combine received so many resolutions of support, letters and invitations to speak, that it would be tedious to document them all here. One important feature of this interest which is worth emphasizing is the way that it led people to make new connections across unions, across sectors and across the workplace and the community. Newcastle upon Tyne is a good example with which to illustrate the different ways in which interest was expressed and these connections made. In general, besides cities with a large Lucas Aerospace factory, it has been cities faced by sharp decline and crisis where the interest in the Plan and in the Combine Committee has been greatest.

Don't let the North-East die

What then were the various connections made by trade unionists in Newcastle with the ideas expressed in the Lucas Aerospace workers' alternative Plan? The first contact was made in the early days of the last Labour government, when many shop stewards in large corporations expected, as did many Lucas Aerospace shop stewards, that the Department of Industry would support their initiatives. On Tyneside, shop stewards from the shipyards and from Vickers created an organization, the Tyne Shop Stewards' Conference, to discuss, and to make use of the promised new industrial policies. The Tyne stewards believed that these policies could only have any real effect on the major corporations if they were backed up by multi-union, multi-plant combine committees, so the problems of building such combine committees were central to the regular meetings of this organization. Members of the Lucas Aerospace Combine came to two of these meetings in 1975 and 1977 to speak about their experience and later to talk in more detail about the Plan.

This latter meeting aroused especial interest among shop stewards in the power engineering industry on Tyneside. The stewards at C.A. Parson's, with the support of the National Power Engineering Industry Trade Union Committee, had just won a major campaign to bring forward the "Drax B" power station, thus securing jobs, if only temporarily. However, these stewards realized that employment could not be guaranteed if they continued to rely only on conventional power-station orders. The CEGB already had a considerable excess generating capacity and it was unlikely that further orders could be brought forward, like Drax B. Nor would the minimum 2GW-per-year ordering programme needed to keep the industry alive be achieved. Other options would be necessary. The Parson's stewards were particularly interested in the potential of "combined heat and power" (CHP), a system for reclaiming the waste heat from power stations to meet local heating needs economically and cheaply.[8] A national system of CHP would also create many jobs for both the power engineering and construction industries. The Parson's stewards became one of the mainstays of a national CHP campaign, while the stewards at Clarke Chapman's, the Gateshead boilermaking company, developed a plan along the lines of the Lucas workers' Plan.[9]

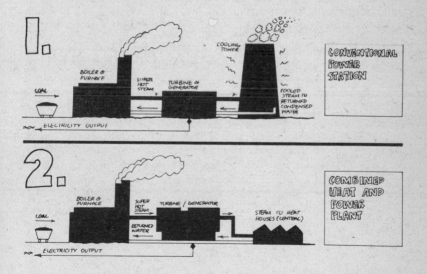

Soon, interest in the idea of workers' plans spread via the Newcastle Trades Council and forums such as the Trade Union Studies Information Unit and the Tyneside Socialist Centre, from stewards in manufacturing industry to activists in public-service unions. In 1977 Newcastle Trades Council first passed a motion recognizing the wider relevance of the ideas behind the Lucas Aerospace Plan. From that point on, the Trades Council maintained regular contact with the Combine Committee and appointed a member of the trades council executive, Bob Murdoch from the AUEW-TASS Committee at C.A. Parson's, to take special responsibility for the Lucas Aerospace Corporate Plan and the issues it raised.

In 1978 the Trades Council and the Socialist Centre organized a series of discussions on the wider relevance of workers' plans at which several Lucas Aerospace stewards spoke. Leaflets explaining the relevance of workers' plans to the problems of Tyneside were distributed to every trade-union branch affiliated to the Trades Council. John Darwin, vice-president of Newcastle Trades Council and a member of NALGO, explained the background to the Trades Council interest in the Lucas initiative:

> Some of us on the Trades Council were already, by 1976, arguing that today's unemployment was not the result just of a temporary downturn in the trade cycle. It was permanent and structural within our present economic system. Once you realize that, then all the traditional defensive policies we relied on in the '50s and '60s are inadequate. Something more positive is necessary; something which also shows in a credible vision a different way of organizing production.
>
> The Lucas initiative was the first well worked out example of this. It was important to be able to illustrate that there was another way of understanding the economy.

This approach began to influence some members of the city council and several of the researchers working for the council. By 1978 the council was willing to provide finance and resources for shop stewards' committees to carry out social audits of threatened closures and to develop alternative proposals. All too often, however, this recognition of the importance of analysing management's strategies, and of developing trade-union alternatives, came too late to help build up an effective resistance.

While the search for more radical strategies to fight the decline of industry in the North-East was the main impetus for widespread interest in the Lucas Plan, the issue of workers' and user control over product decisions aroused interest among public-sector trade unionists. The Newcastle branch of the National Union of Public Employees (NUPE) heard from Trades Council discussions that the Lucas workers were proposing several medical products. Alex McIntosh, secretary of the branch and a member of the NUPE national executive, explained why his members thought that the Lucas workers' approach was relevant to the National Health Service:

> We thought that the Lucas Aerospace proposals would mean making health equipment under workers' control or, at least, with workers monitoring what was going on. That would mean the prices would be lower and the designs would be more appropriate since health workers would be more involved. Also the equipment would be done just for the NHS or other health services, internationally, not for the private sector. We wanted NUPE to be in a position to extend collective

bargaining in the health service to influence purchasing and investment. This would help the Lucas workers and others extend collective bargaining in industry.

The Newcastle NUPE branch passed a resolution along these lines which was also approved at the northern Divisional Council of NUPE. As with many of the seeds sown or fertilized by the Lucas example there has not yet been the organizational strength and political confidence to translate the idea into action.

Activists in the tenants' movement were another group in Newcastle for whom the Lucas Plan illustrated ideas which were becoming important in their own work. They developed the idea of "workers' and residents'" plans:

> A workers' and residents' housing plan is not another conventional or paper plan but a combination of action and research to fight for alternative policies. These would involve finding out how additional resources could be harnessed and existing resources better used to meet the needs and priorities of workers (e.g. in Direct Works Depts) and residents. It is both a means of fighting cuts in public spending, redundancies and closures *and* laying the foundations of a socialist housing policy by the labour movement. [South Shields Trades Council, *Demolishing the Myths: Housing and Jobs in South Tyneside.*]

In 1978 local tenants' groups in Newcastle joined with the shop stewards at C.A. Parson's, the power engineering company, the local Socialist Environment and Resources Association (SERA) group and the Right to Fuel Campaign to press for Combined Heat and Power.

In these developments within a locality and in the earlier examples in different sections of the engineering industry it is possible to discern the emerging shape of a new trade unionism. It is a trade unionism with a positive alternative strategy for the industrial resources or public service resources concerned, and one which builds the basis for democratic control over those resources. This new trade unionism is producing, slowly, a shift in the ways trade unions organize at the base. In particular it is creating contacts across unions, across sectors and between workplace and community-based organization, in other words strengthening and extending the *horizontal* relations of the labour movement. However, while the ideas expressed in both the Lucas Plan and the multi-union shop stewards' Combine Committee help to stimulate these "horizontal" connections, they pose difficult problems for the divided national, "vertical", trade-union structures. For this reason interest and support for the Plan was far more widespread at the local and shop-steward level of the trade-union movement than at a national level.

Nevertheless some of this support among local activists has had an impact within national unions. In addition, many of the Lucas Aerospace shop stewards themselves pressed for the support of their own union.

Several of them were active in the regional organization of their union and so were in a good position to campaign for support.

Support from national unions

The Transport and General Workers' Union was probably the most responsive. The TGWU stewards at the Lucas Aerospace Shaftmoor Lane factory in Birmingham moved a resolution at their branch calling on their union to give full support to the alternative Plan. This was passed and sent on through the different levels of the union, with the result that in 1977, at the TGWU's bi-annual conference, the General Executive Council recommended that the union support the initiative of the Lucas Aerospace stewards and encourage similar initiatives elsewhere. One section of the executives' report on "military spending, defence cuts and alternative employment" gave delegates full details of the alternative Plan. Conference delegates passed the executives' recommendation and since then the TGWU has given much verbal and propaganda backing to the alternative Plan, publicizing it in the *Record* and using it in educational material.

AUEW members did not find their leadership quite so responsive. Among the Combine delegates were two leading AUEW members, one of whom, Ernie Hunt, was to become a full-time official in Birmingham, and the other, Danny Conroy, had been a delegate to the annual meetings of the powerful AUEW national committee for over twenty years. Danny is a stickler for trade-union procedure. He was quick to take the Corporate Plan to the district committee for discussion and support. Ernie Hunt did the same several months later. In both districts the Plan was well received. In Birmingham they asked a member of the Combine, Jack Gunter, to present the Plan at an AUEW shop stewards' quarterly meeting attended by 324 shop stewards. At Burnley the district committee supported the Plan and instructed the secretary to put it before the union's executive with a recommendation to support it. Nothing was heard from the national office. Looking back, Danny Conroy feels "a bit guilty" that he did not keep pressing the executive: "but I felt nobody at national level really cared, and we were very busy locally." However, two years later — by which time the Corporate Plan was very well known — he kept hearing attacks on the Combine for having "gone over the heads of the trade-union procedures". Lord Scanlon himself made this point to Danny Conroy. Danny describes what happened:

> I always remember saying to Scanlon, "Well, that's your fault because we sent you the Corporate Plan through the district committee, through the strict trade-union procedures and you did not act upon it." To his credit he checked and he came back after three months and said, "What we have done is absolutely unforgivable, you sent it through the union structure and we had ignored it for two years."

Eventually in May 1978 the AUEW national conference passed a resolution supporting the Plan. However, this was too late to affect the crucial negotiations between the company and the Confederation of Shipbuilding and Engineering Unions which began in early 1978. As we shall see this inertia on the part of the AUEW, the leading trade union in the Confederation of Shipbuilding and Engineering Union, was one of several factors that made it much easier for management to play the official trade-union leadership off against the Combine Committee and thereby avoid national negotiations about the Corporate Plan.

The experience with the AUEW was discouraging to other stewards. The GMWU branch at the Lucas Aerospace works in Liverpool had participated enthusiastically in drawing up the Plan, although at that time they did not see much point in taking it through their union machinery. Dick Skelland, a GMWU shop steward, explains:

> With the Plan we were only carrying out union policy anyway: we were taking seriously the unions' paper on commitment to opposing redundancies. So we didn't see the need to get further approval. Also we thought it might delay things and get us bogged down. They didn't get very far with the AUEW, did they? We didn't have faith that we would get any further. In addition we sensed that the regional council, not really knowing anything about it, would come to a negative decision which we'd be bound by. So we campaigned for the Plan more directly.

Nevertheless the Combine Committee secretary did send a copy of the Corporate Plan to David Basnett and received a letter back saying that he was reading it "with interest". This interest, however, did not lead to any practical support in the major conflict with the company in 1978.

Staff unions

Turning now to the white-collar unions, in AUEW-TASS, the Corporate Plan was supported at several levels. On 29 April 1976 the regular annual conference of TASS delegates from every site within Lucas Industries agreed "to support the basic concepts of the Corporate Plan and recommend and encourage support for the ideas contained within that scheme." The delegate conference followed up this support with a commitment to incorporate aspects of the Plan in the June 1976 wage claim. As a result the claim submitted by TASS on 9 June stated:

> We would ask the Lucas group to what end it is putting this additional sum of money (i.e. wages saved by pay restraint) and whether in the circumstances that our nation finds itself, it is prepared to use some of this money to develop socially useful products.

This claim took the "social contract" at its word and applied it to collective bargaining. It would have involved a wage increase made up in part of cash and also of a guarantee that the firm would contribute directly to the production of the Corporate Plan proposals. For example, the TASS committee in Lucas Aerospace called for a 40 per cent increase in the production of kidney machines at the Neasden plant. The company refused to negotiate over this part of the wage claim. In February 1977, in response to a major redundancy threat, the Lucas Industries TASS National Negotiating Committee gave its support to the Corporate Plan and urged the government to take action "to secure its realization". Later that year aspects of the Plan were again integrated into the annual wage claim.

In the meantime, leading TASS members of the Combine had been presenting the Corporate Plan to TASS at a national level. On 14 June 1976 a working party of the TASS national executive, consisting of TASS-sponsored MPs, full-time and lay officials, heard Mike Cooley and Frank Hyde from Wolverhampton give a detailed presentation of it, complete with slides. The working party recommended that the executive should support the general approach of the Plan. This recommendation seems to have been accepted, for on 3 September the Combine received a letter from John Forrester, then the Deputy General Secretary, saying:

> I can also advise you that the ultimate decision of the Executive Committee was to accept the general concept of the Plan.

Forrester added:

> This is valuable to me, in the sense that I can now feel free to ultilize the initiative shown by the shop stewards when I am representing TASS.

However, this was not the end of the matter. Support for "the general concept of the Plan" turned out to mean different things to different people in TASS. The late John Forrester clearly thought it meant practical support; and on several occasions he himself gave such practical support. Other leading officials seemed to interpret "general" as excluding specific practical support. For example, although the TASS delegation at the 1978 Labour Party conference voted with everyone else to "applaud that initiative of the Lucas Aerospace stewards", earlier that year a circular was sent to Lucas TASS representatives signed by the General Secretary, Ken Gill, asserting: "Contrary to statements widely circulated the 'Corporate Plan' is not the official policy of TASS." This was at a time when vital negotiations were beginning over 2,000 jobs, a time when the Corporate Plan needed all practical support it could get. This lack of practical support from the TASS leadership also left leading Combine Committee members wide open to victimization by the company. The company have always been able to justify the harassment of Ernie Scarbrow and finally the sacking of Mike Cooley, on the grounds that they took too much time off on "unofficial business", that is on the Corporate Plan. Never once has TASS been prepared to come back at the company and say that in fact the Plan or even "the general concept of the Plan" has the union's official support.

An underlying reason why the Lucas Aerospace Combine was treated with suspicion if not outright hostility by several influential national officials of TASS was because of past political conflicts within TASS involving a leading member of the Combine, among others.

Conflicts within AUEW-TASS

From the Combine's point of view these conflicts should not have been important: it seemed extraordinary that a union should react to a Combine committee of sixty or more delegates, representing thousands of members, in terms of political disagreements with one delegate. However, since TASS's response not only to the Combine but also to the Corporate Plan is an important thread running through the Lucas story, we need to provide an outline of the conflicts within TASS in the late 1960s and early 1970s, which concern individuals but are about fundamental differences in approaches to trade unionism. They involve a clash of principles and ideas regarding the nature of leadership, the value of the initiative and self-activity of the members and the meaning of democracy. Some of these clashes apply also to the Combine's relation to other parts of the official trade-union and Labour Party leaderships. However, the distinctive feature of the response of the TASS leadership is that its roots lay in an intense political struggle within the union. As a result, the response of several members of the TASS leadership to the Lucas Aerospace Combine Committee took a very factional personal form. The object of hostility in the case of Lucas Aerospace was Mike Cooley, though other dissident members of TASS in shop stewards' committees elsewhere have also been the object of similar hostility.

Mike Cooley, as a member of the Communist Party until 1970, had been part of a long campaign by members of the Communist Party and Labour Left to turn TASS into a militant union of the Left. But in the late '60s at least two important conflicts developed within the Broad Left, as this group was called. First, disagreements grew within the Communist Party over China and the Soviet Union. Cooley and others were sympathetic to the ideas behind the cultural revolution in China, and believed that the Maoist emphasis on strengthening the base and reducing the power of bureaucratic superstructures applied to the labour movement in the West. Disagreements over these and other issues led Cooley and others to leave the Communist Party.

These divisions were significant for the internal politics of TASS, because several of those who left the Party were leading members of TASS, and by this time the Communist Party was in a very influential position in TASS. The split in the Party contributed to another source of division. An opposition within the Broad Left believed that the Communist Party's strategy within the union was increasing the power of the appointed full-time officials at the expense of the lay members and their elected representatives. Mike Cooley was a leading spokesman of these critics. He was elected president of the union for 1971–2 and in his presidential address and New Year message he warned delegates of what he saw as an erosion of union democracy. He also opposed the appointment of Ken Gill (also a member of the Communist Party) as assistant general secretary. Ever since that time, several leading figures in TASS have been hostile towards Cooley and anything with which he is associated. Perhaps they feared that he and others would provide a focus of opposition to the Communist Party's position within the union (though it is important to add that many Communist Party members outside the TASS leadership have been supporters of the Lucas Combine Committee's ideas). In many petty ways they have tried to undermine Cooley's influence. For instance, after his year as president, they excluded him from committees on which the president customarily sat. They refused to reprint a booklet he wrote on Computer-Aided Design, in spite of considerable demand for it. And, as we shall see, they were halfhearted, to say the least, in their attempts to defend him when he was harassed and finally sacked by Lucas management in 1978 and 1981.

The response of the other staff unions was less hostile, but equally half-hearted. APEX's response to the Plan was also ambiguous until 1978. Alf Deane, the APEX delegate to the Combine from Burnley, summed it up: "In general public statements and when talking to you privately they say it's a great thing, but when it gets down to the nitty-gritty of fighting for it to be implemented they back off." Deane's APEX branch at Burnley was involved in the Corporate Plan since its inception. It is one of the only APEX branches to be part of a multi-union staff and shop-floor stewards' committee. National APEX officials have discouraged their members in Lucas Aerospace from becoming involved in the Combine Committee.

In the case of ASTMS, it was not until March 1978 that a resolution in support of the Plan reached the national executive. The main reason for this was that ASTMS members, with a few exceptions such as John Swarbrick at Liverpool and Walt Rendall at Bradford, had never been involved in the Combine Committee or the Corporate Plan. There was no tradition of trade unionism among the supervisors at Lucas Aerospace, and it has only been in the last five years that they have joined ASTMS in large numbers. Moreover, when the Combine drew up its Corporate Plan, supervisors' jobs seemed secure, and most of them believed that the company would look after them. As it happens, this view was very short-sighted, but at the time it meant that they were lukewarm towards the plan.

Several ASTMS branches outside Lucas, in the Health Service and the computing industry for instance, thought the Plan was an important precedent. The London Divisional Council of ASTMS passed a lengthy resolution calling on the union to support the Lucas Plan and other similar initiatives. In particular, they suggested that ASTMS members should provide "marketing and management know-how not only to Lucas workers but to any other groups of workers whose factories are threatened with closure, and where plant and machinery could lend themselves to similar conversion to other uses for our economy and services". This was followed up in 1980 by support for the ASTMS national conference and by several weekend schools during which Lucas Aerospace stewards have explained the ideas and problems involved in developing alternative plans and in building combine committees jointly with shop-floor workers.

"Lucas Aerospace stewards are given every welcome at Whitehall College [the ASTMS college]," commented John Swarbrick. ASTMS has donated funds and given other forms of support to CAITS, the research centre created by the Lucas stewards in 1978. Members of the ASTMS research department have also been supportive. But as with the TGWU, in spite of this support, ASTMS did not exert any significant pressure on the company and the Labour government.

In the first two years after the Corporate Plan was launched, this ambivalent national trade-union response was not put to the test. Management's rationalizations were defeated, as we have seen, by strong local shop stewards' committees making use of the Corporate Plan according to local conditions, and backed by the national Combine Committee. In 1978, however, the national union executives via the Confederation of the Shipbuilding and Engineering Unions had control of national negotiations over redundancies at Lucas Aerospace. Their paper support was then put to the test, as we shall see.

In the Labour Party
Support from the Labour Party was also put to the test over these negotiations. In the meantime, support within the Labour Party constituencies and among backbench MPs was extensive. The 1976 Labour Party programme gave explicit support to the campaign of the Lucas Aerospace stewards, as an example of the possibilities of defence conversion.[10] In 1978 the Labour Party conference took up both the defence and the industrial policy aspects of the Plan, giving unanimous support — including the support of all union delegations — to a resolution which included a call on the government to enter into a planning agreement with Lucas Aerospace on the basis of the Plan and to take into public ownership, through the National Enterprise Board, the parts of a company affected by non-implementation of the Corporate Plan. But, like most Labour Party conference resolutions, this had little direct bearing on the actions of the Labour government. As Denis Easton, an AUEW steward from Bradford put it, "We had every support short of actual help."

Political choices for the alternative technology movement
In the meantime it was not only the rhetoric of the Labour movement which was being put to the test by the Lucas Aerospace Combine's alternative Plan. The Plan also tested the strategic sense of the alternative technology (AT) movement — a network of groups, some carrying out experiments with windmills and solar collectors in their back yards, others more concerned with campaigning against nuclear power and for more ecologically sound forms of technology.

Conflicts were already beginning to develop within the alternative technology and ecology movement. In part this was a result of the oil crisis.

The oil crisis meant that all kinds of official bodies, from transnational corporations through government departments to the Royal Family, became interested in alternative energy technologies. This interest from the establishment raised all the political questions of control over technological change which are often ignored in a movement united around technological forms. The Lucas Aerospace workers took this questioning further by taking several alternative technology ideas out of the realms of apolitical utopias. By using and modifying alternative technologies in their resistance to redundancies, the Lucas stewards were showing how the design of technologies and the choice of technologies involves bitter struggles over power, not simply over different technical "fixes".

Some parts of the AT movement had in fact already begun to realize that the key issue was not so much the hardware itself as the politics of production, distribution and control. An editor of the radical AT magazine *Undercurrents** gave an indication of the thinking going on:

> Small may be beautiful, but is small fascism beautiful? It is quite possible to envisage a future society in which widespread use is made of wind energy, methane, organic farming, geodesic domes, and all the other alternative technology clichés, but which is thoroughly repressive in a social, political and cultural sense.[11]

The emphasis within the AT movement had been gradually moving away from individual "self-sufficiency" in remote communes and towards "community-scaled technology", i.e. technologies suited to more conventional living situations. There was also a shift of interest taking place from "the technology of consumption to the organization of production".[12] So for several reasons the Lucas campaign fell on fertile ground, at least as far as the more radical part of the AT movement was concerned. At the same time it led to conflicts and shifts within that movement.

Many AT activists responded enthusiastically to the fact that the Lucas shop stewards were trying to make technological choices a part of collective bargaining. Yet some of these enthusiasts did not fully realize the power struggle which collective bargaining involves. This became clear when a group within the AT movement, the Future Studies Centre, organized a conference in 1975 of over six hundred environmentalists, conservationists, and alternative technologists to discuss "Industry, the Community and Alternative Technology". The Lucas stewards' Plan was going to be the centrepiece of the conference. But the organizers, under a policy of "political neutrality", had also invited members of Lucas management. This naive — no doubt well-intentioned — act totally transformed the nature of the conference and in the longer run triggered off a trans-

---

* *Undercurrents* magazine, which at the time had a circulation of around 6,000, produced one of the first major reports on the Plan in September 1975. And subsequently, over the next five years, it provided its readers with a blow-by-blow account of the progress of the campaign.

formation of the AT movement. The last thing that the Lucas stewards could do, when management was announcing redundancies and refusing to negotiate over the Plan, was discuss the Plan with management in an atmosphere of "political neutrality". The Combine wrote the conference organizer a firm but polite letter of refusal:

> We hope you will not think this rigid or doctrinaire of us. The harsh reality of our actual experience at the point of production has taught us some bitter lessons. Even at this moment our members at Hemel Hempstead are fighting to *retain* the only non-aerospace product at their site. . . . In these circumstances for management to attend a conference to discuss our initiative for the "right to work on socially useful products" seems to us to be hypocrisy of a very high order. By their *deeds* shall ye know them.

With the centrepiece gone, many conference participants felt they had to discuss the framework; and that meant discussing the social and political direction of the AT movement. To some extent the result was polarization, with the radical rump forming a new organization — the Network of Alternative Technology and Technological Assessment (NATTA) — which held its first conference, with representatives of the Combine attending, in April 1976. Other developments occurring around the same time, such as the "Green Bans" of trade unionists in Australia, also influenced the direction of the AT movement.[13]

These and the Lucas Aerospace Plan triggered off a shift among many alternative technologists towards closer and more politically coherent alliances with working-class organizations based both on the workplace and the community. In the last two years the campaign against nuclear power has given an added urgency to these alliances and helped to open up further debate in the trade unions about the control of technology.[14] There has been an interesting dialectic in all this. While trade-union organizations, such as the Lucas Aerospace Combine Committee, clearly helped to politicize the AT movement, the politicized wing of the movement is now, through organizations such as the Socialist Environment and Resources Association,* and NATTA, an important catalyst in further politicizing union debates on technology and energy.

Neither bombs nor the dole but conversion

Another movement which both welcomed and was influenced by the Lucas Aerospace shop stewards was the disarmament movement, the impact of which among trade unions was weakened by the problem of unemployment in the arms industries. After all, it was rearmament which ended the

---

* Of all the environmentalist groups it was SERA who championed the Lucas cause most enthusiastically — organizing several local conferences addressed by Lucas stewards. It also took on some of the general publicity work from the Combine — setting up a special Lucas support group, convened by Mike George, who was later to become the co-ordinator of CAITS.

appalling unemployment of the 1930s. Those who defended high defence spending repeatedly played on this vulnerability in the peace movement's arguments. For instance, in the first two years of the 1974–9 Labour government, the Defence Minister, Roy Mason, refused to implement the disarmament policy agreed by Labour Party conference on the grounds that the cuts called for by conference "would cost 350,000 jobs and lead to the destruction of key sections of manufacturing industry". Incidentally, this was at a time when the Labour government's deflationary policies towards the welfare state and sections of industry was leading to unemployment of over one million. However disingenuous the arguments of the defence hawks, they did stick, especially within the trade unions. For although trade unions and Labour Party conferences alike repeatedly passed general resolutions calling for cuts in military spending, the unions never used their considerable strength to press for their implementation. In effect most trade unions merely paid lip-service to disarmament.

Some trade unions were concerned to overcome this conflict between disarmament and full employment. As long ago as 1929 the Transport and General Workers' Union took the initiative in setting up a committee to examine the economic consequences of disarmament consisting of the TUC, the NEC of the Labour Party and delegates from the parliamentary party. In 1931 this committee made recommendations which included: "That alternative work of suitable character not at present available to industry should be provided." The problem then was not lack of good intentions, it was rather that the precise mechanisms of converting from arms to civilian production were never worked out at any level of the trade unions, and as a result there was never any pressure from the shop floor to keep trade-union leaders to their good intentions. The Labour Party manifesto of 1974 contained the same general commitment without any detailed strategy. The statement on disarmament ended with the lame assurance that "alternative sources of employment will be sought where possible by taking on contract work and research for outside industry. . . ." Few trade unionists working in the defence industries could have been very convinced by being relegated to such an offhand afterthought.

The Lucas Aerospace shop stewards provided a way out of this impasse facing the disarmament movement. In fact they did more. They reversed the whole way of seeing the relationship between disarmament and unemployment. The Lucas Plan implied that instead of the problem of alternative employment being seen as a residual problem to be cleared up after the other decisions about disarmament had been taken, the possibility of liberating the skills and energies of defence workers for socially useful production became part of the positive case for disarmament.

Not surprisingly, as soon as news of the Lucas workers' Plan spread[15] among the numerous groups within the disarmament movement the Combine Committee was flooded with requests to speak and write articles. Few conferences on disarmament would have been held since 1975 without a speaker from or on behalf of the Lucas Aerospace shop stewards' committee.

Of all the ways in which the different organizations had responded to the Plan, this response from the disarmament movement was the one which least surprised the Combine Committee. For they too, along with trade unionists throughout the aerospace industry, had sensed the problems facing the peace movement so long as it merely preached against weapons from on high, without getting down to the details of conversion.

Said Terry Moran from Burnley:

> We welcomed the support of the disarmament organizations, because we had always felt that disarmament or jobs was a false choice. As part of the Aerospace Liaison Committee we'd supported campaigns against the cancellation of military products. But we'd rather not be in that position. The disarmament movement had failed to come up with an alternative. But once the workers themselves had proposed something detailed and credible the peace groups gave us a lot of support.

Following the launching of the Corporate Plan, several organizations and many individuals within the peace movement took the initiative to spread the ideas of the Lucas stewards. In particular the Campaign Against the Arms Trade (CAAT) made work on conversion a top priority. CAAT in effect acted as an information and campaigning centre for the Combine Committee within the peace movement (internationally as well as in Britain). Several religious groups, including Quakers, industrial chaplains and the New Dominican monks, have all given support to the Lucas Plan. The industrial chaplains organized a "week of reflection" upon the Plan at their college in Selly Oak, and many of them have been active in their unions extending support for alternative plans.[16]

The co-operative movement also saw much in the Lucas workers' approach that they welcomed, even though the Combine Committee had made clear that a workers' co-operative was not their aim; they were more concerned with challenging management in the centres of economic power.

While generally supportive of the idea of co-operatives and co-operation as a long-term goal, the Lucas Combine tended to see them in the present as a last-ditch option unlikely to be successful against the pressures of markets dominated by the major corporations. They felt that at this stage isolated workers' co-operatives would be vulnerable, insecure and unable to survive the hostility of private capital unless workers accepted worsened pay or work conditions.

However, the Lucas initiative clearly demonstrated that workers had the potential for self-management, and so it was taken up as valuable evidence by the co-operative movement. Several fledgling co-ops approached the Combine — and later CAITS — asking for ideas for new products, and the parts of the co-operative movement provided a medium for spreading the idea of socially useful production and workers' plans to a wider audience.

Socialist organizations were mixed in their responses. The Socialist Workers' Party initially reported the Combine Committee's plan enthusiastically. Later it tended to associate the Lucas campaign with attempts to set up workers' co-operatives and therefore as a doomed "island of socialism" in a sea of capitalist competition.* They did not have an agreed analysis, but the comments they published tended to see "workers' plans" as diversions from more traditional shop-floor struggles and from building a revolutionary party. (See for example Dave Albury's article "Alternative Plans and Revolutionary Strategy" in *Socialist Review* and Mike George's reply the following issue, 1980, and "Is Lucas island all at Sea?" in *Socialist Worker*, 11 November 1978.)

Socialist Challenge was supportive, running a major feature on workers' plans in October 1978, while *Militant* ran an article entitled "Lucas workers show what could be done" (19 December 1975). *Big Flame* produced a discussion pamphlet on alternative plans for a special conference on "Alternatives to Unemployment", and the Lucas issue was reported and discussed in most Left "science" journals such as BSSRS's *Science for the People* and *Radical Science Journal*. The labour movement press — *Tribune, Labour Weekly, Voice of the Unions*, etc. — all ran articles on Lucas.[17]

Undoubtedly all these movements helped to sustain the extensive media interest in the Lucas Plan and contributed to the build-up of pressure on MPs to campaign for the Plan in Parliament. Among the 170 or so MPs who have in one way or another expressed support for the ideas in the Plan are many who did so in response to public interest and pressure from diverse groups within their constituencies. And we shall see in Chapter 15 that this degree of public interest, which included but went beyond trade-union interest, meant that government ministers felt that they had to be *seen* to be taking action in support of the Lucas Aerospace Corporate Plan. In the end government ministers could not simply congratulate the Lucas stewards and show them the door, for the stewards kept coming back and a large number of people were watching intently. And drawing conclusions for the future.

---

* See "Capitalist profit: the fatal weakness of co-ops", *Socialist Worker*, 1978.

14 An idea come of its time. . . .

"Lucas stewards ring the world with meetings." When the *Burnley Express* ran this headline, it was telling the literal truth. The international response was extraordinary. It further demonstrates that the Lucas workers were expressing, with particular confidence and practicality, what many were already thinking. The greatest international interest came mainly from two groups: trade unionists facing structural unemployment and loss of control of the introduction of new technologies; and disarmament groups facing up to the problems of halting and reversing the momentum of the military establishment.

Individuals in these organizations would hear about the Lucas Plan through the press or through British contacts. Frequently this initial interest was followed up by a visit to Britain to talk to Lucas Aerospace shop stewards and/or an invitation to the Combine to send a small delegation to spend a week or so speaking at meetings throughout the country. Just to give an indication of the extent of the Combine's travels: two delegates went to Italy at the invitation of the Italian metal workers' union (FLM); a young AUEW member from Burnley went to Vienna at the invitation of the European Youth Conference on disarmament. Four delegates went to West Germany at the invitation of the Free University of Berlin and also spoke at meeting organized by I.G. Metall — the German Metal Workers. Trade unionists at the Saab plant in Linköping and shipyard trade unions at Gothenburg helped to arrange meetings in Sweden for Combine delegates. On several visits to the USA, stewards have spoken particularly with members of the Union of Automobile Aerospace and Agricultural Workers (UAW) and the International Association of Machinists and Aerospace workers (IAM). Combine delegates have also been to Norway, Holland (several times), Denmark and Canada. Two Combine members spent a fortnight talking at trade-union meetings in Australia. And Mike Cooley was also invited to represent the Combine on a delegation to China, but management would not allow him to go — even though Bernard Scott, then chairman of Lucas Industries, had visited China several months earlier.

A list like this does not convey adequately the extent of the international contact and mutual influence. It is often easy to feel overwhelmed by the apparent strangeness of making international links, when there are so many problems involved in building or keeping going even local and national organizations. The Lucas stewards themselves, six years ago, would never have imagined the possibilities which existed for international contact, and the benefits of forging such links. They were often surprised at the extent to which their problems were shared on an international scale. To illustrate this we will look at the background to the interest in the Lucas Plan in the United States and, in less detail, in West Germany and Sweden.

The United States: the Lucas Plan strikes a chord
In the United States, two aspects of the Corporate Plan aroused interest: its implications for defence conversion and its emphasis on resisting the brutalizing features of modern capitalist technology.

By the time the Plan was launched in Britain in early 1976 a new interest in defence conversion had emerged in the United States. In part this was a response to the general economic recession following the end of the Vietnam War. Also, disarmament activists found that the end of the war did not mean the end of arms contracts. Many anti-war networks moved on from the campaign against the government to take on the private companies which benefited from the Vietnam War and which continued to sustain the military machine. The interest of these anti-war campaigners in conversion often came out of bitter practical experience with the university-based peace movement and its lack of realistic, strategic thinking. Dave McFadden from the Mid-Peninsula Conversion Project (California) describes an experience fairly typical of the pressures which led disarmament activists towards an interest in conversion:

> In 1974 I was involved in a demonstration against the B1 Bomber. As we went past the factory where it was being produced the workers came out in full force and jeered at us. It was after that experience that I vowed never to go on a demo against a weapons system unless some way had been found of involving workers in developing alternatives to secure their jobs.

McFadden and others who were beginning to work on the details of conversion with trade unionists in the arms industry had very little experience on which to build. There was "Sword into Ploughshares", the broad brushstrokes of a conversion plan drawn up in 1969 by the late Walter Reuther, president of the Union of Automobile Aerospace and Agricultural Workers (UAW). And there was the work of Professors Seymour Melman and Lloyd Dumas from Columbia, which had been used to draw up proposals for legislative backing to conversion projects.* But that was all. None of this previous work provided a basis for anti-war activists to build alliances with industrial workers which could challenge the military-industrial complex now, without waiting for legislation which would anyway be inadequate on its own. In 1977 word began to get around about the Lucas workers' Plan. Anti-war activists and Left trade unionists who had talked about conversion now had a practical example to point to. It was never as widely known about as in Britain, but its trade-union origin had especial importance in the United States, where links between the disarmament movement and the trade unions were even weaker than in Britain.

---

* The Mathias-McGovern Alternate Use Planning Legislation.

For these reasons the Lucas example helped to get conversion or "alternative use" issues discussed seriously within those unions with members in the defence industries, especially in aerospace. In the case of the union which organizes the largest number of aerospace workers, the International Association of Machinists and Aerospace Workers (IAM), this impact was considerably helped by William Wimpisinger, the new leader of the normally conservative IAM. Wimpisinger, a socialist in the Reuther tradition, has been consistently promoting discussion about alternatives to military production ever since he became leader of the IAM. There is now an experimental educational class starting within the IAM on "alternative use planning" and control over new technology. As the idea of conversion has gained ground within key sections of both the IAM and UAW, the implications of alternative plans have been developed beyond defence conversion to the issues of technological unemployment, environmental pollution, and the organization of work itself. Thus, although initially the interest in the Lucas Plan in the US arose from its relevance to defence conversion, as it was discussed and "unpacked" it was applied to the very same problems which in England were its main impetus: structural unemployment and workers' lack of control over technological change.

One illustration of this wider relevance of the ideas behind the Lucas plan is the welcome given to Mike Cooley by the UAW local 600 in Detroit. This is the trade-union branch which covers the River Rouge Ford plant and is probably one of the largest trade-union branches in the world. During 1978 they had been working with Harley Shaken, a researcher for the UAW, on the consequences of new toolroom machinery for the skills of the toolroom workers and their control over the labour process.

DETROIT CITY COUNCIL

Testimonial Resolution

Lucas Aerospace

Detroiters have experienced the hardships of poverty, the devastation of plant closings, the loss of jobs through automation, and currently, the spectre of large-scale permanent unemployment for Chrysler Workers.

The Lucas Aerospace Workers in Britain have refused to accept the painful contradiction between a society that wastes its human resources, and have refused to accept unemployment as the price they must pay for technological change.

We in Detroit can learn a valuable lesson from the Lucas Aerospace Workers' Plan, in moving the production process and the society in a positive and humane direction.

Through Harley Shaken the River Rouge workers became interested in the ideas of the Lucas stewards about new technology and unemployment. The Ford workers felt the Lucas Aerospace workers' ideas to be so important that they pressed the Detroit City Council to make a presentation to Mike Cooley as a representative of the Lucas Combine Committee. The inscription (see insert on previous page) in effect sums up reasons why the Lucas Aerospace Combine Committee had such an impact on the other side of the Atlantic.

West Germany: "The Lucas Plan points to a way out of the impasse"
In Europe too the interest in the Plan came from both disarmament groups, rejecting the false choice of disarmament or jobs, and industrial workers facing structural unemployment and decline. In West Germany, for instance, Lucas shop stewards found that several local leaders of I.G. Metall were very keen to discuss an alternative to arms production that would also stem the growing threat of unemployment. The threatened closure in 1975 of the VFW factory in the town of Speyer brought the two issues together and also led to contact with the Lucas Combine Committee.

The livelihood of the town was almost entirely dependent on the survival of VFW, which made mainly military equipment. Because of this dependence and because of strong trade-union organization in the VFW factories, the workers and citizens of Speyer organized one of the most militant campaigns to be witnessed in post-war Germany. An occupation was maintained for twenty-four hours a day for twenty days. The climax of the campaign was a demonstration organized by "citizens' committees" alongside the trade union, I.G. Metall. The campaign was for the existing jobs to be kept. That meant jobs on the Multi-Role Combat Aircraft. But the leaders of the campaign sensed the short-term nature of their campaign to keep the MRCA. Willi Weber, the I.G. Metall chairman in the factory, was very clear about this in an interview at the time: "There is no long-term advantage in arms production. In fact there is far too much arms production in Germany and the Western World." A year later Weber and his colleagues came, with the help of a group of film-makers, to England to speak to members of the Lucas Aerospace Combine Committee, and a representative of the Combine went to speak to workers in Speyer. The Lucas Plan touched on exactly the problem which Weber and his colleagues sensed during their magnificent and partially successful campaign to save their factory: "The Lucas Plan may not be a complete formula but it has taken the disarmament movement out of a cul-de-sac," commented Weber in the film. A film was made about the connections between conversion in Germany and the Lucas Aerospace Plan, and the experience of workers from Speyer was used to illustrate these connections. The film was made in 1977; since that time it has been shown regularly as part of the educational programme of I.G. Metall as well as being used by the disarmament movement, the Green Party and other radical movement in Germany. I.G. Metall adopted a policy of encouraging conversion plans at its national conference in 1977. In the last two years this has led to work on such plans in several shipyards. Moreover, the I.G. Metall have created two research centres to carry out work on alternative plans, one in Berlin and one in Hamburg, inspired partly by the Lucas experience.

Swedish workers develop their own plans

In Sweden, the conversion aspect of the Plan was taken up by trade unionists producing fighter planes at SAAB. In 1978 trade unionists at the large SAAB plant in Linköping contacted the Combine Committee to discuss alternatives to the fighter planes on which they normally worked. Orders had come to an end and new orders were not yet in the pipeline. The manual workers at SAAB wanted to start producing telechiric devices (which SAAB had the facilities to make) instead of pressing for more military orders. The technical staff, on the other hand — or at least their representatives — were keen to continue working on the fighter planes. So the manual workers independently waged a vigorous campaign, as there was no joint organization. They drew directly from the ideas of the Lucas Plan. As a result of discussion with Lucas stewards, these Swedish workers succeeded in making their management contact Lucas management with a view to collaborating on the production of telechiric devices. Lucas, however, never informed the Combine Committee of this contact. The Combine heard about it from the trade unions in SAAB. The initiative did not come to anything, partly because new fighter plane orders at SAAB rather took the wind out of the campaign in Sweden and partly because of the total lack of response from Lucas management in Britain.

Another group of workers in Sweden who made contact with the Lucas stewards were shipyard workers in Gorhenburg shipyard, Götranken. Together with researchers based at Gothenburg University they had begun to explore what alternative proposals could provide a focus for resistance to redundancies in shipbuilding. They produced an extensive list of ideas, for example floating fertilizer and ammonia factories to avoid the pollution problems of such factories on land, as well as plans for desalination factories in Third World countries and several other ideas. These proposals acted as a focus for a struggle which at least delayed the redundancies and cut down the numbers involved, though it did not save all the jobs. This initiative is an interesting contrast to the campaign at SAAB because the proposals were drawn up entirely by white-collar workers, although manual workers were involved in the campaign for implementing them. In 1977 two delegates from the Lucas Combine went to Gothenburg to share their experiences with the shipyard workers.

While these delegates were in Sweden a third group of workers, women from the Algot Nord factory in Skelleften, began a campaign around similar principles to those of the Lucas Plan. The fashion-wear factory where these women worked was going to close. The women desperately needed the jobs and were keen to try anything to keep the factory open. They had heard about the Lucas Plan on radio programmes and in the

press, and they travelled nearly eight hundred miles to hear a talk that
Terry Moran from Burnley and Mike Cooley from Willesden were giving
near Stockholm. Soon after they had returned to Skelleften they and their
colleagues started to draw up their own alternative plan for protective and
utility clothing as a basis for their campaign to keep the factory open. They
did this in a very direct, some might say naive, way. They contacted wood-
choppers, slaughterhouse workers, steelworkers, miners and hospital
workers asking them what kind of special clothing they needed. At first
people laughed. The Algot Nord women talked to them, explaining what
they were trying to do, and soon they were convinced. As a result the
women received detailed replies from thirty-seven sources. Their campaign
was only partially successful. They failed to make the government (the
textile industry is nationalized in Sweden) keep the factory open itself, but
at least they were given the factory and an initial grant to start a
co-operative. All the twenty or so women who had fought so hard kept
their jobs; the co-operative is still going and slowly expanding to this day.
    The three groups of Swedish trade unionists who made contact with the
Lucas workers illustrate a response which was widespread in Sweden. In
fact it is probably there that the ideas of the Lucas Plan have gained the
most response. There have been several television films and radio programmes on the Lucas Plan, and also two books, one of which is now into
its second edition. Part of the explanation for the particularly favourable
response which the ideas of the Plan received in Sweden lies in the fact that
trade unions there have managed to include a wider range of issues in
collective bargaining than in Britain or West Germany. Job evaluation,
work study, and employment decisions are all to a varying extent covered
by collective bargaining. This has come about not so much as a result of a
greater militancy on the part of Swedish trade unionists, but rather the
contrary. For although the Swedish trade-union movement is strong in
terms of membership density, it is also highly centralized and relatively
"orderly". For these reasons management in the past have had little fear of
from militant shop-floor-based organizations taking their own initiatives
independently of agreements made by their officials. An extension of
collective bargaining has not therefore been seen by management as the
threat to management prerogatives which British management perceive it
to be. The recession, however, brought sharper conflicts of interests, and
with them, the need for trade-union policies within collective bargaining
which expressed workers' distinct interests.
    The Lucas workers' Plan, reflecting its origin in a trade-union
organization with a far greater tradition of militancy and independence
than was usual in Sweden, provided a vivid example of exactly such
policies. The Lucas Plan contained both a long-term strategy and more
immediate bargaining proposals which were based on entirely different
priorities from those of management. Moreover, these priorities enabled
trade unionists to call the bluff of government and management claims to

social responsibility. This was especially important in relation to the government, because a high proportion of the economy is state-owned and it is widely assumed that the government is morally obliged to guarantee jobs.

Shared heresies gain expression

It is clear from all the diverse responses across the industrialized Western world that the Lucas stewards were saying something fundamental about the direction in which the productive system of these countries was heading, and at what cost to the majority of people. Perhaps the common implicit theme in responses to the Plan was the challenge to the idea of "progress" which justifies the momentum towards ever greater powers of destruction, towards increasingly and indiscriminately capital-intensive forms of production. The Lucas shop stewards' Plan gave people greater confidence to stand back, take stock and ask, "Is this the kind of progress we want, that marches carelessly over our livelihoods, our skills and our dreams?" There is everywhere a strong conventional wisdom that "you can't stand in the way of progress" even if it destroys you. There is even a feeling that to object would be selfish, parochial and ultimately futile. The impact of the Lucas Plan lies partly in the fact that its concreteness, and coherence gave others confidence to express openly their silent scepticism. These heresies have, of course, been expressed before by individual scientists and technologists. But as soon as they do so they are quickly marginalized with rumours that they are going senile, or their views are deliberately suppressed. David Noble, Professor of History of Science at MIT, gave three vivid examples from the United States.[1]

The first example is of a former president of the American Society of Mechanical Engineers (ASME) and a manager at General Electric called Dexter Kimball, who gave a speech in 1932 on the meaning of technological progress. In his speech he acknowledged the problem of technological unemployment and urged a shorter work week and ameliorative social legislation. He also, most heretically of all, suggested the option of slowing down the rate of progress, towards increasing automation and mass-production. Such a suggestion, however, overstepped the limits of acceptable discourse. It questioned the ideology of progress. When the ASME published the speech, this last paragraph was deleted and in its place was substituted: "Finally, whether industrial progress be slow or rapid, these new methods are here to stay."

Fifteen years later another scientist, Norbert Wiener, received similar treatment when he dared to ask questions about the social consequences of his work. He was the father of cybernetics (which wedded computer and servo-mechanisms and paved the way for the automatic factory). In 1947 he published a letter in which he announced that he would no longer publish his work out of fear that it would inevitably get into the hands of "irresponsible militarists". Two years later, Wiener went further; deeply concerned about the probable social implications of the applications of computers and servo-mechanisms to workers in industry, he refused to do any consulting work for companies getting into this field, such as General Electric. At this point in his career, when he was voicing his alarm about the social consequences of so-called progress, people started to talk about his approaching senility.

The third heretic was John Parsons, the inventor of numerical control and, as such, the originator of computer-based manufacturing. In 1965 the editor of *American Machinist* interviewed Parsons and asked him what he thought should be the best technological path to travel over the next ten years. Parson replied, to his interviewer's astonishment, that he thought there should be a moratorium on all new technological development, that instead of developing new gadgets we should learn first how to use more effectively what we already have. Noble describes the response: "A moratorium!" the editor exclaimed. "If I write that in my magazine everyone will think I'm crazy." Parsons suggested that the editor instead simply quote him as saying it. "But then they'll think you're crazy." The editor never printed the interview.

As we shall see, both the leaders of "progress" and their political allies have tried in a similar way to defuse the Lucas shop stewards' challenge by describing them as "mavericks" and by denying them any kind of legitimacy. However, they have proved more difficult to outlaw than isolated scientists. The reason is not simply that the shop stewards are part of a collective; rather it is that they are a collective which represents those on whom the smooth running of the wheels of "progress" depend. This challenge has given confidence not simply to dissident intellectuals but to others who, like the Lucas stewards, make possible the day-to-day normality of "progress". Moreover their questioning of the direction of this "progress" arose from within the very process of making these wheels go round. They consequently are able to see the other directions in which the wheels can go; and the ways they can be redesigned. So their questioning of the glib optimism of the conventional views of progress was not fatalistic. It could help directly to mobilize for change.

The problems accompanying success

There was, however, a contradiction in all this. For while the very nature of the Combine Committee's trade-union base and history gave the Plan its wider impact, it also posed problems for how this impact could be followed through. It meant for instance that all the Combine Committee delegates had considerable trade-union responsibilities in their own factory or section: negotiating on wages, bonus rates, health and safety, overtime and so on. Some had more local responsibilities than others. Senior stewards from shop-floor unions, for instance, were involved in domestic wage negotiations for sometimes as long as six months in the year, involving sometimes weekly meetings with management preceded by detailed preparatory work and requiring regular mass meetings. Moreover, only about three of the Combine delegates had had any experience of public speaking beyond mass meetings in their own factory. A further problem was that the Combine had very little money to finance educational material and visits beyond their own locality. In 1976 there was £2,000 in the deposit account (from the Burnley strike fund) and £750 annual income from affiliations and sales of *Combine News*.

How did they cope with all the requests to speak, to supply information, to respond to the media, and to campaign for the Plan within the company and with the government? In the first few weeks most of the speaking was done by the most experienced delegates. But soon other delegates were being thrown in at the deep end, as Brian Salisbury, a TASS representative from Birmingham, recalls:

> Ernie and Mike arranged for BBC television to come to the factory and interview me. I felt I made a real mess of it. But it made me want to get on top of the Plan. I was a terrible speaker, like most people I'd never really thought I'd got anything to say. But I went ahead, and the leading people in the Combine encouraged me. Eventually I really felt I was able to communicate with people. I felt I was getting through to them when I spoke. It was a tremendous lesson. And it gave me more ability and confidence on other union issues.

Salisbury's experience seems to have been fairly typical: being thrown in and finding that in spite of initial doubts, you can swim after all.

As the interest in the Combine Committee and the Corporate Plan grew, delegates began to consider how to spread the load and involve new stewards. First they divided the country so that different plants took responsibility for different regions. This also meant that some of the plants less involved in the Combine were encouraged to play a more active part. Where possible an experienced speaker would take someone who was new to the Combine, and would then, after several meetings, encourage them to do the initial speech. This did not always work. Stewards still felt reluctant to introduce meetings. So the Combine executive tried another idea. Mick Cooney, not himself one to be hesitant about speaking, explains the background:

> Most shop stewards can handle the foreman, but are a little frightened of higher management. Yet once they've had to deal with higher management they're no longer afraid. Also they meet government ministers and see through all the mystique. And once you've cut through the mystique, they're away. It's the same with addressing strangers. . . . We had the idea that a slide show with a tape would mean that a lad who has never done it before would be able to present the slide and tape. Then once the dialogue had started they'd be in their element.

But things like tape and slide shows require money, as do a lot of the speaking visits themselves. At first the Lucas stewards only asked for the bare minimum from the groups they visited, even though an evening meeting usually meant the loss of an afternoon and sometimes a morning's pay. But it was difficult to sustain and widen the involvement on this basis.

Various *ad hoc* improvements did not solve either the financial problem or satisfy the growing publicity, research and information needs. So the Combine executive began to look for outside help. A small network of sympathetic researchers had already been established through the Science and Technology Advisory Committee and the Corporate Plan. In March 1976 the Combine asked the secretary to explore ways in which this could be made more permanent.

A new use of academic resources

There followed nearly two years of thinking, discussion and finally negotiations which led in February 1978 to a new phase in the Combine Committee's campaign for socially useful production: the founding of a centre based at North-East London Polytechnic bringing together academic researchers with industrial and later public-sector workers. In many ways the discussions leading up to the formation of CAITS (Centre for Alternative Industrial and Technological Systems — no one will own up to inventing the name!) also helped to clarify and make more explicit some of the principles behind the Corporate Plan.

One of the things which had struck combine delegates as they thumbed their way through technical journals and talked to sympathetic academics was the extent of the tie-up between the management of the major private corporations and the universities and polytechnics. They found that research projects, laboratories and sometimes whole departments were jointly funded by corporations with the more or less explicit understanding that the research is orientated to meet the needs of "industry", as defined by management. Symbolizing these understandings are the representatives of management who sit on the governing bodies of universities and polytechnics.

In the past many of the shop stewards involved in the Combine Committee had tended to treat the universities as somehow apart from industry and industrial conflict, ivory towers which the tax-payer sustained because the pursuit of knowledge was in some mysterious way a Good Thing. Once the Combine stewards had cut through the mystique, they looked at the resources locked up in academic institutions in a new light. From their visits to polytechnics and universities as speakers, and in some cases from their own or their children's experiences, they knew what resources were available. They considered that as tax-payers and members of the surrounding community they had a right of access to these resources: to office space, to libraries with periodicals which public libraries cannot afford, to workshops without management supervision and to contact with people from many different disciplines.

Out of its past work with sympathetic academics the Combine had begun to evolve some principles by which the practical skills of industrial workers and the generalizing skills of academics could be most creatively combined.

These principles involved a rejection of the assumption, built into our education system, of an equation between linguistic ability and intelligence and a recognition instead of the tacit skills which come from experience. Mick Cooley illustrates the point with an example from the work of aerospace engineers:

> We have ordinary maintenance fitters who go to London Airport if a generator system is causing a problem. The whole aircraft might perhaps be grounded because of it. One of these fitters can listen to the generator, make a series of apparently simple tests — some of the old fitters will touch it in the way a doctor will touch a patient — and if it is running, will be able to tell you from the vibrations whether a bearing is worn and which one.
>
> The decision may be far more profound in many ways than that which an academic scientist might make, yet if you asked those "ordinary people" to tell you how they reached that decision, they could not do so in the usually accepted sense.

The philosopher of science, Michael Polanyi, has attempted to show the importance of this tacit knowledge, as he puts it: these things "we know but cannot tell".[2] Polanyi left it at that. He treated tacit knowledge as unsusceptible to conscious understanding, and therefore tended towards a conservative irrationalism. The Combine Committee, however, starting from a commitment to social change, were concerned to understand these tacit skills in order to be able to generalize about the social conditions under which such skills could be fully exercised and developed.[3] This required co-operation with academics whose work and training enabled them to generalize and theorize.

However, they were wary of being dominated by academics, whom they suspected of having a tendency to appropriate the knowledge of others rather than engaging in joint work. So from its founding in February 1978 CAITS was controlled jointly by a representative of the Engineering faculty of the polytechnic, Richard Fletcher, and a representative of the Combine Committee, Mike Cooley. The CAITS advisory committee, too, contains both professors and shop stewards. Also the people who worked at CAITS have already tried to relate theorizing and practical activity in a way which makes it possible for industrial workers and academics to co-operate. This has usually meant that the theorizing and the generalizing involved in a project is done as the work progresses. The process by which the Corporate Plan itself was drawn up also illustrates this principle. If full political/ theoretical agreement and clarity about all the implications of the Plan had been a precondition for beginning, then the Plan would never have got off the ground. Yet a reflective process has gone on through the discussions at Wortley Hall, at the sites and at the meetings and conferences based on the Corporate Plan. And this reflection on a common experience has led to much greater political agreement at a higher level of understanding than existed prior to the Plan.

One area in which the Combine believed it would be especially important for CAITS to carry out joint work was prototypes of the Plan's proposals. It was increasingly clear that the company was not going to provide the resources for such prototypes, and the Combine on its own, without positive government support, did not have the strength to force them to do so. Yet the existence of prototypes would strengthen trade-union bargaining positions for new products in the future and would enhance the credibility of the Plan in the eyes of the membership. In these respects the Combine was not thinking only of its own needs but of the usefulness of developed prototypes for trade unionists elsewhere needing positive bargaining positions with which to resist redundancies. The importance of access to facilities for working on the hardware of the Plan was one factor which led the Combine to approach North-East London Polytechnic. This polytechnic has extensive research and development laboratories along with workshops equipped for testing and manufacturing a wide range of engineering and other products. Another point in its favour was that engineers from NELP, in particular Richard Fletcher, had already worked with the Combine Committee on one of the products in the Corporate Plan: the road-rail vehicle. Full development of a prototype of this vehicle would be one of CAITS's first projects. The Dean of the Engineering Faculty, Jim Proctor, took the Poly's claims to social responsibility literally, and was also keen on the idea of CAITS. He expressed this belief in his speech at the opening of CAITS in January 1978:

> NELP is especially pleased to be involved in this development since it matches the approach the Polytechnic has taken since it was first established in 1970, that of an outward looking organization which wishes to use its intellectual and material resources to help to solve problems of social value presented by the outside world.

It later turned out that when such social involvement required taking sides in social conflicts, as inevitably it would, the leading members of the board of governors took fright and did their best to "delete" CAITS from the Poly's facilities. But that was not until 1980; and CAITS survived. At first all went well, with the Poly providing the hardware and the office facilities. The Joseph Rowntree Charitable Trust provided the initial funding, and in February 1978 CAITS began its work in a pocket-sized office with one worker: the Centre's co-ordinator Mike George. A second worker, Jane Barker, was recruited a few months later.* These two CAITS researchers and organizers, the two co-directors and the advisory committee had an ambitious brief:

---

* At the time of writing, there are four people working full-time at CAITS: Mike George, Jane Barker, Dot Lewis and Dave Pelly.

To assist the Combine Committee in the development of various Lucas Plan products, and to help to develop the economic and social arguments to support the shop-floor-led demand for industrial conversion and diversification.

To act as a clearing house for the Lucas Corporate Plan and promote the development and application of socially useful products. To establish expertise in the field of socially useful products, and make this available to other groups. To engage in the promotion of design, development, prototype manufacture, production and marketing of "alternative" products. Also to assist in the development of more socially desirable, non-hierarchical organizational forms of industry.

To assist in establishing small-scale co-operative ventures and community industries in the East London area.

CAITS has rapidly become known internationally as a source of information on workers' plans in the UK; it has been bombarded with requests for speakers, documentation and films and has played host to many hundreds of overseas visitors, students, researchers and journalists as well as trade unionists. The creation of CAITS was in these ways the Combine's first step to overcome the pressures which the interest aroused by their Combine Plan placed on their day-to-day trade-union responsibilities. CAITS made it easier for the Combine to carry out joint work with other trade unionists, researchers and sympathetic activists in different campaigns. In this way it enabled the Combine Committee to follow through the wider political ideas which it had stimulated. There was, however, still a tension involved in keeping the right balance at different times between the Combine's more traditional trade union activities and the activities connected with the Corporate Plan.

At times, between 1977 and 1979, the Combine did neglect some of its work on wages and conditions. The main reason for this was not so much the visits abroad and public meetings across Britain but rather that the Combine secretary and several members of the executive were spending the greater part of their energies trying to get some practical support from the government. This seemingly straightforward objective proved much more difficult than the Combine had anticipated.

15 Up against institutions whose time is past

Labour ministers

> "The Government looks to those who work in industry to make industrial democracy succeed so that it may make the contribution that is needed to improve the efficiency of our industries and the prosperity of the country. [From the Labour government's White Paper on Industrial Democracy].

Were not the Lucas Aerospace stewards doing exactly what the government said it wanted from those working in industry? Was not the Corporate Plan an exemplary case of workers making a contribution to the "prosperity of the country" — if that phrase refers to the standard of living and job security of the majority of the country's people? The Combine certainly took the government at its word. On 28 November 1975, even before the Plan was made public, Ernie Scarbrow wrote to Eric Varley at the Department of Industry to explain the Combine's proposals and their wider relevance to the problems facing Varley's department, and to seek the government's advice and support:

> Central to our concern is a desire not to find ourselves in a year or two in a "Chrysler situation". . . .
> The point in writing is to formally request a meeting with you and representatives of your department; in order that we can present the plan to you formally, discuss its contents in some detail and consider ways in which it could best be implemented. . . .
> We feel it would be particularly desirable at this stage to have a discussion with you so that you are aware of the overall plans we have in mind rather than your department be continuously confronted with a series of isolated problems at each of the individual plants.

Labour governments frequently complain about trade unionists being irresponsible and apathetic. For instance at the end of 1976 Jim Callaghan, in a private letter about planning agreements, said:

> I regret to say that we have also faced a lack of enthusiasm for, and lack of knowledge about, planning agreements amongst many local shop stewards — which companies have naturally used as an argument for moving slowly.[1]

How did the government treat a group of workers keen to make a positive and socially responsible contribution, keen to make planning agreements work and to avoid hopeless situations like the Chrysler collapse? Would Varley or one of his ministers meet the stewards in order to understand the details of their proposals and to use Lucas as a case to educate and enthuse stewards elsewhere? A meeting with the Combine seemed to be the last thing that the government would consider. Ernie Scarbrow describes what happened during the two years following the Combine's initial approach to the government:

Varley passed us on to Gerald Kaufman. And we tried to pin him down on something quite specific, and then he passed us off to his deputy, Huckfield. And we've had a whole mass of correspondence with Huckfield, and now he no longer writes to us, it's his secretary that writes to us.

From late 1975 to mid-1977 the different messengers from the Department of Industry carried the same message. Gerald Kaufman, 22 December 1975:

I hope you will now be able to proceed . . . by having talks with your management about the plan, and then sending a copy to me when your discussions are complete.

Scarbrow then sent to the Department of Industry a letter from Lucas Aerospace management which refused yet again to meet the Combine Committee, even on a tripartite basis (that is, with the government). In his reply of November 1976 Kaufman asserted:

I have been firmly of the view that the proper place for the examination of your ideas must be, at least initially, within Lucas Aerospace. I understand discussions are taking place within the normal machinery.

And after Scarbrow had for the second time told the Department of Industry that *no discussions of the Corporate Plan were taking place* (even the Burnley negotiations over the heat pump were not then in progress), Kaufman wrote on 24 December:

Let me repeat our understanding; this is that for some time the company and its employees have been examining a number of the suggestions in your plan within the normal consultative machinery.

By this time "the employees" felt they should come to the House of Commons and explain their case. On 1 March 1977 seventy of them packed into a House of Commons Committee room. The delegation included staff and manual union representatives from every site. If anyone would know whether discussions were going on they would, as they were the people with whom the consultations were supposed to be taking place. They spent the whole afternoon explaining to the MPs, including Les Huckfield from the Department of Industry and Albert Booth from the Department of Employment, that the company had wanted to divert the Corporate Plan proposals into local consultative discussions; but that they, the workers' elected representatives, were insisting on negotiations. A month later, however, the Department of Industry was still refusing to consider the Combine's proposals on the grounds that discussions were already taking place within the company. Les Huckfield to Chris Price on 4 April 1977:

My understanding is that the more promising ideas put forward in the "corporate plan" are in fact already being discussed within the Works

Council structure that has been set up in the various Lucas Aerospace Divisions.

Huckfield and the other Industry ministers seemed prepared to accept the company's word,* and leave it at that, hoping no doubt that the issue would die away. Labour MPs in constituencies where Lucas Aerospace workers lived were more inclined to listen to those workers and to investigate further the company's claims. Jeff Rooker, a Birmingham MP, wrote to the chairman of Lucas Industries on behalf of twelve or so other MPs expressing their concern that the company was not giving the stewards' proposals the attention they deserved. The company responded quickly and a meeting was held on 17 March 1977 in the House of Commons with three senior directors, the deputy chairman and two other directors. Audrey Wise, one of the MPs present, gives her personal impression of the meeting:

> The company representatives assured us that they were anxious to diversify, and that they didn't need the Combine to tell them, but when we tried to pin them down to what new products they were thinking of, they became extremely vague.

Jeff Rooker describes two details of the meeting which he found particularly disturbing, first: "It took us over half an hour of cross-examining to discover they weren't actually talking to the authors of the Corporate Plan." Secondly, the company gave away their real motives and priorities when they handed round to all Labour MPs a list of fourteen ways in which the government could help Lucas Aerospace with orders for aircraft. "That is," commented Rooker, "they came to lobby us on behalf of the Company with its existing product set-up, whereas we specifically asked to talk about the problems of future recession in the industry and diversification using the skills and technology of the Company."

National Economic Development Organization

Towards the end of 1976 the government had launched its much vaunted Industrial Strategy, "to regenerate British industry". Eric Varley had written to the chairman of every major British-based company asking him what steps the company intended to take to implement this strategy. The "strategy" was intended to be "tripartite", involving the unions as well as the company and government. However, neither the government nor the unions did anything, beyond talking, to ensure that the "strategy", such as it was, had any impact on company-level decisions. The Lucas Combine tried to give the Industrial Strategy a cutting edge. Ernie Scarbrow wrote the following letter to Whitney, the Lucas Aerospace personnel director:

---

* And the concept of "work councils" which the TUC and Labour Party both oppose.

You will know that Eric Varley, Secretary of State for Industry, has written to Mr Bernard Scott as Chairman of Lucas Aerospace, asking him what steps the Company intends to take in respect of the implementation, at company level, of the Government's "Industrial Strategy". Because of the tripartite nature of this agreement all unions have been asked to become involved in the implementation of this planning strategy at company level.

The point in writing is to request a meeting with the Directors in order that the Combine Committee can explore the means by which this planning could take place.

Whitney again refused to meet the Combine. At the same time the Chairman of Lucas Industries was telling the *Sunday Telegraph* that Lucas had no interest in the government's plan for industry. "You cannot plan Lucas," he asserted (*Sunday Telegraph*, 19 July 1976).

In the face of this intransigence the Combine tried to enlist the support of the TUC, the government's partner in the Industrial Strategy. This move came up against another reason for not discussing the Plan. In one of the nice, friendly letters to which the Combine were getting accustomed, David Lea of the TUC Economic Department, after stressing that "the TUC fully share your concern", went on:

Government and employer representatives took the view that Lucas Aerospace did not fall within any of the 39 sectors identified in the Industrial Strategy and therefore the issue could not appropriately be pursued in that form.

On this basis very few multi-plant, multi-division companies could be brought into the Industrial Strategy. And indeed the TUC did not accept entirely the government and company argument. But the TUC were not prepared to take the issue any further on their own. David Lea's letter to the Combine ends up with the by now familiar message:

We suggest that you again approach the company on this matter. . . . The views expressed in this letter should be drawn to the attention of the company, and should you encounter further difficulties, please do not hesitate to contact us again.

The TUC

Lucas management, however, remained unmoved. The company's next reply to Scarbrow not only insisted that they would not meet the Combine in the future but also denied that there had ever been any regular contact with the Combine in the past. Scarbrow went back to the TUC. This time he wrote more to draw the lessons of management's response than with any expectations of practical support. Management's refusal to discuss company plans with the Combine Committee means, Scarbrow argued, "that when a group of workers are sufficiently well organized, at an industrial level, to attempt to put into practice what the TUC is advocating, large monopolies like Lucas simply show contempt for both you and me."

You would have thought that by now a Labour government and TUC who were serious about their Industrial Strategy, based as it was on job creation and the involvement of trade unions in strategic planning, would have got round a table with the authors of the Corporate Plan to discuss the problems of implementing it. There were several possible courses of action which could have been taken immediately. For example, the government could have taken the very minimal step of using its own resources to initiate a feasibility study of the product lines in the Corporate Plan. Such a study would have included discussions with several government departments who would be the major customers for some of the products. On the basis of this study the government could have then used all its powers to ensure that those products that were viable on commercial and/or social grounds were developed and brought into production. It could have made all future financial assistance conditional upon reasonable progress being made to introduce products in the Corporate Plan. When it came to carrying through its wages policy the government had seen no problem in making financial and other forms of support to private companies conditional on their compliance with government policy. Why could not the principle be applied in relation to the Industrial Strategy? Another option suggested at the time by people sympathetic to the Combine Committee was that the NEB could be instructed by the Secretary of State to undertake manufacture of some of the products in the Corporate Plan. Such NEB units should, it was argued, be in the immediate vicinity of existing Lucas factories. These are just some points that could have been discussed, had there been an ounce of determination to get something done.

Department of Industry

At this stage one of the main obstacles to getting something done lay in the entrenched relationships between the Aerospace division of the Department of Industry and Lucas (along with all other Aerospace companies) and in the ministers' reluctance to challenge the advice of these civil servants. Of all sectors of British industry, aerospace had, and probably still has, the closest relations with the government. Aerospace is one of the only industrial sectors in which the government has been directly involved throughout the post-war period. Even in the 1950s, when direct government involvement in industry was minimal, the Aerospace industry, including Lucas, was receiving special government help. Throughout the 1950s and most of the '60s there was a special government department responsible for the aerospace industry. The Aerospace Division of the Department of Industry of the 1970s inherited the close relations built up by previous Air Ministries. One indication of the close relations between the Department of Industry and Lucas is an easy interchange of leading personnel from the department to the company and vice versa. In 1978 John Williams, deputy chairman of Lucas Aerospace, was seconded to work as the right-hand man to the chairman of the NEB, with special responsibility for British Leyland (incidentally a major customer of Lucas Industries). More significant, though, were the movements of Sir Anthony Part, who until June 1976 was Permanent Secretary at the Department of Industry. In an interview with *The Director* in January 1975 Part mentioned that he wished to go into industry or commerce when he retired from the Civil Service. *The Director* thought this might at first be difficult:

> Unfortunately there are complications here, owing to the Civil Service rules about retired top bureaucrats going into firms with which they have had official dealings . . . it doesn't look as if there'll be many firms which don't fall into that category for Sir Anthony Part.

Certainly, Lucas did not fall into that category. As Permanent Secretary, Part would have had contact with Lucas at least since the Department of Industry in 1969 gave Lucas £3 million to carry out the initial rationalization of the Aerospace components industry in 1969. But this kind of complication did not slow Part down in the rapid fulfilment of his desire to be an industrial baron. By October 1976, three months after leaving the Department of Industry, he took up his seat on the Board of Directors of Lucas Industries. A very useful man to have around at a time when the company was under fire from shop stewards who earlier had been encouraged by Part's *bête noire* Tony Benn. The Combine Committee has always wondered what role Part played, behind the scenes, in the discussions with the Department of Industry between 1977 and 1979 (and probably earlier).

It was the civil servants involved in these close relations who gave Kaufman his advice on Lucas Aerospace. And their advice came from consulting the management of Lucas Aerospace. No contact was made with the unions concerned either at a national officer level at this stage or a shop-steward level. Moreover, these civil servants would have been extremely resistant to any proposal that might imply directly contradicting Lucas management's opinions. For example, the idea of the Department of Industry carrying out an assessment of the Corporate Plan would imply that Lucas management could be wrong. Even such a modest and moderate initiative as this went directly against the deeply-entrenched traditions of the Department of Industry. It would have required a minister strongly committed to the involvement of shop stewards in industrial strategy to override advice from such quarters. In fact, judging by the fate of Tony Benn, the one minister who did have such a commitment, it would have required a lot more than a strong political will on the part of an individual minister.

Gerald Kaufman, who was responsible for Aerospace, showed little sign of any faith in the capacity of shop stewards to draw up plans for industry:

> You really are quite often in the position where the shop stewards in the company can only see the tree trunks because by definition they

are very low down. They are grassroots workers' representatives and they can't see the wider problems.

However, he showed considerable respect for trade-union leaders: "There are some people with exceptional ability in the Confederation" (of Shipbuilding and Engineering Unions).

The Confederation of Shipbuilding and Engineering Unions

And it was to these "exceptionally able" men that the buck was next passed. By mid-1977, Labour ministers at last had acknowledged the company's refusal to discuss the Corporate Plan. However, instead of the government using its powers directly to set up a meeting with the Combine, ministers sent the Combine Committee off to the Confederation of Shipbuilding and Engineering Unions. This had now replaced the company's consultative machinery as the "proper channel". Ministers asked MPs sympathetic to the Combine Committee to encourage it to make contact with the Confederation. Les Huckfield wrote to Jeff Rooker (22 June 1977):

> It is our very clear understanding in the Department that the CSEU would respond in a positive way to requests from the Combine Committee to take up their problems providing of course, the Combine Committee uses the established trade-union machinery.

An innuendo is creeping in here: that it is the Combine Committee which is at fault for not using "the established trade-union machinery". Since this criticism of the Combine Committee becomes an important factor — even a scapegoat — later on, it is worth commenting on its accuracy at this point.

First, what is "the established trade-union machinery"? It could mean simply the district and national structure of each union. In this sense of term, Combine delegates had already put resolutions in support of the Corporate Plan through the established trade-union machinery of at least the three main unions concerned, the AUEW — Engineering Section, AUEW-TASS and the TGWU. With different degrees of responsiveness and enthusiasm each of these unions adopted the general approach of the Corporate Plan as union policy.

If by "established trade-union machinery" is meant the procedure of the Confederation of Shipbuilding and Engineering Unions then the matter is more complex; and it is by no means self-evident that the Combine Committee should have taken the Corporate Plan through the Confederation executive, although once they were directed by the government to take this course of action, they immediately did so. Neither is it self-evident that, assuming the issue should have gone through the Confederation at some point, it was the Combine's responsibility alone to pass it through. National union executives can get issues on to the agenda of the Confederation executive, and items can be submitted through District Confederations. A proposal brought by a national union executive is likely to get on to the agenda with far more speed and a greater possibility of success than a resolution from a district Confederation. Proposals to support the Combine's Corporate Plan had reached three union executives by mid-1977. If these executives felt the issue should be taken through the Confederation then they had every opportunity to do so. Moreover union leaders themselves frequently improvise beyond the formal procedures of the Confed. For example, they have got together in an *ad hoc* way in response to major redundancy crises such as British Leyland.

There are two important differences between these cases and Lucas Aerospace: first, the Lucas Aerospace shop stewards were proposing action *before* a major redundancy crisis broke. Their Plan was an attempt to *anticipate* management plans with positive bargaining policies. Most trade-union structures are reactive, and the Confederation perhaps more deeply so than any other. Secondly, the role in which trade-union leaders were brought into most of the redundancy crises of the late 1970s was to negotiate the final redundancy settlement, when whatever shop-floor resistance there had been had petered out. In the case of Lucas Aerospace they were being required to support a shop-steward initiated campaign. A third factor explaining why union leaders did not improvise to provide that support is that the leadership of the union with the largest number of members in Lucas Aerospace — AUEW-TASS — was hostile to the Combine Committee and other more sympathetic unions such as the TGWU and ASTMS had not at that time (1976–7) recognized the importance of the alternative Plan.

Against this background of unresponsiveness and inertia on the part of the trade-union establishment, what explains the sudden insistence, in June 1977, that the Combine should go through the Confederation in order even to *discuss* the Plan with a government minister? Gerald Kaufman explains why he refused to meet the Combine and insisted they must go through the Confederation:

> The Combine was in no sense a body which was representative of the workers on the shop floor. It was a self-selected group of people who decided that there was a job that had to be done, but they represented nobody but themselves. They were shop stewards but they were not elected as members of the Combine Committee. I am not knocking them. I am saying that there was no compulsion on anyone to deal with them any more than to deal with any other group of shop stewards who decided to get together on a factory basis.
>
> Now in the case of the Combine, what they did was to get something going and to get a small group of Members of Parliament *pretty well all of whom are no longer Members of Parliament* to take an interest and put pressure on, get resolutions, debates taking place and they created a problem for both the management and the Confederation.
>
> Since I believed the initiative they took was worth examining I wanted to see how that could be furthered.
>
> It was quite plain to me after very early meetings with the trade-

union leaders, *particularly Ken Gill and TASS*, there was no way of getting it furthered except through the Confederation. [Emphasis added.]

Ken Gill was centrally involved in the Confederation-government negotiations over Shipbuilding and Aerospace, the two industries for which Kaufman was responsible within the Department of Industry. Kaufman was concerned to maintain good relations with the Confederation and with a leading negotiator like Gill in particular. Also, as chairman of the CSEU Aerospace committee and General Secretary of the largest single union in Lucas Aerospace, Ken Gill's views had considerable authority within the Confederation's executive.

Why was Gill so insistent that government ministers should not meet the Combine other than through the Confederation? If it had been the result of a genuine concern to carry out the support which TASS had at different levels given to the Corporate Plan, then he would have taken action through the Confed or informally at an earlier stage. After all, a sub-committee of the TASS executive had recommended support for the Plan early in 1976. It would seem from TASS leadership's failure to take such an initiative, while at the same time insisting that the Confederation was the proper channel, that Gill was using the Confed more as a means of controlling the Combine's initiative rather than helping it.*

The Confederation structure (more because of its history than because of any conscious design) provides an ideal mechanism for a trade-union executive wishing to control a multi-union shop stewards' initiative to which it is hostile but which, on its own, it cannot control. For the Confederation can take action only with the agreement of all major affiliated unions. In effect a union closely associated with a particular case has the power of veto, although the details of the discussion and votes on the Confederation executive are never made public. Thus a determined executive of a single union can negatively determine the response of all the Confederation unions to a shop stewards' initiative, especially if the executive representatives of the other unions do not have any especial interest or information on the issue. Yet at the same time that union executive is not directly accountable to its shop stewards for what it has agreed on the Confederation executive. No minutes of any TASS committee ever reported the approach TASS was taking on the Confederation executive to the Lucas Corporate Plan. TASS representatives in Lucas Aerospace, for example, were never told that the Confederation Aerospace Committee wrote to Lucas Aerospace Management three times between July 1977 and January 1978; neither were they told of the content of these

---

* We have written to Ken Gill asking to discuss these and other issues concerning TASS's relation to the Lucas Aerospace Combine Committee. He has not replied.

letters. These letters eventually led to a meeting between Ken Gill and the management of Lucas Aerospace in January 1978 at which no Lucas Aerospace workers were present and about which they were never informed. Yet, as the next chapter will tell, this meeting was the beginning of negotiations over the company's major rationalization programme.*

At the same time as the Confederation was contacting the company, and the company was, when it suited them, agreeing to meet Gill, the Combine Committee, on Huckfield's instructions, was writing to the Confed. It wrote on three separate occasions between June 1977 and the end of the year. *These letters did not even receive an acknowledgement.* The first letter expressed pleasure and relief that the Confederation might provide a way out of the impasse. Three months and no progress later, the Combine felt they had merely gone down another dead-end street. Their secretary wrote:

> It is with surprise and disappointment that I must record that I have not even received from you an acknowledgement of that letter, although I wrote to you three months ago. To your committee, this may be just another routine matter, but to those of us here in Lucas Aerospace it is a matter of whether we will lose our jobs or not.

Even this condemnation did not elicit a reply, an apology or any communication whatsoever. When Jeff Rooker questioned Ken Gill about this lack of communication Gill commented that "there has been a lot of sickness at the Confederation". It is rather odd that the correspondence of an organization which claims to be important enough to control all contact with government ministers depends on a sick General Secretary. No one knows why the letters were not answered. Ernie Scarbrow suspects that it was not deliberate but rather an indication of what a completely run-down organization the Confederation had become, until resurrected and "ordained" by the Labour government and trade-union leaders as the most convenient way of conducting negotiations between themselves, more often than not without the involvement of "lay" representatives.

Planning agreements and government priorities

These attempts to get the government to follow up the Lucas workers' Plan were going on at a time when government ministers and civil servants were working out what to do about "planning agreements", a major part of the Labour Party's industrial policy. The Labour Party Conference had intended planning agreements with major corporations to be compulsory if necessary. But the 1975 White Paper on industrial policy, followed by the 1975 Industry Act, made them voluntary. Progress towards such voluntary planning agreements was very slow indeed. Only one was ever signed with a private company, Chrysler. Since Callaghan put some of the blame for

---

* They got to know about this meeting and these letters through a television researcher who interviewed Gill on the same day as he met the Lucas Aerospace management.

this on lack of interest from shop stewards, the implication was that he and his government would support and encourage expressions of interest by shop stewards. The experiences of this chapter indicate that no such idea had ever entered into ministerial or civil servant thinking. A note passed on to a sympathetic MP of a Department of Industry meeting on planning agreements indicates that ministers' main concern, as far as planning agreements were concerned, was how to be seen by the Party and MPs to be doing their best, while at the same time doing nothing that would unduly upset the CBI and its more powerful member companies.[2] In this thinking the national unions were a subordinate consideration. Shop stewards did not even figure in the discussions.

A similar order of priorities can be seen in the negotiations and deals which began in March 1978, when Lucas announced a major rationalization programme.

16 A lost opportunity

By January 1978 two years had passed since the Combine had made its first approach to the government. During this time Lucas management had not been standing still with its rationalization programme. In February 1977 they had announced that 1,100 workers were "surplus to requirements", and they proposed to cut 500 jobs in Liverpool, 300 in Burnley and 300 in Birmingham by August 1977. The majority of these jobs were saved after a combination of local pressure, as in Burnley, backed by a national overtime ban, a ban on sub-contract work outside the group and a threat to withdraw labour throughout the sites. The alternative Plan provided a strong argument for sustaining this resistance, and management retreated.

However, this merely delayed management's plans. They learnt lessons from their defeat and drew up new rationalization plans that took fuller account of the resistance they would meet, including the political support which the Combine had gained. In July 1977 Lucas had appointed a new General Manager, James Blyth. His background, record, and his short stay (three years) seem to indicate that he was brought in to get a particular job done: to carry through the unfinished rationalization which had begun in 1971, but had foundered on the resistance mounted by the Combine Committee. Unlike the previous General Manager, Blyth had had no experience of Aerospace or indeed of Engineering. He was an arts graduate whose career had included employment with Maxwell House, US Oil, Lucas Batteries and Mars. What he lacked in engineering experience he had made up in proven ability to carry through major rationalizations. This is what he is remembered for at Mars and at Lucas Batteries. And he was quick to start work on preparing a major rationalization for Lucas Aerospace. "Too many people and too much factory space"; this was James Blyth's summary of the state of affairs at Lucas Aerospace. On 16 March 1978 he announced that 2,000 jobs were to go. The main points of the announcement were:

(i) the closure of the Victor works in Liverpool and the movement of most of the Liverpool work to Birmingham (1,400 jobs to go).

(ii) The closure of the existing Bradford and Shipley sites and the movement of most of their work (on generating systems, gas turbine engineering and control gear) to Hemel Hempstead.

(iii) The only part of the Bradford works to stay would be the manufacture of actuators. A new factory would be built for this work, employing 400 out of the original Bradford workforce of 758.

(iv) The closure of the Coventry foundry (46 jobs to go).

(v) Reduce Willesden to the Sting Ray project only (this was work subcontracted from Marconi's). The closure of the Bashley Road section (43 jobs to go).

(vi) The closure of the industrial ballscrew division at Hemel Hempstead (68 jobs to go).

The company's line of argument to justify these redundancies had shifted somewhat from the line they put out to justify their refusal to negotiate over the Combine's Corporate Plan.

One of the company's main points in response to the Corporate Plan was a denial that the Labour government's defence cuts "had affected Lucas Aerospace to any great extent". The company's argument was that markets in the aerospace sector were buoyant and likely to continue to be so and that consequently there was no need to diversify. Jobs would be best secured by sticking to the existing product range. It therefore intended "to remain primarily in the aerospace sector, both civil and military; in defence products and as opportunity permits, to further its involvement in the nuclear field".

In contrast, at the press conference announcing the closures in 1978 the company said:

> There is perhaps not a full understanding around of just how Britian has declined as an air-freight manuafacturer . . . the actual number of aeroplanes we have built (since 1963) has halved and these we are sharing mainly with contractual manufacturers.

and the 1977 Annual Report had commented:

> the continued recession in demand for civil aircraft and the defence cuts in the UK of recent years has naturally affected the company.

The Combine's worst fears were confirmed. The events which followed further intensified their anger.

On 20 March, four days after the announcement, a meeting was held between James Blyth and Ken Gill in the New Ambassadors Hotel. What exactly went on there or in any of the subsequent private meetings we will never known, and neither did the Combine Committee or any "lay representatives" at the time. Gill never told the Combine or any TASS representative in Lucas Aerospace of the meeting. Whatever the detailed discussion, three months later, on 12 June 1978, Gerald Kaufman* announced a deal whereby Lucas was given £6 million to build a new factory to retain 500 of the original 1,400-strong workforce in Liverpool. In the year of a possible general election, a year when unemployment was over 12 per cent in Liverpool, a year when the government was allowing British Leyland to close a five-year-old factory in the Speke estate of Liverpool, it was important for Kaufman to be seen to be doing something to soften the blow of a highly publicized closure on Merseyside. And the emphasis certainly was on being seen. The announcement came in answer to a "planted" question from Sir Harold Wilson about unemployment in Liverpool.** In the announcement the emphasis was on the company

---

* Kaufman had been put on to the Lucas Aerospace problem essentially to clear up the mess left by Varley and Huckfield.

** The site for the new factory is Wilson Road, Huyton.

"opening the new factory". It did not mention the fact that the 500 "new" jobs were far outweighed by the loss of 950 jobs. The shop stewards at Liverpool distributed a leaflet which gave a more accurate impression:

> If the company had gone to the Industry Minister and said, "We wish to take 950 jobs away from Merseyside, please give us £6 million," the answer would have been swift, rude and to the point. They now seem to be achieving the same end by the simple ploy of first declaring a complete closure with the loss of 1,450 jobs, and then allowing themselves to be persuaded to relent by the offer of what is believed to be a £6 million subsidy towards a new £10.5 million plant employing only 500 people. The factory is supposed to be for machining work only, that is a factory without a product, a superior jobbing shop.

This £6 million deal was not the end of the matter, because management and government were not the only ones putting pressure on the CSEU. The shop stewards' Combine Committee had followed up the announcement of the drastic redundancy plans with what amounted to a challenge to the CSEU. A meeting of the full Combine Committee, including a section of the manual workers who had started to meet separately, put out a unanimously agreed statement that they would resist the redundancies with industrial action. The Combine hoped that this resistance could be organized with the full support of the CSEU; but they were prepared to take action independently if necessary.

A combination of factors pressured the CSEU into activity: growing pressure from MPs and from the regional and national trade-union organizations (for example the North-West TUC and the TGWU); the removal of responsibility for Lucas Aerospace from the CSEU Aerospace Committee — chaired by Ken Gill — to the CSEU Engineering Committee; the appointment of a more efficient CSEU general secretary and finally the relentless letters, lobbying and industrial pressure of the Combine Committee. The CSEU responded by calling a meeting in Birmingham of shop stewards from all sites and all unions in Lucas Aerospace. At that time this kind of company-wide shop stewards' meeting was a rare initiative for the CSEU. Such CSEU-sponsored meetings were beginning to take place in the shipbuilding industry and have since occurred in the power engineering industry. The Combine Committee welcomed this meeting, thinking it was the beginning of a campaign by the Confederation to resist the redundancies. However, when the seventy or so delegates arrived and saw the agenda they were not so sure.

The first forty minutes of the meeting were taken up by managing director James Blyth presenting his case with slides, graphs and simplified pamphlets. Representatives who had attended the Combine Committee meeting in December comprised a good three-quarters of those present and they had prepared a proposal to put to the conference. Once the slide show was over, the mood of the meeting quickly changed as Ernie Scarbrow went to the microphone and moved a resolution declaring total opposition to the further rundown of Lucas Aerospace in the UK. He proposed that all movement of work or equipment between plants be blacked and all sub-contracting banned. The motion also demanded a parliamentary enquiry into how the deal was arrived at by the Department of Industry. It concluded by calling on the CSEU to support these measures and make contact with the French trade unions to prevent any further work leaving the UK.

Combine News

The resolution was carried overwhelmingly. The CSEU national officials then proposed that a meeting be arranged between themselves, the company and the government. The conference agreed subject to an amendment that the proposed meeting include "lay" representatives, i.e. shop stewards. A further conference was held in June 1978, followed by a meeting with Blyth. The June conference moved that a committee be elected to investigate management's proposals and draw up their own alternatives. After some argument about numbers — the Confederation officials wanting a smaller committee than the delegates — a committee of fourteen was elected from the conference. It was further agreed that two technical advisers could be co-opted. At the meeting with management, Blyth agreed to provide all the facilities necessary. He also accepted that while the committee did its work the company would undertake to maintain the *status quo*. At the time Blyth did not imagine that any of this would upset the agreement he had come to with Kaufman and Gill earlier in the year. He even said as much in an interview with *The Engineer* in June 1978:

> A Lucas spokesman told *The Engineer* that nothing dramatic was expected. He claimed that Lucas's plans to close the factories had not been affected and the working party just represented the next step in

the negotiating procedure. This was confirmed by the Department of Industry.

Perhaps one reason why he was so confident was that the Department of Industry and the Confederation would be in charge of the final tripartite meeting. The fourteen lay representatives would be little more than observers; and anyway the basic agreement had already been reached with government, so the tripartite meeting was hardly likely to be a serious negotiation. Finally, Blyth underestimated the capabilities of the fourteen-man committee.

The fourteen-man committee was made up of at least one shop steward from each major union and each major site. The sites most affected by the company's proposals, Liverpool and Bradford, had two representatives. About two-thirds of the fourteen were from the shop floor, the rest were from staff unions. All except two of the committee members were from union committees affiliated to the Combine Committee.

The committee should have started its work in July 1978 but this was delayed by arguments over the two people the committee unanimously agreed to co-opt as technical experts. The two people nominated were Mike Cooley and Phil Asquith. The personnel manager, Alan Whitney, told the Confederation that they were unacceptable, the main reason being the association of these two with the "unofficial combine committee". The Confederation conceded to Whitney's veto, but the fourteen shop stewards did not. An angry exchange of letters and phone calls took place over a three-month period. The company formally won its point, but *de facto* Cooley and Asquith acted as the fourteen-man committee's technical experts. At last, at the beginning of November, the committee went on the road, spending six weeks on visiting every site, interrogating management and talking with the local shop stewards.

A unique investigation

Management were totally unprepared for the sort of interrogations which the fourteen shop stewards put them through. Central management had given the stewards a pretty free rein, expecting that the more information they gave to "lay" representatives the more bogged down they would become. At times the committee members themselves felt in danger of being overwhelmed by the information: "I had mixed feelings when I saw the boot load of information we had collected," said one of them. But they had a very clear idea of what they were trying to do; Gordon Sugden, an EETPU steward from Bradford, sums it up:

> Our purpose in collecting the information and writing the report was to show our members, the officials and the media — as a way of reaching the great British public — the selfish and irresponsible way in which our company is managed. We wanted to show that the redundancies were not necessary. We wanted to say, "Look, we the workers have a solution, an alternative, we've got to do something about it."

John Swarbrick from Liverpool ASTMS gives a vivid description of how the committee carried out its interrogations:

> When we got to a site we'd sit down with the trade-union reps. We'd ask them the problems they had, and what questions they'd asked management about the rationalizations. We found local reps on their own often got fobbed off. We had information from the other sites so it was easier to see when we were being conned. Then, always with senior union reps from the local site, we would see local management. Management would often start off, as is their wont, assuming they were in charge. For example at one site they began the meeting saying, "Well, are you all here? Are there any apologies?" The co-ordinator of the committee said very cuttingly, "We don't ask for apologies from your side or determine who comes from your side. Similarly you have no control over who we bring. Sit down and behave yourselves." Another time management expected to be able to adjourn and prepare the answers as soon as we'd asked the questions. But we soon put a stop to that. The styles of management were very different. The Engineering Management Division were aggressive, blustering and often quite stupid, the corporate clones! We got more out of them than they realized. The Electrical Division were very professional. They gave the impression they were telling us a lot; but often it was half truths. Information from trade-union members in the Costing and Technical departments often contradicted management's waffle. For example management told us there were no markets for a small gas turbine. Members in the Costing department told us of a very large order from the Post Office which had been turned down.
>
> The whole experience was quite new for all of us. For nearly six weeks we were investigating and going round the country full time. What I learnt during those six weeks makes my twenty-six years on the site seem like nothing.

The success of the fourteen-man committee, backed by the industrial sanctions, to get information out of the company, contrasted dramatically with an earlier attempt by the shop stewards (in December 1977, following Blyth's tour of the sites) to operate the "disclosure" provisions of the 1975 Employment Protection Act. Despite going through the official procedures as outlined in The Code of Practice, which stipulate that the information should be made available within fourteen days, they did not receive any answers to their questions about the company's plans.

If extracting the information was a major challenge to the normal hierarchy within the factory, the way it was written up was a challenge to the normal hierarchy within higher education. The committee, remember, was a CSEU committee, but the CSEU had none of the resources necessary for fourteen people to write up a lengthy report. Such facilities would have involved room enough for fourteen people to write and discuss over a period of two weeks, a good library, access to back-up research, typing help and photocopying equipment. What was needed were the sort of facilities normally available only at academic institutions, and for the use of academics alone. This was a situation where CAITS came into its own. It was here that the fourteen-man committee and their two technical advisers spent a fortnight of intense work and discussion drawing up the report, which with appendices came to over three hundred pages. Tommy Quirk, the GMWU convenor at Liverpool, explained what the experience had meant to him:

> At first I did not feel that I could write up reports and things like that. During the first two days I felt like going home. But by the time of the last two days I felt I could go on forever. My confidence had really been lifted. And we worked as a very good team. Without the mix of technical and manual workers I don't think we'd have done anything like as good.

The report *was* good. It made detailed criticisms of the company's arguments and then went on to make alternative proposals for "Turning Industrial Decline into Expansion", as the title of the report proclaimed. It was not as wide ranging and political as the alternative Corporate Plan; but it had a more specific focus.

To illustrate the argument of the report: one of the company's justifications for the redundancies was that there was a prolonged down-turn in the aerospace market. The report of the fourteen-man committee presents, in detail, a different picture. They analysed international market trends and documented many of the orders for which Lucas had refused to tender, including a massive order from Boeing for GG 220 gas turbines. These refusals were the consequence of trading agreements with Dowty, Plessey, General Electric and Bosch. The information on the refusals came from trade-union members in the marketing and costing departments of different sites.

One justification Blyth gave for the closure of the Victor works was that the whole fuel-control systems business "is moving from hydro-mechanical to electronic systems". The fourteen-man committee's report answers that:

> In our view this is a deliberate attempt to mislead and confuse. An engine fuel system can never be electronic — unless it is possible for fuel to flow through a chip. What is meant is that the *control* of the engine system is electronic; the major components of the system must, of course, remain hydro-mechanical.

They then show a picture of a typical engine fuel system with electronic controls, illustrating that it has to be predominantly hydro-mechanical. The inscription on the system says, "Pierburg. Lucas Aerospace", which leads to the next step in the shop stewards' analysis:

> In practice what appears to be happening is that the company is reducing the level of hydro-mechanical work in the United Kingdom. . . . It seems to us that major parts of this work are being sent to the

Continent (Pierburg is in West Germany) and the impression is being conveyed in Britain that this reduction in workload for hydromechanized equipment stems from the change in technology.

So we see how a change in production levels in the UK factories is presented as the result of uncontrollable market and technological forces when in fact it is a result of a conscious management strategy.

It might well be that this is the necessary route to competitive success for Lucas Aerospace as an international aerospace company; but the stewards were not arguing on the premise that what is good for Lucas Aerospace is necessarily good for those who work for it. One reason why the shop stewards did not accept this premise is because they believed, on the basis of their Corporate Plan, that there were alternatives. These alternatives could well have cut into the profits of Lucas Aerospace, but looked at on a social balance sheet, taking into account the social costs of unemployment and the economic and social benefits of the products, they would have been economical.

Some of the fourteen-man committee's alternatives were for immediate implementation. But the shop stewards' brief was also to suggest alternatives that would provide jobs with a long-term future, and jobs which would not be saved at the cost of jobs in other plants or companies. The report suggested products for Liverpool which could have given these works a secure future, and could have even led to the creation of new jobs. These products included the GG 220 gas turbine for which Lucas had recently refused to accept orders; fuel control systems; coal-fuelled gas turbines; coal combustion fluidized beds; and the full-scale production of the heat pump, for which there was already a prototype at Burnley. For each of these products there were wider social arguments and evidence of new markets as well as the case for job creation. The two types of turbines proposed were especially economical in their fuel consumption. And the heat pump, as we have seen, provides a particularly cheap form of domestic heating.

These products would take some time to establish at Liverpool. In the meantime, Liverpool could produce kidney machines, for which the Victor works were easily adaptable and for which there was a clear social need. A section of the report went into detail about the kind of kidney machine which medical experts considered to be most beneficial to patients. In connection with all these products the Lucas stewards made contact with workers producing similar products in other companies to work on a more co-ordinated strategy of workers' plans to avoid workers' proposals for one company putting workers in another out of work.

The tripartite "negotiations"

With these arguments as well as continuing industrial sanctions, including bans on overtime, on sub-contracting and on the movement of work from Liverpool or Bradford, the CSEU negotiators and the government were in a potentially strong position when they met the company on 9 February

1979. However, the negotiating team of national full-time officials made little use of the shop stewards' report. Mick Cooney, the Burnley convenor, who was at the negotiations as part of the fourteen-man committee, commented:

> The only official who gave an inkling of having read the report was Alex Ferry (the CSEU General Secretary). One official said to me that he had just been told to come the day before; he wanted to be filled in on the background there and then! There were two meetings in the course of the negotiations and different officials turned up for each one. How could they make the most of the bargaining weapon we'd given them?

It seems that serious bargaining was not the purpose of the tripartite meeting. The Department of Industry had a prepared package which the national union officials were ready to accept. The Department of Industry's proposal involved giving Lucas another £2 million in order to save an additional 150 jobs in Liverpool and Bradford together. The fourteen-man committee said this would be unacceptable to their members and they forced an adjournment.

At the next meeting this stand by the fourteen-man committee resulted in a further 150 jobs being offered. All but one of the committee reasserted that their brief from the delegate conference which had elected them was to prevent any loss of jobs — the extra 150 would still mean a loss of 650 jobs. The one shop steward who found the additional 150 acceptable was the AUEW convenor at the Liverpool factory; his members were going to fill the jobs that were saved. It was GMWU members whose jobs would be lost. The lack of unanimity of the fourteen-man committee, which was anyway in a subordinate role to the national officials, enabled the official negotiators to reach agreement.

Kaufman presented the agreement as the government giving Lucas in total £8 million to "create" 800 jobs in Liverpool. He also implied that the deal involved serious steps towards implementing the Corporate Plan: "management agreed to set up a joint working party with the unions to see whether any of the stewards plans' could be implemented".[1] Moreover, the problem of the company's refusal to talk to the Combine Committee was "resolved", says Kaufman, "after a series of private meetings when the shop stewards were included in an official team set up by the Confederation". Kaufman was pleased with the way it looked. "The party could see we had made the effort", he concluded in his description of the Lucas Aerospace negotiations in his book *How to be a Minister*.

The Combine Committee and the CSEU conference of delegates from Lucas Aerospace called in April 1979 to hear the results of the negotiations considered the outcome in a very different light. To them the agreement meant that 650 and 350 jobs would eventually be lost in Liverpool and Bradford respectively. 47 highly skilled jobs and an award-winning research and development team at Shipley had already been allowed to go, as had 43 jobs at the foundry in Coventry. And an opportunity to create jobs in two areas crying out for industrial development was lost.

Moreover, all this was costing the taxpayer not only the £8 million grant but also £5 million which was the estimated cost of the company's redundancies and their multiplier effects throughout the economy. Lucas was a company which was already subsidized to a considerable extent, through £75 million deferred taxation in 1978 and £10 million in grants between 1971 and 1977. A minister at the Department of Employment himself admitted that with the £8 million alone the number of jobs which his department could create through its various schemes was *9,000*.*

As to the Alternative Products Group of two representatives from the company, one government official, one independent management consultant as chairman, and two shop stewards: even the agreement itself made it clear that whether the discussions would lead to anything would depend on Lucas Industries using its "best endeavours". As we shall see, the shop stewards were hostages unable to back up their arguments with the kind of power that would require management to negotiate. Not surprisingly, then, the CSEU conference of delegates from Lucas Aerospace described the agreement as "bitterly disappointing". Against the advice of the Confed national officials the delegates overwhelmingly passed the following resolution: "The basis of the agreement falls very far short of the policies decided upon by this delegate conference." The conference then was only willing to endorse the basis agreement if certain conditions were complied with. These included:

a) That there is a clear understanding by all concerned that the objective is to retain the entire workforce in its present geographical areas and that there is an ongoing commitment from the CSEU to this objective. Furthermore, that the "status quo" is to remain until such time as this delegate conference is satisfied as to the Company's sincerity and responsible approach in these matters of restructuring, and the implementation of the spirit and intention of the "Basis of Agreement" with respect to introducing alternative work.

---

* From *Hansard*: 1979
MRS AUDREY WISE (COVENTRY, SOUTH WEST): To ask the Secretary of State for Employment, how many new jobs he anticipates could be created for a sum of £8 million, using the various mechanisms at his disposal.
MR JOHN GOLDING REPLIED:
The relevant special employment measures to support new jobs for which I am responsible are designed to provide temporary employment opportunities for the unemployed through the Special Temporary Employment Programme and to provide temporary support for expansions in employment through the Small Firms Employment Subsidy. Assuming that the £8 million was divided equally between these two schemes the number of new jobs supported would be about 9,000.

b) That a fourteen-man committee must be ongoing with facilities to monitor every aspect of the Company's restructuring activities including the monitoring of all sub-contract work both internal and external.

c) That this fourteen-man committee is required to report back to this delegate conference at regular three-monthly intervals.

d) That this delegate conference elects the two persons for the alternative products group, these two persons to be responsible at all times to the fourteen-man committee and be subject to instant recall and removal.

To everyone at the conference and to most people reading this it would look like a very serious modification of the agreement, arising from anger and dissatisfaction at the compromise involved. But this is not how the Confederation wanted to understand it. They reported in the minutes of their executive that: "The Conference had eventually accepted the agreement reached on 14 February 1979 at the tripartite meeting chaired by Mr Gerald Kaufman subject to certain safeguards being secured from the management", and also in their annual report:

A further Delegate Conference was convened on 15 March 1979, and was approved with certain reservations. The Delegate Conference also appointed two lay representatives to serve on the Working Group on Alternative Products.

No hint of the seriousness of the conditions laid down by the Delegate Conference. Neither did the National Confed tell Blyth the nature of the consultative conference decision. They just hoped the anger would die down.

Conflicting assessments of the realistic

There is no doubt that both the Confederation and Kaufman were sincere in believing they had got a good agreement and had done the best they could. One official revealed the standards by which officials at that time were judging redundancy agreements when he said to Mick Cooney, as they took the bus to Euston together after the negotiations, "I wish I'd got that sort of deal at Speke. I seem to spend all my time selling jobs these days." Kaufman was not so frank. In his presentation of the agreements there was an element of the hypocrisy common among Labour ministers trying to satisfy what they consider to be the unrealistic demands of party conferences and constituencies. But the difference between his and the Confed's assessment of the outcome on the one hand and the shop stewards' majority assessment on the other has to be explained by something far deeper than hypocrisy, though it does have something to do with different assessments of what is "realistic". The explanation for these different assessments lies in the way that the Department of Industry and the CSEU leadership accepted management's basic objectives for Lucas

Aerospace. The following extracts from an interview with Kaufman indicate the Department of Industry's acceptance of Blyth's view:

> Q: The shop stewards feel that they could have taken on the company industrially and saved all the jobs?
> Kaufman: That would have wrecked Lucas Aerospace, there is no doubt about it, all the jobs in Lucas Aerospace.
> Q: You mean that Lucas management would have closed down Aerospace?
> Kaufman: Lucas Aerospace the company would have become unviable. It is as simple as that. Lucas Aerospace as a company was on the verge of becoming unviable because of the delay in implementing their restructuring plans. And in that case they would have just had to close the whole thing down. Now the Confed in my view very sensibly decided that that was not a risk they wanted to take. . . .

At another point in the interview:

> Q: It was not clear from the agreement whether all the jobs were saved or not.
> Kaufman: No, all the jobs were never going to be saved. One of the things that the Confed Conference put forward was that all the jobs should be saved and that was never on. I worked out a formula whereby the Confed could make an agreement and the agreement was made on that basis.

Lucas Aerospace management also described this mutual understanding, not in an interview but in their Annual Personnel Report for May 1977-8, where they say:

> It is clear that national officers of unions and the Department of Industry are aware of the Company's policies and the CSEU is dealing effectively with this unofficial body [referring back to a previous mention of the Combine Committee].

The agreement itself, particularly over the new machinery factory in Liverpool, also showed clear signs of mutual understanding. The idea of a machinery factory in Liverpool, employing machinists alone — the proposal in the agreement — had already been hinted at favourably by Blyth himself at a meeting with MPs in April 1978:

> Of the direct operatives at Victor, we need about 250, perhaps 300, out of 1,400 people. If we could supervise them effectively from 100 miles away and run the factory as a 300-people machine shop, it would be smashing. But we have a huge overload. It is a 220,000 sq. ft. factory.

What better solution from Blyth's point of view than a new purpose-built machining factory, three-quarters paid for by the government, and rent free for five years?

Kaufman could have used the Combine Committee's Corporate Plan as a very effective way of resisting the company's implied blackmail. But in effect the company was able to turn to its own benefit the pressure which the government was under over the Combine Committee's plan. This was partly because of the close relations between Lucas Aerospace and the Department of Industry. The other explanations lie in the lack of seriousness with which Labour ministers viewed workers' initiatives, especially the initiatives of the unordained, the "lay" representatives. This dismissive approach was reinforced by the protective structures of the trade-union establishment.

The Alternative Products Group

The Alternative Products Group was greeted as a breakthrough by press reports and by Gerald Kaufman. The implication of some initial reports was that at last the company was prepared to discuss seriously the stewards' Corporate Plan. The Alternative Products Group was undoubtedly an outcome of the public and political pressure on Lucas to consider the proposals of the Corporate Plan. And it was an unprecedented kind of committee: a financial analyst and a marketing analyst from Lucas, a representative from the Department of Industry, a management consultant from Henley College, two shop stewards from Lucas Aerospace and a chairman who was Engineering Consultant for Lucas Industries, discussing three trade-union proposals for products and three company proposals. The stated purpose of the committee was to identify a suitable product(s) which Lucas Industries would "use their best endeavours to manufacture on Merseyside, so as to create or preserve jobs". The committee spent just over £30,000 of Lucas funds on this product evaluation. However, the catch in the project was that management were not bound to follow up the committee's proposals, neither were they obliged to treat the two shop stewards in any formal sense as trade-union representatives with full facilities for reporting back to their members. As Gerald Kaufman stated: "The spirit and intention of the agreement is all important — without that there can be no agreement."

The spirit and intention of the members of Lucas management on the Working Group itself seems to have been one of commitment to finding mutually acceptable products. The intention of the top management in Lucas Aerospace and, in the background, of Lucas Industries, however, seems to have been to marginalize or ignore the Working Group, once the initial fanfare of publicity had died down. There were several expressions of this negative spirit on the part of Lucas Aerospace management:

* Lucas Aerospace management refused to recognize or provide time off and facilities for the fourteen-man committee to which, according to the CSEU Delegate Conference resolution, the two shop stewards on the working group were to report.

* In one of James Blyth's six-monthly visits round the different sites he told senior staff at the Liverpool site that "the working party is just a meaningless appendage to the agreement" and irrelevant to the situation at Liverpool.

* Management at all Lucas Aerospace sites, with the exception of Burnley, would not allow Phil Asquith and Mike Cooley to report back to the shop stewards on the discussions of the Alternative Products Working Group, even though at the Alternative Products Working Group itself all agreed that such reporting back facilities should be allowed.

* Mike Cooley received warnings on two occasions from Lucas Aerospace personnel management that he was "taking time beyond that which is felt to be reasonable for (his) involvement in the New Products Appraisal Teams". On one occasion the Willesden personnel manager took the warning to Mike Cooley's home at 9 pm and handed it to Shirley Cooley. Ewan McEwen, the chairman of the Working Group and Lucas Industries' most senior engineer, had to write on two occasions to the Lucas Aerospace personnel director explaining that it was for the Working Group not personnel managers to decide how much time a member of the Working Group required.

* After a year's work the Working Group wrote a lengthy memo along with their interim report to the chairman of Lucas Industries, asking for close liaison with the board of Lucas Industries in order that decisions could be made about investment. No substantive reply was ever received.

* In June 1980 Lucas Aerospace management sent a notice of dismissal to Ernie Scarbrow, the co-ordinator of the fourteen-man committee and the secretary of the Combine, because Scarbrow refused to move from Willesden to Hemel as the company had wanted.

This last move led the fourteen-man trade union committee to ask Mike Cooley and Phil Asquith to resign from the Working Group. How could they continue as trade-union representatives on a working group whose work assumed mutual trust when management was trying to sack one of their colleagues? Asquith and Cooley resigned on 4 June 1980 and a few months later the rest of the Working Group wound up its activities.

Could the Working Group have led to the implementation of any of the Combine Committee's proposals to save jobs? Or was it doomed from the start? Those with power in Lucas Industries clearly regarded the Working Group as an insignificant and even slightly irritating concession to the political pressure built up by the Combine. One small indication of this disregard for the Working Group came to light later, in May 1981, when management tried to move Mike Cooley from his engineering job. The reason they gave was absenteeism and they listed absences during 1980. They included in the list at least eight of the days when he attended the Alternative Products Working Group! One reason why Lucas Aerospace management could marginalize the Working Group was because the Lucas Aerospace shop stewards had in effect been left on their own once the agreement was signed. The stewards were on their own because the CSEU officials assumed, until too late, that Lucas management would act according to the spirit of the agreement. Phil Asquith contacted the CSEU at the end of April 1979 telling them of management's refusal to enable a fourteen-man committee to meet and explaining the shop stewards' problems with reporting back. When Alec Ferry replied he insisted that management would act in good faith. Phil Asquith and Ernie Scarbrow persisted with their complaints. Eventually Ferry recognized that there was a problem. On 4 June he wrote to Ernie Scarbrow, after a conversation with Alan Whitney (the Lucas Aerospace personnel director) about the company recognizing a CSEU fourteen-man committee, that "we are going to have problems in getting Lucas to recognize the fourteen-man committee." He admitted that this and other issues raised by Scarbrow "certainly throw up the question of management's good faith and I will therefore discuss the matter with Roy Grantham on the basis of your suggestion that a meeting be arranged with Lucas Management". The meeting never took place. It was arranged for three different dates and then cancelled by the CSEU because national officials concerned could not be present. Here then is yet another small indication of how inadequate established trade-union structures are for achieving negotiations over trade-union proposals rather than in reaction to management proposals. If the trade unions could have backed up their representatives on the Alternative Products Working Party by insisting that management provide proper facilities for reporting back, then the possibility of genuine negotiations through the working party would have been put to a real test. It seems likely, however, that Lucas management created the working party knowing that they would not face any such embarrassment.

A change in government on 3 May 1979 meant that the company avoided the embarrassment of any political limelight that the discussions on alternative products might have attracted under a Labour government. The Labour government's ability to hold the company to "the spirit of the agreement" — whatever that was — was never put to the test. And the company no longer had to make concessions to the political influence of the Combine's Corporate Plan. On the contrary, in the abrasively anti-union atmosphere of the Thatcher government the company could move more directly to undermine trade-union strength. Moreover, the Combine Committee, after being entangled for three years in the ropes of Confed procedures and the red tape of the Department of Industry, were in no position to stand up to this new offensive.

A reckoning

The Combine and the local shop stewards' committees had been able to prevent any compulsory redundancies since the agreement, so far. But the original intention behind drawing up the plan had been more ambitious than preventing compulsory redundancy: the Combine had seen the plan as part of a strategy to prevent "natural wastage" and to create new jobs. The outcome of the resistance to Blyth's rationalization is therefore in part a defeat. And the action of the government and parts of the trade-union leadership lie behind that defeat. But their action and non-action do not fully explain the defeat. Looking back, there were weaknesses in the Combine's own organization which made the defeat possible. Some might argue that their whole strategy was at fault; that they should never have made serious approaches to the government in the first place. For it was this strategy of pressing for government support that entangled the Combine in the procedures of the CSEU. Against this argument it is clear that the government, and therefore the CSEU, would have got involved whether the Combine wanted it or not. Even as it was, they got involved mainly at management's behest. Sustained resistance to redundancies in major corporations unavoidably become national and political. The Combine were consequently in a relatively strong position for having prepared the political ground within the Labour Party and among MPs. It was this political pressure on the government, together with the Combine's industrial pressure on management, which forced management to negotiate and finally make serious, though inadequate, concessions.

The Combine's weakness arose not in its basic strategy but in aspects of its organization. In particular the site organization at Liverpool was divided and even the leading stewards of unions that were involved in the Combine from Liverpool had not kept the membership adequately informed about the Combine and the negotiations. There had been enough commitment to impose industrial sanctions throughout the negotiations. But not enough to follow the lead of the Combine and refuse to accept any loss of jobs. This problem could not have been overcome by the Combine alone. However, its existence indicated that there were failings in the Combine's communication with the trade-union members at some of the sites, which should not rely entirely on the effectiveness of individual delegates. This is a problem which has faced many of the combine committees which developed in the 1970s.

The Lucas Combine in fact was relatively strong on internal communications. The fact that they had not overcome this problem illustrates how serious it is. The difficulties facing shop stewards' combine committees including the Lucas Combine Committee, in the '80s was to confirm this.

PART V: NO COMBINE IS AN ISLAND

17 The Combine on the defensive

Under the Labour government, the company had attempted to contain the strength of factory trade unionism. Under the conditions created by a Tory government it has tried to break that strength.

Lucas management have made use of the recession to carry out a massive rationalization of its Electrical Division in the UK while expanding investments in Korea, Brazil and Spain. Over 8,000 jobs have gone in two years at its Birmingham and Burnley Electrical factories. One of the five Girling factories has now been closed and over 2,000 jobs have gone in CAV. Several strong shop stewards' organizations have been broken up in the process. In Lucas Aerospace the problem has not been redundancies — at least not yet;* with the new cold war there has been no shortage of orders for military aircraft systems. But Lucas Aerospace management have not been slow to make use of the atmosphere of crisis and doom in the rest of Lucas Industries. They have refused to negotiate on wages in both 1980 and 1981 and have tried, without success, to avoid negotiations on the introduction of new technology.

They justify this approach with talk of the company being unable to afford higher claims. But they use extremely conservative accounting techniques which seriously understate the company's profits. For example in the interim results 1980/81 for Lucas Industries, which showed a loss of £27.47 million, the company placed 50 per cent of its capital expenditure and £12 million closure and redundancy costs against current profit, rather than against reserves. If the more usual historic accounting techniques had been used, the balance sheet would show something nearer a £12 million profit. Yet the £27 million loss was a much more useful statistic for convincing trade-union negotiators that there was no option but to carry through another 4,000–5,000 redundancies at Lucas Electrical and to impose a 5 per cent non-negotiable wages offer on the whole workforce in Lucas Industries. Meanwhile in the City, Lucas shareholders received a very different impression of the company's fortunes. In the month after the announcement of the "disastrous" interim results, a share in Lucas Industries rose from 166p on 26 March to 234p on 27 April. The profits of Lucas Aerospace were rising rapidly during 1980 and '81 after three years during which profits were low.

To a large extent these doom tactics worked. The redundancies were successfully carried through in Lucas Electrical, and after sporadic but impotent protests, the non-negotiable wage offer was imposed in 1980 and 1981. Throughout this period the personnel management of Lucas

---

* The announcement in February 1982 of over 1,000 redundancies at Burnley indicate that this is changing.

Aerospace continued its attempt to marginalize the Combine by refusing to meet it and attempting, eventually successfully, to sack or harass its leading delegates.

The Combine's strengths and weaknesses

The past year's involvement with the CSEU had had a contradictory effect on the strength of the Combine Committee, who had put all their energies into making the CSEU negotiations work. In effect the Combine had submerged its identity into the fourteen-man committee. For instance, no issue of *Combine News* came out during 1978–80. The Combine met during

this period, but more as a pressure group within the negotiations than a group taking its own initiatives. The experience with the government and the CSEU revealed obstacles facing the Combine which many stewards had not fully anticipated. Some, like Gordon Sugden at Bradford, were disheartened and demoralized:

> Of course the Combine is what we want ideally. But it goes against our own union's constitution. And each union is just concerned with its own membership. It'll take a long while to change that and to base the unions on combines.

At Bradford this kind of pessimism led the stewards to propose to the shop-floor workers that they disaffiliate from the Combine. But at a mass meeting the members voted overwhelmingly to renew their affiliation. Danny Broomhead, the AUEW steward who reluctantly had put the recommendation to the mass meeting, explained the vote this way: "They believed that they owed the Combine their jobs." These contradictory responses at Bradford illustrate the way in which, although the Combine's organization had been weakened during the CSEU negotiations, the credibility of its ideas had grown.

Another factor explaining the Combine's position was the contradictory pressures involved in the campaign for the Corporate Plan. We have already touched on the tension between following up the widespread enthusiasm for the Plan and maintaining a strong trade-union base through bad times as well as good. John Routley, an electrician from Birmingham who became active in the Combine in 1980, put the problem like this: "It's a bit like winning £1 million on the pools, spending it on a medical research centre and then being evicted for not paying the £6 ground rent." He did not mean it was wrong to start the "medical research centre" in the first place. But the experience of the Lucas stewards contains lessons for others who are embarking on similarly political and far-reaching initiatives: that they need all the time to be consciously nurturing their more limited trade-union base; that is, making sure they pay the ground rent.

Many shop stewards, in Lucas Aerospace as elsewhere, had became accustomed throughout the 1960s and early '70s to take their members' support for granted. Members too would tend to leave their stewards to get on with the negotiations and not expect to receive detailed reports on what was going on. During the boom years this did not seem to matter. Support for militant action did not usually entail taking many risks. But during a recession and a Tory government this lack of adequate communications has undermined the ability of many shop stewards' committees to overcome the fears and lack of confidence of their members on even very basic issues such as wages and conditions. On an initiative like the Combine's alternative Corporate Plan, lack of a constant flow of information, explanation and discussion is even more damaging. Without this constant reporting back, the stewards who are closely involved in such a new and radical initiative can gather a momentum of their own, out of touch with their members. Sometimes this happened in Lucas Aerospace. The mistake was usually recognized and a flurry of leaflets and bulletins would result, but at some sites this was too late. This unevenness in communications with the membership contributed to the problems facing the Combine in maintaining the solid base built up during 1969–76.

A third source of weakness was the split of several manual workers' committees from the Combine. We have referred to the origins of this in Chapter 11, but in order to assess the Combine Committee's position in the face of management's new confidence we need to analyse this division in more detail.

Unity against the divided grain

To put this split in context, it is worth reminding ourselves of how unusual permanent unity is between the staff and the hourly paid in the engineering industry. This can be illustrated by recalling the conditions under which, in the history of the Combine, staff and shop-floor unions managed to over-come the gulf which in most companies is normally bridged only in an irregular *ad hoc* fashion, if at all. In the Willesden, Burnley, Wolver-hampton, Birmingham, Bradford and Hemel Hempstead factories — the major sites where unity has at different times been achieved — the unions came together for the first time in the course of a major struggle, or in the face of an extreme threat to the whole workforce. The resistance to rationalization and closure at Willesden; the parity strike at Burnley; the redundancy campaigns at Wolverhampton and Birmingham; the threat of closure at Bradford; the action to save the industrial ballscrews at Hemel Hempstead; all these were struggles which lifted the activity of the shop stewards and their members, staff and shop-floor alike, out of the normal routines of trade-union organization where sectional concerns tend to pre-dominate, on to a level where cohesion between staff and shop floor was the only way to win. By stressing the extreme situations in which co-operation has occurred we do not want to imply that such unity occurs spontaneously whenever the threat is dire enough. In all the examples we have referred to, the dramatic moments of unity on a mass scale would not have occurred without the hard work of a small core of trade unionists supported morally and materially by the existence of the Combine Committee. The point of stressing the circumstances in which unity has come about is to emphasize how rarely it occurs as a natural consequence of day-to-day trade unionism and how much it goes against the grain of the established trade-union structures. The implication is that when trade-union activity gets back to its routine tasks, the weight of the established trade-union structures, with all their different priorities, vested interests and historical distrust, can be overwhelming. The exceptions to this in Lucas Aerospace and elsewhere are when the new unity has been somehow institutionalized and/or where there remain workplace leaders among both the hourly-paid and among the staff who trust each other and have a strong belief in the long-term benefits of staff/shop-floor unity.

The origins of the split

In Wolverhampton, Willesden and Liverpool in the late '70s both these factors were absent. For instance in Wolverhampton, as we have seen, the co-operation achieved through the redundancy campaign was not consoli-dated by the creation of a joint organization. Moreover, two of the trade unionists whose work had helped to prepare the unity of of the redundancy campaign left the factory. Consequently there was little to counteract the bitterness which shop-floor members felt towards TASS members when TASS failed to support the indexing campaign. After the collapse of the indexing campaign this bitterness fuelled the arguments of two other convenors who disagreed with the policies of the joint Combine.

At Liverpool John Mottram, the AUEW convenor since 1975, had had little commitment to the Combine. He believed that a separate committee of manual workers, with recognition from the company, was the way forward for manual workers. And he was convinced that the company would provide facilities and recognition for such a committee; something which the company would never, especially after the Corporate Plan, give to the joint Combine. Mottram's election as convenor reflected a change that had taken place on the Liverpool site since Dave Gough, the AUEW convenor who was committed to the Combine and to a united organization, had left in 1973 to become an AUEW District Official. Gough's resignation was followed by the break-up of the joint AUEW and GMWU shop stewards' committee in 1974, itself a product of personality clashes more than anything else (which both individuals concerned, Stan Kelly of the GMWU and Mike Reynolds of the AUEW, now regret). This in turn contributed to a sectional and weak trade unionism on the site which favoured the election of an AUEW convenor, Mottram, who lacked any commitment to the principle of unity across unions. The Liverpool AUEW leadership found an ally in Jim Cooney, the AUEW convenor from Willesden, who by 1976 had drifted away from the Combine. Cooney's personal change was important because he was in a completely dominant position within the small seven-man shop stewards' committee. No mass meetings were (or are) held where arguments could take place and questions could be asked. Neither was Cooney under any pressure from the union locally. Although the North London AUEW district had a militant tradition, this had been eroded over the years by the decimation of the engineering industry in the area, and by the defeat of even the most militant struggles to save jobs.

Whatever the exact reasons for Cooney's behaviour, there is no doubt that management played some part, initially covertly and through individuals, in bringing about the split. For on 4 May 1977 every manual workers' committee in Lucas Aerospace received a letter from J. Mottram, the Liverpool convenor, calling them to a meeting on 12 May. They were assured that the company would give them paid time off and cover expenses.

At first many manual workers' committees were wary of the initiative. The Bradford stewards were suspicious of the financial side of it. Dennis Easton, the AUEW convenor, commented on this:

> It is interesting that the company is prepared to fund the manual workers to go down to Birmingham four times a year. They are prepared to do the same for staff. But only if they are separate. When you think about the cost of a day's wages, the loss of production, the expense of travel and meals; for thirty and more people four times a year. That's not cheap. The fact that management are prepared to pay this out shows that they know what they are doing. They are keeping a nice dividing line by encouraging us to meet only separately.

Stan Kelly, a manual worker himself, was sure that there was something behind it, beyond the criticism of the Joint Combine that it did not meet the needs of manual workers. He felt the Combine had bent over backwards to take account of the specific problems of manual workers.

> I and others had put forward the straightforward solution to change
> the constitution so that manual workers — and any other section —
> could meet separately to discuss their own special problems, and yet
> still be part of the Combine Committee on other issues of concern to
> all. But those who seemed determined to split would not accept that as
> a solution. So there must have been something more than just a
> resentment towards staff.

Mick Cooney, AUEW Convenor at Burnley, who also believed that the
split was unnecessary from the point of view of the interests of manual
workers, recalls:

> They would always try and blame the joint Combine for things that
> hadn't been done. But in fact the manual workers had met manage-
> ment by themselves without staff and they'd accepted pathetic offers,
> so they only had themselves to blame. Cooney would come up to me at
> Wortley Hall and say, "Mick, you're being led up the garden path."
> He was clearly trying to break things up so I'd have nothing to do with
> it at that stage.

The manual workers' committee established

Although the origins and the initial leadership of the manual workers'
committee are important for assessing the position of the Combine
Committee they could not be the sole determinants of the Combine's
response. For once the manual committee was formed and granted full
facilities by management it became a semi-official part of trade-union
organization in the company. Several manual stewards' committees were
sceptical of the manual committee's effectiveness, but nevertheless they felt
obliged, as manual-worker shop stewards, to attend its meetings. As a
result several site committees became affiliated to both combines. The
Burnley committee, which in fact represented the largest number of
manual workers, has however kept its distance from the manual workers'
committee.

As a result of gaining a semi-official status the manual workers'
committee came to encompass a wide range of views. For instance its two
founding convenors were critical of the Corporate Plan, but by the middle
of 1979 the committee included many delegates who supported the joint
Combine Committee's polices on redundancies. Consequently, although
the manual workers were to meet separately on wages and fringe benefits,
when it came to fighting redundancies they looked to the joint Combine for
a lead. For instance they joined the Combine's lobby of MPs in early 1977;
they responded to a call from the joint Combine for a meeting to discuss
the strategy for resisting Blyth's redundancy plan in 1978. And throughout
the campaign which followed, including the CSEU delegate meetings and
the work of the fourteen-man committee, the majority of the manual
committee supported the Combine's proposals. When the fourteen-man

committee's report was finished the Liverpool AUEW committee and the Wolverhampton shop stewards' committee made financial contributions to CAITS, fully aware of its close connection to the Combine Committee.

However, the experience of working together in the CSEU fourteen-man committee did not overcome the split. The importance of the experience is rather that it illustrated how in fighting redundancies even the most conservative shop stewards recognized that, against all their instincts, a strategy was needed which went beyond sectional trade unionism. If a lead was given in this direction most of them followed it. Leading members of the joint Combine believe that the issues which demonstrate the limits of sectional trade unionism will in the long run provide the key to overcoming the divisions. Moreover, the kind of issues which required this united trade-union response — the introduction of new technology, the restructuring of companies and whole industries — would be on the agenda of every shop stewards' committee in manufacturing industry for the 'eighties.

Willesden: the front line falls

Before the Combine was in any position to take up these issues it had to overcome a major weakness in its internal organization. The infrastructure and the communications that kept the Combine together were too dependent on what was left of its support at Willesden, and particularly on Ernie Scarbrow, the secretary, backed up by Mike Cooley, the newspaper editor. Willesden was in a sense the front line of the Combine Committee. For instance during its first seven years, three out of the six officers of the Combine came from Willesden. As we have seen, many other individuals became active in the Combine Committee, in spreading the ideas of the Corporate Plan, in campaigning against redundancies, in running the pensions campaign, and leading their own site committee on principles learnt partly through involvement with the Combine. However, the stronger sites like Burnley and Birmingham were slow to move into the front line themselves; consequently, in spite of the growth of the Combine, the basic responsibilities of co-ordination and following up Combine decisions remained with Ernie Scarbrow. One reason for the slowness of others to take on and learn to carry out these responsibilities was that the sum of Ernie's work was invisible. As Terry Moran from Burnley says:

> There was a lot about Ernie's work that we'd taken for granted. He'd really made things happen. We would take decisions at Combine meetings and things would happen as a result: but all the time Ernie had been there making the connections which made decisions flow into co-ordinated action.

Not surprisingly, management seems to have made a target of the Willesden leadership. Management had harassed Ernie Scarbrow since 1971 for his trade-union activity; on several occasions the Combine had had to organize threats of industrial action to defend him. In June 1979 management tried again to remove him from his trade-union base at

Willesden. They told him he had to leave Willesden and go to Hemel Hempstead. Scarbrow refused. Management kept up the pressure, sometimes going to extreme lengths to get him to move. For instance, three days after his wife had died and on the very day of her funeral, management wrote to Ernie yet again, even adding: "It may be that recent events allow you to come to a different conclusion. Perhaps we could discuss this matter again in a short while."

In November the company changed tactics; they offered an alternative job, not a product engineering job but a Refurbishment and Repair Supervisor's job which in fact had already been unsuccessfully advertised. Again Scarbrow refused on the grounds that it was not suitable for his qualifications and it would put him outside the area covered by his union. The TASS office committee at Willesden and the TASS Lucas National Negotiating Committee supported him in his refusal to accept the supervisor's job, as did the Combine Committee. But management had clearly calculated that they could get their way. On 5 December they gave him his notice, telling him his employment would terminate at the end of January. It produced an angry response from all the Lucas Aerospace sites, whether affiliated to the Combine Committee or not, and from many of those trade unionists, socialists and disarmament activists who had at one time or another gained confidence and inspiration from the Lucas Aerospace shop stewards. But it was a difficult issue on which to win support for industrial action. For management had made Scarbrow's move part of a more general rationalization of work between Willesden and Hemel. Several other engineers at Willesden were prepared to go to Hemel. Shop stewards in the other sites therefore feared that their members would not accept it as a clear-cut case of victimization and would be reluctant to take action. As a result the campaign to protect Ernie Scarbrow's position did not have the force behind it that it needed. Site committees protested and threatened but they did not take action. The final outcome of this pressure was a compromise: Scarbrow was given a job at Willesden in an area covered by TASS but it was not the job he was qualified for. He was under constant surveillance by management and he had only inadequate facilities for his trade-union work.

The difficulties of regrouping

Scarbrow accepted the compromise, but he knew within himself that he could not stay at Willesden for long on that basis. So with this in mind, and concerned that the new secretary would have time to work himself gradually into the job, in May 1980 he resigned from the secretaryship of the Combine and shortly after retired from his job. He had been secretary without a break for eleven years. During these years he had accumulated a combination of widespread trust, skills at organizing and communicating, and a thorough understanding of the company, its strategy and its strengths and weaknesses. These aptitudes were difficult to pass on to a new secretary in a short period of time. In a long-established trade-union organization, with the stability and even stagnation that comes of being accepted and recognized by employers and the government, as well as by fellow trade unionists, the responsibilities, contacts and skills of a secretary are fairly easily passed on. They are codified and explicit. They are the subject of trade-union courses and manuals. By contrast, in the case of an unofficial combine committee, lacking support from established institutions, always having to improvise and move forward in order to survive, the trust a secretary builds up for the combine tends to depend considerably on the trust for the individual concerned. And because his or her skills have come from improvising rather than operating explicit rules, these skills will tend to be tacit and intuitive. There are no trade-union courses on combine committee organization, nor handbooks on the problems facing a shop steward when he or she take on the job of co-ordinating many different factory committees across the country. The transition from one secretary to another in the Lucas Combine Committee was therefore a difficult one. No one has yet settled into it for longer than a year. It was also a difficult time to be taking over the secretary's job: a time of retrenchment and reconstruction in the face of fierce attacks. Looking back and drawing lessons for others faced with similar problems, many Combine delegates feel that they should have spread out Ernie Scarbrow's pivotal job earlier, when the vulnerability of Willesden first became apparent.

Brian Salisbury, Combine secretary in 1980 and 1981, explains the lesson they learnt: "We should think more strategically about who does what job. It's not just the personal qualities of someone which is important but also the strength or weakness of their site organization." Salisbury had not been secretary for six months before the management took another swipe at the trade-union organization at the Willesden site.

The sacking of Mike Cooley

On 6 May 1981 management told Mike Cooley that he would be sacked if he took time off, even if unpaid, without prior written agreement. In the course of the previous year he had taken thirty days' unpaid leave to work on the ideas of Corporate Plan and the design of human-centred technologies at CAITS and at UMIST; and to lecture and discuss the social implications of increased automation.*

On 13 May Lucas management told Cooley that his present job as a

---

* The fact that a technologist could be sacked for taking time off to engage in this kind of critical intellectual activity points to an area in which issues of civil rights and freedom of speech need urgent consideration. At a time when technological development is increasingly under the control of major private corporations it becomes very important that those employed by these corporations should have time and resources to discuss the social implications of their work. Such an extension of the value of critical discussion from the universities to the factories would require very much more generous provisions for time off for education than are presently contained within the Employment Protection Act.

design engineer no longer existed because the Ground Support Equipment section where he worked was closed, to make way for the Sting Ray project at Willesden. They offered him instead a training officer job in the Personnel Department, even though there were several vacancies advertised for design engineers on the Sting Ray project and all his colleagues in Ground Support were given comparable design jobs on the Sting Ray project. Cooley, learning from Scarbrow's experience, believed that management was trying to demoralize, harass and isolate him. With the advice and the full backing of the TASS committee at Willesden and the local TASS official, Cooley rejected the training officer's job. Management responded by giving him his notice. A campaign began to build up: a one-day strike took place among TASS members at Willesden on 9 June and a national one-day strike of TASS members was threatened throughout Lucas Industries on 26 June if management did not withdraw Mike Cooley's notice. On 18 June management told TASS officials that the company would not withdraw the sacking. The one-day strike was called. 88 per cent of all TASS members in Lucas Aerospace and CAV came out on strike. In Lucas Electrical and Girlings, however, the vast majority of TASS members stayed at work.

On 23 June management, presumably concerned that the campaign might gather momentum, but confident it could be nipped in the bud, told Cooley to get off the premises — for good. The same day TASS members at Willesden voted to come out on strike immediately. In the meantime the Combine Committee executive had met to discuss what action the Combine could take to back up TASS in the campaign. In the past, when attempts had been made to sack Combine members, the Combine had taken a lead in organizing the action. It had not waited for the official procedures to be exhausted. This had always been effective until the recent harassment of Ernie Scarbrow. The Combine felt it had let Scarbrow down. Learning from this that they were unable to take on the company by themselves, they gave every support to TASS. There was also a feeling among some delegates that the antagonism which TASS had shown in the past towards the Combine had been overcome by the Combine's attempt to work through the CSEU. Moreover, the TASS local official in Birmingham, Bob Parsons, had shown considerable determination to win: "Lucas are going to find that they are not dealing with the engineering section [of the AUEW] like at British Leyland," he had said on Birmingham radio. And Chris Darke, the TASS official who covered Willesden, put up a strong case in negotiations with local management. The Combine executive decided to go back to the sites to call mass meetings of TASS members, to explain recent developments and prepare people to take action; to request help from the shop-floor unions as soon as TASS had given a lead; to put out a daily bulletin reporting the latest developments and to organize a campaign through Parliament, the press and the wider trade-union movement.

This wider support hardly needed organizing. Telegrams, letters, phone calls of solidarity were flooding into Cooley's home and the TASS head office, and protest letters must have been piling up in the office — or dustbin — of the chairman of Lucas Industries. After the event, TASS head office has been dismissive of this support, referring to it in their report of the affair as "international interest among academics and other groups". In fact the most important international support came not from academics, but from trade unions who had recognized the relevance of the Combine Committee's work to their own problems. William Wimpisinger, president of the IAM , sent a telegram "on behalf of the officers and members of the International Association of Machinists and Aerospace workers in the United States and Canada" condemning the sacking. The telegram goes on:

> From this side of the Atlantic we have followed the work of Lucas Aerospace Combine shop stewards' committee closely and are well aware that the untiring efforts of Mike Cooley to save jobs and alert working people to the dehumanization of new technologies has earned him deep respect in the international trade-union movement.

The secretary of I.G. Metall, the largest union in West Germany, wrote a letter to Ken Gill, general secretary of TASS, offering to help put pressure on Lucas. The secretary of the Swiss metal workers' union wrote offering support and further support from Switzerland came from the Technical Section of the Builders' Union. Pino Taliazuckhi wrote on behalf of the officers and members of the FLM, the metal workers' union in Italy.

The FNV, the industrial trade union in Holland, sent support as did the engineering and construction section of the GPA in Austria. It was not only metal workers' and technical workers' unions who were sending support. Harry Isaksson wrote on behalf of the miners' union in Sweden. The General Secretary of the chemical workers' union in Austria wrote on behalf of his members. Much of this international trade-union support, though morale-boosting, could have little effect on the management of Lucas. But some of it could have: especially important was the support coming from workers in Lucas subsidiaries or Lucas's customers in Europe. A telegram came from the Workers' Assembly at the Lucas CAV Condeisal Plant in Southern Spain, asking what action they could take. A telex came from the Solidarity committee in Kience, a Polish region where Lucas had part ownership of two companies. Workers in the West German Pierburg subsidiary of Lucas Aerospace threatened to take action. Technical workers at Ford's Cologne threatened to boycott Lucas car components and to press the rest of the company to do the same. The TASS national leadership, however, warned against such action, arguing that it "would simply mean redundancies in UK factories and more work for the German manufacturer Bosch" (J. Tuckfield, assistant general secretary of TASS).

On the domestic front, the TASS leadership showed the same unwillingness to give a lead. The offers of practical support were potentially even more decisive. They could have had crippling consequences for Lucas. At the major sites of Lucas Aerospace's two main customers, Rolls Royce and British Aerospace, TASS office committees wrote to their management threatening to boycott Lucas products and personnel.

"If this problem is not quickly resolved satisfactorily then we shall request that our members and colleagues boycott Lucas Aerospace products especially where there are suitable alternatives," wrote Peter Ward, secretary of the TASS divisional negotiating committee at British Aerospace, Preston. Shop stewards at the Burnley Lucas Aerospace site had immediately told management that they could expect industrial action if the sacking went ahead. Peter Flynn, an AUEW shop steward at Burnley, reported: "We were ready to call a mass meeting. But the senior TASS reps said the issue was going through their procedure, so we held back expecting them to get something going." These threats would lead to practical action only if a strong lead was given by TASS in Lucas Aerospace and nationally. However, weaknesses at the Willesden site gave the TASS leadership an excuse to back off the campaign.

On 29 June the Willesden members voted against continuing strike action. This clearly did make the campaign much more difficult, but it was a development which TASS representatives throughout Lucas Aerospace had anticipated. For they knew that their Willesden colleagues were in a very weak position.

The first source of weakness was that their jobs were dependent on a sub-contract from Marconi's on which they had already completed much of the design work. This led many of them to feel that as Kurt Nebel, a section leader at Willesden, said, "If we went on strike for long, we'd come back and find our jobs gone, no mistake about it."

Secondly they would not be able to depend on the more powerful shop-floor unions to come out on strike with them. The split between TASS and the AUEW shop stewards' committee at Willesden was so deep that the manual workers ignored the TASS picket lines and carried on work as usual. Moreover, not only were Willesden members industrially weak, but their confidence and morale were low. The company was suing them for £43,000 (£1,000 each) following a dispute in January that year when TASS members imposed an overtime ban in protest against the closure of the Lucas Girling factory on Merseyside. Furthermore, many of the TASS members had been there for over fifteen years, some seven or eight were nearing retirement age; if they were sacked as a result of continuing industrial action they would lose their pension rights and redundancy money.

For these reasons the TASS committee in Lucas Aerospace had devised an alternative strategy to get action started by TASS members elsewhere in Lucas Aerospace so that they could then ask all those unions who had expressed support elsewhere in the aerospace industry to take action. Their strategy involved withdrawing key parts of the Lucas group and financing the strikes with a £1 levy on all TASS members in every Lucas factory and contributions from the union centrally. Once strike action had started elsewhere, the NNC would then ask the Willesden members to join the strike.

At its meeting on 3 July, the TASS Lucas National Negotiating Committee (NNC) agreed to this strategy. However, the TASS national executive did not accept the NNC's recommendation. Instead of backing a strategy to overcome the insecurity of the Willesden members, it appears to have used this weakness as an excuse to avoid an effective campaign. The local TASS official for Willesden was asked to obtain an immediate guarantee from the Willesden members that they would go on strike if others came out. This, the Willesden members felt, was against the spirit of NNC recommendation, which implied Willesden would consider strike action *after* others had come out. They voted against giving such a guarantee.

Meanwhile TASS NNC members were trying to identify key sections willing to come out. It was hard, partly because of holidays, but more fundamentally because of the insecurity felt as a result of massive redundancies taking place elsewhere in Lucas Industries. Nevertheless several key sections did vote to come out. They were at Wolverhampton, where the TASS organization is strong and trade-union principles well established, and at Shaftmoor Lane. These would have been the trigger to start action in other unions and in companies like Rolls Royce and British Aerospace. However, the TASS executive, on the basis of reports from full-time officials, rejected the NNC's proposal.

The TASS leadership, however, did not leave it at a rejection of the NNC proposal; perhaps in order to cover their tracks, to ensure the blame was laid elsewhere, they called instead — against the advice of TASS representatives in Lucas Aerospace — on the Willesden members to come out on strike. TASS offered them full financial support, but that missed the point. It was their jobs the Willesden members were frightened of losing, not a few weeks' pay. And so, predictably, the Willesden members voted against strike action. Their vote was as much in anger against the way the TASS leadership had dealt with the whole issue as anything else. This was made clear by a statement signed by thirty-five of the forty members and sent to the TASS executives. It included the following:

> Although the EC were fully aware of the vulnerability and inherent weakness of this site and its inability in the present circumstances to influence Lucas, they deliberately ignored the recommendation of the NNC to bring out key sections of TASS workers who were fully prepared to carry this fight in Lucas.
>
> Bearing in mind the complete lack of publicity emanating from our EC and officials, culminating in a deafening silence from the General Secretary, we have grave doubts as to their integrity on this matter.

These Willesden TASS members along with other aerospace members of the NNC urged the TASS executive to reverse its decision and reinstate the original proposal of the NNC. However, the general secretary took an action which whether intentionally or unintentionally undermined this possibility: he instructed the full-time official whose area included the Wolverhampton plant to meet with the members to reverse their decision to strike. The Wolverhampton office committee and Aerospace NNC members strongly objected to such a move being made without the approval of the NNC. The objections were ignored. The official came in, thanked the members for their offer of strike action and told them it would no longer be necessary to take it up. So by the time the NNC met on 14 August — four days after Cooley's notice had run out — the basis for arguing for the original NNC strategy was no longer there. There would in any case have been little chance of expressing it, for the meeting was simply informed of the executive decision; no vote was taken. The executive decision was final. And so too was the sacking of Mike Cooley.

This experience brought to the surface all the anger about the role of the leadership of AUEW-TASS in failing to support the Combine Committee's initiative. Many leading lay officials within Lucas Aerospace resigned their union positions in protest and disgust. Ron Mills, a long-standing AUEW-TASS activist in Birmingham, summed up their attitude:

> If the TASS hierarchy had supported the Corporate Plan from is first presentation to the union executive and instructed Lucas Aerospace management that it was official union policy, then Lucas would have had to allow Mike Cooley and others all the time they needed on official union duties. Exactly the same principle applies to Ernie Scarbrow. Both would still be working at Lucas.

In many respects the explanation for the attitude of AUEW-TASS is very specific. However, in their reflections on the company's sacking of Mike Cooley, the Combine reminded itself of the general lessons learned in their ten-year history: that, as the Combine secretary's report put it: "Any Aerospace problem which is left to an individual union to fight has less chance of being successful than being tackled by the Combine as a whole." But what state was the Combine in? Could it live up to the practical implications of this conclusion?

Trade-union organization at the sites

The lack of cohesion at a national level is not the whole picture of trade unionism in Lucas Aerospace in the early 1980s. At site level there was, with three exceptions, a remarkable degree of unity. It is at this level that the lasting organizational contribution of the Combine Committee can be seen, by comparing the state of trade-union organization in most of the sites when they first joined the Combine with the organization which now exists in the same sites. Burnley provides the most striking contrast. When the AUEW shop stewards first joined the Combine a joint organization was emerging with the GMWU, but there was virtually open warfare with the Sheet Metal Workers' Union; and as for staff, "We never had any time for them" was the general attitude summed up by AUEW steward Jim Fleming. By 1979, however, all the shop-floor unions and all the staff unions except ASTMS (supervision) were members of one joint staff/manual committee with a staff member as chairman and a shop-floor member as secretary. This committee meets once every month in work time with the recognition and support from the district CSEU. Staff and shop floor now negotiate together on all issues that affect the factory as a whole: for example new technology, payments for movement of work, and redundancies. Only the national agreement between the CSEU and the EEF prevents them from negotiating jointly on hours and holidays. This joint committee represents 1,900 shop-floor workers and over 500 staff workers.

Trade-union organization in the Birmingham factories showed a similar improvement during the site's seven-year involvement with the Combine. When Birmingham shop stewards began to attend the Combine in the traumatic aftermath of the Rolls Royce crash there was no regular contact with the staff unions and no co-ordination across the five Birmingham factories. Yet in 1979 when trade unionists faced new attacks from management they were in a much stronger position to resist. Joint staff and manual committees met on every site, with differing degrees of formality, but in all cases with CSEU recognition. New technology is the main issue over which they negotiate. These separate factory committees meet together quarterly through the joint/manual Liaison Committee. Only ASTMS (supervision) is not involved in the Liaison Committee. The different factory committees in Birmingham tried to get CSEU recognition for the Liaison Committee in order to secure facilities for regular meetings and when necessary for negotiations, but the Birmingham District CSEU supported by the national CSEU executive insisted that only factory committees could be recognized. The Liaison Committee went across factory committees and was therefore according to CSEU definitions an "unofficial committee" and destined to remain so. In the absence of this recognition, the Liaison Committee is unstable and could easily collapse again, if for instance one group of stewards fail to win their members' support for a jointly agreed initiative.

Bradford is another site where trade-union organization has developed from a joint manual shop stewards' committee lacking any regular contact with staff unions into a joint manual and staff committee with CSEU recognition. Again, ASTMS (supervision) is not involved, although informal contact is maintained. At Hemel Hempstead too the manual stewards and the staff unions have come closer together particularly in the last four years, over the company's rationalization plans and more recently over new technology. A joint staff/manual committee now meets regularly,. A similar development has occurred at Luton. The only major site (that is a site with over 1,000 workers) without a joint manual staff committee is Wolverhampton. At Wolverhampton the situation now is only a slight improvement on the divided trade unionism of the late 1960s. In three of the smaller sites, Netherton, Coventry and Liverpool, there is at least regular informal contact which is an improvement on the situation when the Combine first began; but no lasting joint/staff/manual committee has ever been established.

Wages and new technology: uneven progress

The success of the Combine in rebuilding itself on the basis of the unity that had been achieved at site level has been uneven. On wages, the attempts at co-operation between staff and shop floor foundered on the different negotiating arrangements, the tendency born of insecurity to protect differentials and preferential bonus systems over-zealously, and the fear that action over wages would further jeopardize jobs. The Combine Committee's policies for ensuring trade-union control over the rapid introduction of computer-based machinery in 1980 and '81 met with more success. In this area the different procedure and structures of national trade unions were not such a problem. One reason was that at that time *there were no* established procedures for trade-union negotiations over the introduction of new technology. The national unions were having to improvise and experiment as much as the Combine Committee. In fact the Combine, with the help of CAITS, had probably done a lot more strategic thinking on some of the issues raised by new technology than many national unions. Moreover, the mutual dependence of staff and shop-floor workers in the attempt to control the introduction of new technologies is particularly obvious. Shop-floor workers need from the staff information about the computer-controlled manufacturing machinery and its operations; staff need from the shop floor industrial sanctions over fitting and co-operating with the results of the computer-based office machinery. The Combine together with individual unions built on this potential for co-operation throughout 1980–81. They succeeded in co-ordinating a moratorium on the introduction of new machinery at a time when Lucas Aerospace management was hoping to move rapidly to computer-aided design and computer-aided manufacturing systems at major sites.

This moratorium had two objectives. First it was seen as a way of getting management to negotiate centrally on new technology with representatives from all sites and all unions. Management had already stated that it wanted to carry out all negotiations on a site level. But the Combine Committee felt that such a piecemeal introduction of the machinery would weaken the ability of the unions to develop a really effective strategy for controlling the pace and the terms on which the new technology would be introduced. The second objective of the moratorium was to use the time to involve all the shop stewards' committees in drawing up the policies that would be the basis of these central negotiations.

The moratorium lasted for nearly a year in some sites and longer in others. During this period the Combine Committee and CAITS carried out an extensive investigation and debate on the consequences of new technology for workers in Lucas Aerospace and the policies though which the benefits of new technology could be controlled by those who manufacture it, use it and consume its products, rather than those who own it. The moratorium did not hold consistently enough to force management to conduct central negotiations, but it did lead to several good site-level agreements.

New signs of growth — without illusions

This experience illustrates the contradictory poisition of the Combine Committee at the turn of the decade. It was strong on ideas and strategy but weak as a national organization to implement these ideas, although particular sites were able to carry out Combine policies very effectively. The Combine did manage to extend its support in 1980 and 1981 on this precarious basis. Trade unionists who affiliated to the Combine during that period did so mainly because of its ideas; they saw its potential and hoped to contribute to re-establishing its industrial strength. The decision of the Aerospace section of the Lucas electricians' group to join the Combine in January 1981 both illustrates the importance of site co-ordination in drawing groups into the Combine and demonstrates the support for the Combine's ideas as well as an awareness of the Combine's industrial weakness. The Lucas Aerospace electricians had always been part of the Lucas electricians' trade group in Birmingham which went across the whole of Lucas Industries. They had been represented on the Liaison Committee of the Birmingham Aerospace factories but had never been affiliated to the Combine. In 1980, according to their senior steward, John Routley:

> Things started to change; the senior steward who had kept us away from too much involvement with trade-union organization in aerospace was promoted to a foreman and there were a number of new electricians taken on, with some older faces leaving. At the same time the electrical company started to change its approach to the trade-union movement, running parallel to the Tory government's economic strategy. . . . the shop stewards backed by the members started to look for *alternatives* within the aerospace trade-union organization. Indeed interest was growing when they started to hear of the progress the Combine had made. CAITS for example highlighted the positive approaches that the Combine had taken.
>
> It is fair to say that the last twelve months has seen a growing commitment to the Combine from the electricians. This commitment has developed from the understandings reached with other unions on the site via the CSEU committees and the Liaison Committee. We see the Combine as it stands as a "Think tank" which draws on its members at all levels to work out any strategy that is necessary to deal with any problem no matter what it may be. But what it does not have is the ability to carry out that strategy to its full potential. And that

problem boils down to the fundamental problem of industrial strength.

In the absence of this industrial strength, and while it is being rebuilt, the Combine's jointly run research and resource centre, CAITS, has provided an important campaigning base, a source of ideas and a means of organizational continuity. CAITS workers have helped the Combine produce regular leaflets and bulletins for the membership in the factories at a time when management was restricting the facilities and time available to Combine members. It also helped with some of the functions of communication and co-ordination that Ernie Scarbrow used to carry out, while new secretaries were finding their feet. In this relationship between an unofficial organization of elected shop-floor leaders and full-time researchers and administrators based in a centre outside the company, the Lucas Combine has developed at least part of an answer to the problem of lack of resources and facilities independent of the company which has made unofficial combine committees so unstable. Moreover, the work of CAITS has enabled the Combine to spread its ideas, strengthen its connections with other trade unionists and pass on to other combine committees the lessons it has learnt from its difficulties as well as its successes.

18 Making connections

Thursday morning, 24 January 1980, in the upstairs room of a pub near Euston station: forty-six shop stewards from Glasgow, Tyneside, Manchester, the Midlands and London were gathered to discuss what to do in the face of growing unemployment and intensifying attacks on shop-floor organization. The stewards represented multi-union combine committees based in fifteen of the country's major corporations. Combine committees in the power engineering industry, in Talbot, British Shipbuilders, British Aerospace, Dunlop, Vickers, Metal Box, British Leyland and Lucas Aerospace were among those who sent delegates or observers. In most cases these national combine committees, formed in the 1960s and early '70s, had been the extension of strong plant organizations. Now, with the pressures of the recession, exacerbated by government policies, plant organization was being threatened; and several combine committees were finding themselves stranded, without an adequate base of active support.

Against this background, some of the delegates had come to the meeting in a desperate search for an explanation of what was going wrong. "We failed over redundancies," said a senior steward from the Talbot Linwood plant near Glasgow (to be closed eighteen months later). "We put over all the arguments but the membership rejected our recommendation to fight. Where are we going wrong?" Some delegates had hoped to learn from the Lucas Aerospace Combine Committee, which had called the meeting, and had the reputation of being one of the more successful committees. But the Lucas Combine had called the meeting partly out of an awareness of the limits of their successes and a recognition that their achievements were precarious and could be easily undermined unless they worked closely with others facing similar problems. "Through our Corporate Plan strategy we have managed to stave off most redundancies, but we are becoming more and more aware of the need to work with other similar organizations," wrote Ernie Scarbrow in the Combine's invitation to the meeting. In fact, the company's threat to sack Scarbrow himself, coming just after British Leyland had successfully sacked Derek Robinson,* was one of the experiences which led the Lucas Aerospace Combine to call the meeting in the first place. The Combine had never been isolationist in its approach; it had worked with stewards in other parts of Lucas to try (unsuccessfully) to sustain combine committees throughout Lucas Industries; it had just recently imposed industrial sanctions in support of the Rolls Royce workers who were locked out over the national engineering pay claim in 1979; and as we have seen it had been in contact with many other trade unionists in the course of campaigning for the Corporate Plan. However, the problems the Combine had faced in 1979 and 1980 revealed the need for better co-

---

* Derek Robinson, the chairman of the combine committee in British Leyland Motors, was sacked for writing a pamphlet which called for resistance to Michael Edwardes's corporate plan for Leyland.

ordination between combine committees, to improve their organization, to develop stronger policies and to spread their ideas.

The Joint Forum of Combine Committees

The outcome of the January meeting was the "Joint Forum of Combine Committees". As the name "forum" implies, it was organized in a flexible, open way. John Boardman, an AUEW shop steward from Rolls Royce, Barnoldswick, summed up its main advantage for stewards like himself:

> The most obvious benefit . . . is being able to meet people in other industries and from other parts of the country. The interchange of information, ideas, problems and frustrations helps to give us an understanding of a fuller picture.

The Forum did not pretend to be a powerful organization; there were no declamatory calls to action, no rhetorical resolutions which would be forgotten when delegates returned to the factories. The mood was realistic and cautious, but it was not purely defensive. The minutes of the first meeting report contributions which stressed the need for more positive bargaining positions on new technology and pensions. Other contributions talked of "campaigning throughout the branches and district committees for support for multi-union, multi-plant combine committees".

CAITS was asked to act as the secretariat for the Joint Forum. The job of chairing the quarterly meetings, arranging for the meeting place and the provision of refreshments, rotated between the fifteen or so combine committees. In this way every combine came to feel a sense of responsibility for the forum and no one felt it was the property or "front" of any particular organization. The locations of meetings rotated too, which proved to be a good way of bringing in new shop stewards' committees who might not have travelled long distances for their first meeting. Since 1980 it has been held in Leeds, Liverpool, Carlisle, Birmingham, Sheffield and London. In both Sheffield and London the Labour local and county authorities, respectively, provided the Joint Forum with meeting rooms in their vast Town and County Halls. The Joint Forum launched itself publicly in June 1980 with a pamphlet on the case for multi-union combine committees and the principles on which they should be based.[1] Two thousand copies of the pamphlet were sold through the combine committees within a few months of publication, an indication of the acute sense among trade unionists in manufacturing industry of the vulnerability of their traditional trade-union institutions.

"A wealth of information"

One of the sources of this vulnerability is the lack of adequate back-up information and research for stewards who want to devise counter strategies to the centralized plans of corporate management. For instance even the HQs of unions which on paper support combine committees did not know where such committees existed. Jim Murray, a delegate to the Vickers' combine, recalls: "I asked the head of AUEW research for a list of combines some time ago and he said they didn't have one. I also asked the Labour Research Department for details and they found no way of finding out through normal trade-union channels. They ended up sending similar queries to me!" Collecting and disseminating this very basic information was the first job carried out by the Joint Forum. It began to bring together a directory of combines in all their different forms. This is now being produced together with a pamphlet on the problems of organizing multi-union combines.[2]

Another issue on which the information and ideas coming from many trade-union HQs was inadequate was that of pension schemes and pension funds. The Joint Forum with the help of CAITS sent out a questionnaire to the fifteen combine committees who at one time or another attend the Joint Forum, asking them what kind of pension scheme their company had; how it was controlled; whether the trade unions had any trustees; if so how they were appointed, trained and advised; what the relation of the company's pension scheme was with the state scheme; what provisions were made covering change of employment or redundancy; whether pension payments were increased to offset inflation and finally what information the shop stewards could get about the pension funds investment portfolio, and where the investments were made. The results of the questionnaire — from thirteen replies — were collated and distributed to every delegate.[3]

"There was a wealth of information," commented Jim Marshall from the Dunlop combine, "which we could not have gained any other way. No single union research department would have been able to cover such a broad spectrum of experience. The value of Joint Forum is the variety of inputs to its discussions. We got a lot of ideas which helped us in our own negotiations on the Dunlop pension scheme." The kind of information exchanged on pensions had relevance to other issues concerning company rationalization plans and, in the longer run, control over investment. For instance the trade-union trustees on the Lucas Staff Pension Fund discovered that their manager had attended a meeting of all the major institutional investors in GEC, called by Weinstock in connection with his plans for reorganizing GEC. As a result of questioning of their pension fund manager the Lucas trade-union trustees gleaned some useful information about Weinstock's plans which they passed on to the Lucas Aerospace Combine who in turn, through the contacts at the Joint Forum, passed it on to trade-union representatives from GEC. The Joint Forum found that there was considerable scope for this kind of exchange of information since many of their pension funds invested in each other's companies. So far the Joint Forum has only discussed in detail the information on this interconnection between pension funds and company strategies. But they and the speakers invited to discuss pension funds intend in the future to discuss the question of alternative investment strategies: of whether and of how workers can use trade-union representation on pension funds as a lever to press for job-creating investment.

New technology is another issue on which the Joint Forum gathered and disseminated a wealth of information, on the basis of questionnaires leading to discussion and finally a pamphlet.[4] Here again the information-gathering itself triggered off new approaches. Fred Titchen from the Thorn combine described his response to the new technology questionnaire:

> It got me thinking. For instance the question about contact with staff made me change my approach. I'd never thought about involving staff in relation to our negotiations but once I gave it some thought, it was an obvious thing to do in relation to new technology.

Stewards would follow up the results of the questionnaires by contacting each other for more detailed information when they found themselves facing similar problems. Responses were usually quick because they had built up personal contact through the Forum.

The making of contacts across major companies was very important for another reason. It meant that combine committees were in a better position to catch up organizationally with the company mergers and reorganizations which in the past have tended to throw combines into disarray. For example when Vickers took over Rolls Royce Motors, Mike Kenny from Rolls Royce Aerospace (which had been part of a single company with Rolls Royce Motors) describes how he "was able to give the secretary of the Vickers combine names of the convenors in Rolls Royce most likely to be interested in the Combine, and a letter introducing him to them. Now the Rolls Royce Motors stewards are part of the Vickers combine and they come to the joint Forum as well. I don't think the contacts would have been so easy to make, if at all, without the Joint Forum." So, information, ideas and contacts are three of the benefits of the Joint Forum. Another benefit is that it provides support and stimulates and strengthens morale at times when a single combine is not doing too well or is getting a bit complacent. Combines which are not officially recognized always depend on the commitment and determination of a few individuals, who sometimes may get in a rut or reach an impasse; then decline sets in, followed by demoralization and collapse of the combine. Recently this had begun to happen with the Thorn committee. Fred Titchen again:

> After the last Joint Forum, I saw more clearly that we'd been just sitting back. No wonder attendance had dropped. I came back from the Joint Forum with a clearer idea of how to involve more people, get more unions in and strengthen our organization. I think the Joint Forum meetings help keep up morale as well as providing ideas.

For these reasons shop stewards have kept on coming to the Joint Forum even though it costs money in terms of travel and a day off work, and even though it has no official status whatsoever.

CAITS: Education for control

The relation of CAITS to the combine committees involved in the Joint Forum is much more that that of a secretariat, and CAITS's role has been a further factor behind the relative stability of the Joint Forum. In effect CAITS provides a new kind of trade-union education and research which directly follows up the kind of issues which combines bring to the Forum. Just as the Joint Forum is in a modest way filling a vacuum in the established trade-union structures by enabling direct contact to take place between shop stewards facing similar problems, from different unions and corporations, so CAITS is contributing to the education and research needed to confront these problems.

The feature which most of the issues raised at the Joint Forum have in common is that they all go beyond the traditional concerns of collective bargaining. Management's rationalization plans and investment decisions, the control of pension funds, the design and purpose of technological change; these are the issues which the recession and a period of devastating industrial restructuring are forcing on to shop stewards' agendas for the first time in post-war years. Yet until the late 1970s, collective bargaining institutions and their research and educational back-up had been built up on the basis of bargaining only over the price of labour and the terms of the employment contract. Richard Lee, an AUEW steward from the Metal Box combine committee, points out the resulting weaknesses of the trade-union education as far as the needs of stewards in large multi-plant multi-national companies are concerned:

> Normal trade-union education does not educate stewards in what's going on beyond their own plant. You come out of a course knowing how to bargain on day-to-day issues. But you don't really know the company you're bargaining with, what it's up to at different plants, what its investment strategy is, what it's getting from the government. I've never known a shop steward come out of a course thinking he's really learnt how to deal with the company he's up against.

Some parts of the official trade-union movement have been responsive to these needs. Tutors at the TUC Education Unit, for instance, have attempted to remedy the weakness in trade-union education which Richard Lee highlights. The debate about industrial democracy and the extension of collective bargaining, and the development of company-wide trade-union organization, produced a new interest in the late '70s in providing courses that would help shop stewards investigate and respond to company strategies. For example, the Education Unit introduced courses on "Bargaining and Company Information" into their nation-wide programme of local day-release courses. The courses aim to help stewards gain an insight into how management plan and control a company's operation — and to think through what this means for a whole range of trade-union strategies, from pay claims to investment and job security. The focus is on building up a picture of a company as a whole, and countering the familiar arguments with which management tries to play off one plant against another.

The TUC Education Unit also recognized the importance of national courses which can bring together stewards from different plants and unions within the same company. It was hoped that such courses would act as a catalyst for the strengthening of company-wide trade-union organization and the development of new bargaining agendas. However, in the face of restrictions placed by management and a lack of commitment by several individual unions, they have managed to organize by 1982 only four such courses. Moreover, few individual unions have the resources to provide the longer-term research help needed by stewards to follow up these courses.

CAITS and trade-union research and resource centres throughout the country* are therefore meeting a largely unmet research need. In doing so they are pioneering a new kind of trade-union research. It is not research simply as a service from researchers as experts to trade unionists as clients. It is rather research carried out jointly in a way that develops trade unionists' skills, confidence and organization so that the anticipation of management's plans and drawing up of alternative policies become a regular part of their trade unionism.

Creating the conditions for workers' plans

Such an ideal is easier stated than achieved. CAITS's original brief had included the task of "spreading the idea of workers' plans similar to the plan of the Lucas Aerospace workers".

However, very few shop stewards' committees have developed the kind of extensive information network the Lucas stewards had established before they embarked on their alternative plan. One consequence of the lack of such networks is that shop stewards would tend to treat CAITS workers as experts who would provide instant packaged answers, and immediate suggestions for alternative products, as if CAITS was a trade-union equivalent of a management consultant. CAITS, under pressure to get something done, sometimes responded in line with these expectations. But ideally the people at CAITS see themselves as catalytic to workers developing their own alternatives and gaining the confidence and strength to fight for them. This has meant helping combine committees to improve their communication with their members by starting a newspaper; encouraging shop-floor-based combines to involve the staff; providing background information on the strategies of the major corporations so that stewards are able to recognize what their own managements are up to; and initiating discussions of the implications of government policy so that stewards understand their own problems in a wider context. All this has been a precondition for any useful and genuinely workplace-based discussion of alternative plans.

CAITS's work with the Metal Box combine illustrates this well. In the last two years, three closures have taken place in Metal Box with little effective

---

* In 1979 these centres formed "The Network of Trade Union and Community Research and Resource Centres", through which they organize workshops to discuss common problems, co-ordinate joint projects and share a full-time worker to raise funds and ensure a regular exchange of information.

resistance. A combine committee has existed in Metal Box since the 1950s but it has never before had to face up to this kind of rapid restructuring. Its failure to anticipate the closures and develop a strategy of resistance stimulated leading combine members to look for ways of investigating the company's plans. This led them to bring together many plants and unions, including staff unions, to a weekend at Wortley Hall to piece together and to analyse what the company was doing against the wider background of government policy and the international economy. Richard Lee described what happened:

> Mike George (from CAITS) had an overall picture of the kind of strategies adopted by these multi-nationals, so he helped start the discussion along the right lines. People from the different plants would report on what their managers were saying elsewhere. All the company's lies came out into the open. Suddenly people saw how they were being played off against each other. Suddenly we were able to go beneath the surface and piece together what is really going on. That means we're in a much better position to anticipate closures and work out our tactics in advance.

The picture built up so far was then disseminated through the combine newspaper *The Boxer*, calling for more information "which you think will help us put the jigsaw together".

This work of CAITS and the Joint Forum of combine committees illustrates that the idea of "workers' plans" does not necessarily or exclusively involve alternative products. The idea refers to policies based on the needs of the workforce and the community in which they live, drawn up by the workers themselves in whatever form is appropriate to the conditions of the company. Workers' plans make explicit workers' needs and priorities; and increasingly this has come to mean workers not just as producers but also as members of a local community, as fathers and mothers, as future pensioners, as patients and as users. "Workers' plans" involve attempting as far as possible to show the connections between these needs, and how they could be met with the productive and financial resources now under the control of management, the financiers or the civil service. And finally, workers' plans point ahead to the improvements and extensions of workers' organizations which are necessary to fight for control over these resources.

Illustrating the argument with alternative products

Although alternative products are thus only one part of the idea of workers' plans, they are an important part. And they are important as much for illustrating new possibilities as for immediate negotiations with management. A design or prototype of a product which could meet unmet needs, and for which otherwise redundant resources are available, stimulates people into thinking of new ways of organizing production and designing technology to meet people's needs more adequately.

Take the road-rail vehicle, for instance. This featured in much of the media coverage of the Plan; primarily because a small prototype test unit had actually been built at NELP in 1975/76 by Richard Fletcher, with help from the Lucas stewards. The science and technology television programme "Tomorrow's World" had shown an early version on test on a disused railway track, shifting from road to rail at a level-crossing. It aroused considerable interest, for example from the Highlands and Islands Development Board and various overseas governments, including Tanzania. Nearer home, Labour councillors in Burnley were particularly interested in the road-rail vehicle: "It's just what we need to keep some of the branch lines open and to service the more outlying areas. And production of it could provide more jobs for workers at British Leyland and Lucas," commented Councillor Birdshaw. Labour councillors on several other local and county authorities, including Sheffield, London and Manchester, along with local trade unionists concerned with transport, were thinking on similar lines.

Under more favourable political conditions, co-ordinated pressure from workers in Lucas, in British Leyland and in Dunlop and from local authority purchasers might have forced the companies to go into production of the road-rail vehicle; or perhaps a public or municipal enterprise could have been established. As it was, the best that could be done was to modify an existing bus to produce a working prototype. This was done at CAITS between 1979 and mid-1980, developing on the earlier work carried out at NELP by Richard Fletcher. Even the production of this illustrated in a small way the alliance which socially useful production would require, cutting across existing economic units. For instance several local authorities, including Burnley, offered CAITS a bus. The bus which proved to be the right type came virtually as a gift from the National Bus Company: CAITS received, for £500, a bus which would normally cost between £3,000 and £4,000. With the help of a sympathetic engineer in Dunlop, CAITS received free tyres. At least half the components for the bus were made in Lucas Aerospace. In some cases this was the result of sympathetic people in the training schools, allowing apprentices to work on components as one of their projects. In other cases shop stewards simply did the work in the company's time with the company's equipment and material but without the company's knowledge.

The bus was finally tested with great success in July 1980 on the West Somerset Railway with the full co-operation of the West Somerset County Council. Since then the bus has provided mobile agitprop in campaigns against unemployment, on the People's March for jobs and on demonstrations in Burnley, Birmingham and West London for instance. It is fitted out with posters and with a video showing pictures of other socially useful products proposed by the Lucas Aerospace Combine as an alternative to the dole.

The propaganda value of the road-rail vehicle in illustrating that there are such socially needed alternatives was demonstrated vividly on Mayday in Burnley 1979. The Mayday Parade was intended as a parade against unemployment with different shop stewards' committees contributing floats

on themes appropriate to their industry. Every float except for the Lucas workers' float — the road-rail vehicle — in effect identified the workers' interests with the company's competitive success (which in a recession under the present economic system would conflict with the interests of workers in other companies). "Fly the British Flag the World over with Rolls Royce", proclaimed the poster on the back of the Rolls Royce stewards' float, which carried a massive, shiny RB211 engine. "Buy British", "Import controls now" was the message of the flags waved by women on the Thorn's float. In between these two floats came the red road-rail vehicle with "Lucas Aerospace workers' socially useful product" painted on the side.

After the positive experience with the prototype of the road-rail vehicle, the Lucas Combine were keen to gain access to more facilities for work on product prototypes. As well as the propaganda value of these prototypes the Combine argued that the more prototypes there were of alternative products, designed and built to meet the social needs of the producer and the user, the stronger would be the bargaining position of workers fighting redundancies in the future. Moreover, if the prototype work was done with facilities which trade unionists jointly controlled then these prototypes could be of use in job-saving negotiations or campaigns of groups of workers who, given the existing division of labour, do not have the skills to design the alternatives. Centres like CAITS, in or making use of academic institutions, could provide a way of pooling and co-ordinating different design and technical skills which do not exist in equal proportion in every workforce. Such a co-ordination of skills makes it possible to think in terms of alternatives on a local and regional basis rather than simply within a single company with a high proportion of design and technical staff. With this vision of spreading the idea of socially useful products as a contribution to the more general strategy of workers' alternative plans, the Lucas Combine have tried to spread the idea of CAITS to other parts of the country. Students at Bradford University first took up the idea and, together with stewards at the Lucas factory in Bradford and money from the Rowntree Charitable Trust, they started a small research and information centre, the Alternatives in Technology and Employment Centre (ATEC), lodged in the buildings of the Bradford College and with limited access to engineering workshops in the university. In the Midlands the Lucas stewards had a more ambitious project in mind. They wanted to be based in the Engineering Department of a polytechnic or university with full access to engineering workshops and with students working on product proposals, jointly agreed with the Combine Committee or other trade-union groups. They received an initial grant of £60,000 from Cadbury's Trust with which to pursue their ambitions. However, with one exception, the academic institutions were not so liberal about hosting a project associated with shop stewards. The story of the difficulties faced by the Combine in establishing a West Midlands CAITS and of their final success is revealing.

By their seemingly simple request that at least some of the resources of academic institutions should be available to trade unionists, the Lucas stewards were walking into a minefield of vested interests and hidden assumptions about the purpose of education. Often they were taken unawares by what their initial proposals had led them into. The minefields sometimes exploded in their face. Usually they found allies who, in their own way, were questioning the purposes and power structure of the institutions concerned. The initiative of the Lucas stewards gave much great potency to that questioning because it revealed the nature of the connections between academic institutions and private industry; and it illustrated in a very practical way the possibility of a connection with those who work in industry.

Academic hierarchies and conventions

The Combine Committee started in 1978 by approaching Birmingham Polytechnic, where they were already in touch with several of the lecturers. At the same time they began to prepare a proposal to the Inner City Partnership Committee for funds. The Partnership Committee seemed sympathetic to the idea of a research centre exploring alternative products controlled jointly by an academic institution and the Lucas Aerospace shop stewards. A detailed proposal was worked out for siting the centre at Birmingham Polytechnic. Staff from several departments of the Polytechnic became involved. There was widespread interest in and support for the idea — until the proposal reached the deputy director. He would not allow the proposal to go any further unless the Birmingham Chamber of Commerce became involved as one of the controlling partners. This was completely unacceptable to the Combine. Apart from the fact that Lucas Industries was a very influential member of the Chamber of Commerce, the Combine also argued that this reflected a clear bias in favour of management: "If management go to a poly or university with a research proposal, the authorities never insist on consulting the unions before going ahead," commented Brian Salisbury. The polytechnic was under no direct pressure from Lucas managmeent. Rather, this was a case of the covert exercise of power: where an institution — in this case Lucas — has power without having to exercise it because less powerful groups anticipate and defer to it. "Timidity, insipidness and an unwillingness to take a risk, that was the problem at the Poly," concludes Paul Embley, an economics lecturer who worked closely with the shop stewards in formulating their proposal.

Next on the list was the Management Centre at Aston University. Here the problem was not so much Lucas's overt or covert power, but rather the established conventions and self-image of the Centre. At the university, as at the Polytechnic, there was a group within the Centre, led by the leading Fabian Society member and Operational Research expert Professor Steven Cook, who were enthusiastic about the idea of a CAITS-type centre. By this time the Inner City Partnership Committee had lost interest. It was at this point that the Cadbury Trust offered to fund the Centre once the stewards had found an appropriate base. Those in control of the Management Centre were not keen to provide such a base. They had an image they wanted to preserve; and support for shop stewards' initiatives, however constructive, was not part of this image.

"It was very short-sighted," commented Dr David Best, one of Steven Cook's group of enthusiasts, and now on the management of a company in Nottingham.

> Given the state of industry in the West Midlands, I think it's clear that such a centre as LASSCC were proposing could have made a real contribution. In fact the Management Centre did no work whatsoever in the area of job creation or alternative forms of industrial organization. That is sad indictment in an area which has lost 8 per cent of its jobs in the last three years.

Next the Combine tried Warwick, "the Business University" as it has been named, ever since students discovered correspondence between the vice-chancellor and leading industrialists that revealed very close relations between the university and major corporations based in the West Midlands. The Combine Committee knew of these revelations but did not realize how thoroughly the needs of the big corporations had penetrated the university. They over-estimated the autonomy and freedom of the academics who had expressed interest and support for the idea of a CAITS-type centre at Warwick. And indeed there was a lot of support. An initial meeting attracted around forty academics from eight different departments. Three departments, Business Studies, Law and Engineering, all passed motions in support of the project at departmental meetings — though a minority of the Engineering department were not at all sympathetic. Moreover, the Combine felt they were in a strong bargaining position with £60,000 from the Cadbury Trust behind them. Robert Bryer from the Business Studies department helped the Combine to formulate a detailed proposal based on the work and facilities of all three departments. The first indication of the Business University still at the heart of Warwick's sprawling campus came when Bryer was chatting to one of Vice-Chancellor Butterworth's administrative assistants while waiting to take the proposal to the Senate steering committee. The assistant let slip that the vice-chancellor had rung up a member of Lucas management to ask their opinion about the proposed centre. We can only speculate as to what was said at the other end of the phone, but the Senate steering committee rejected the proposed centre.

One fact to bear in mind: arrangements were being made for a senior member of the Lucas-funded engineering research centre at Birmingham University to become "Professor of Manufacturing" at Warwick, bringing with him grants from Lucas for the Warwick Engineering Department.*

In 1970 the staff and students of Warwick summed up their findings on the power of the corporations at that time in the following way:

> Just as the great landed aristocracy of the eighteenth century exerted their power by manifold exercise of interest, influence and purchase, so the new lords seem to infiltrate the command-posts of our society, including our educational institutions, not through any transparent democratic process, but quietly, in unnoticed ways. They apparently share with their precursors the same assumption that this is *their* world, to dispose of by ownership and by right of purchase. These are the people who know other people; who govern by telephone; who are unaccountable because it is always their inferiors who make up the accounts; who put things in each other's laps.[1]

Ten years later, it seems their power continues, and they still govern by telephone. But at least the possibility of a different kind of relationship with "industry" has been illustrated.

Fortunately not all academic institutions are quite like Warwick University. Coventry (Lanchester) Polytechnic (at one point an alternative candidate to become Coventry's university), as a polytechnic funded by a Labour-controlled council, had some interest in furthering good relations with those who work in industry as well as those who own it. This was especially so at the time of cuts in government expenditure when there was the offer of funds from Cadbury's. Cadbury's, to their credit, had stuck with the project throughout. In the summer of 1981, the Midlands CAITS — the Unit for the Development of Alternative products — at last found a base in the Combined Engineering Department of Lanchester Polytechnic. Representatives of the Combine Committee jointly with representatives of the polytechnic interviewed and appointed a full-time co-ordinator, Brian Lowe, a transport engineer who had been a principal lecturer in the Combined Engineering Department. Technically, Lanchester's Combined

---

* He was also to run short courses for members of Lucas and British Leyland management at Warwick.

Engineering Department provides an ideal base for prototype work on new products because it combines at least four different types of engineering. There is also a lot of enthusiasm for the project among students and staff. Brian Lowe felt it had tremendous potential for enabling students to make a real contribution to solving social problems.

> I've always said to students that they can't opt out of society and social problems, but in the past they have not had the chance to be involved. The design and prototype projects they do in their final year normally just get stored away. They are never used because there's no one in the department whose job it is to find groups, trade unions, local authority or management who could make something of them. Academics when they've finished with one lot of students simply go on to dealing with the next lot. I felt through UDAP we could make sure students' work made a real social input.

Altogether sixty-six students are involved in work on products contained within the Corporate Plan, some working alone on one product, others working as a group. Given that students are working on UDAP projects for only part of their course, this is the equivalent of about eight full-time workers. The students certainly seem to find it different from the project work they are used to. Ricardo Robles, a Venezuelan student, describes his feelings:

> I work on designing a prototype of a universal power pack. It would make it easier to pump water and to solve many other agricultural problems in my country. I like doing something where I can see the practical effect it could have. I hope the government in my country will be interested.

Already some of the projects which Lanchester students are working on could have a practical effect. The products on which they are working include a portable kidney machine, auxiliary braking systems and several other products for which a need certainly exists and, with an increase in public spending, purchasing power could also exist. UDAP's main project is the hybrid car, which uses a small internal combustion to drive electric batteries. The result is a low-cost non-polluting small car suitable for city transport. The West Midland County Council has already agreed to provide further funds to develop the car so that a co-operative or municipal enterprise could manufacture it in Coventry: the Coventry Car. Municipal enterprise is not the only option for using products developed at Lanchester. The option especially favoured by the Combine Committee is that of trade unions making use of the prototypes to negotiate for diversification policies that would provide jobs for workers who would otherwise face the dole. This is a difficult option especially at times when it most needed, that is when unemployment is high but therefore trade-union bargaining power is low. A second worker has been appointed to UDAP ideally suited to developing this side of UDAP's work: Jim Shutt, an engineer who until recently was a very active member of the TASS office committee in Talbot Coventry.

So, after three years of negotiating with academic hierarchies which turned out to be no less conservative and jealous of their powers than Lucas management, the Lucas stewards are jointly controlling a project full of promise. The difficulties faced by the Lucas stewards during those three years indicates that, in order to achieve this use of academic resources, people working in those public institutions and in private industry, and the people who use and consume from both, need to organize across those institutions as well as within them. For one reason why the rulers of the established order have the upper hand is that they have strongly bonded connecting links, both formal and informal. No single combine committee can map out the kind of network which is needed to plan for social need and to campaign and fight for those plans. The network will grow out of particular initiatives which then make connections, rather than from any one overview. But it always helps to try to describe and identify the main tendencies of that growth, even if you have to modify your vision in the light of experience.

Popular planning

We have seen how the Lucas stewards have begun to do this with the other combine committees in the Joint Forum. The Joint Forum has begun to work with four trades councils who carried out an inquiry into the industrial policies of the last Labour government, to develop the idea of popular planning for social need on a local level as well as through nationally based campaigns.

In 1981 the four trades councils and the combine committees produced a statement entitled "Popular Planning for Social Need", which invited trade-union and labour-movement organizations to develop proposals and plans that could be fed into and modify the Alternative Economic Strategy being developed by the Labour Party — as well as provide a basis for local initiatives. Local plans are already being discussed with trades councils and community groups, while several Labour-controlled local authorities have begun to develop their own plans for local employment and industrial development — drawing on several ideas in the original Lucas Plan.

Thus the idea of worker and community plans has begun to spread. In the very difficult conditions of the 1980s the Joint Forum, backed up by CAITS, and other resource centres linked to the initiatives of trades councils and Left local authorities, are in effect preparing the ground for a trade-union challenge to corporate power which will be in a stronger position not only to grasp the opportunity of a more expansionary government but to sustain its momentum when such a government retreats.

VI: CONCLUSIONS

19 The limits of collective bargaining

The first question to ask in any assessment of the Combine Committee's plan is, how successful has it been in achieving its own ends? It had its origins in the fight to save jobs. In this the Combine's campaign between 1975 and 1981 was remarkably effective. Instead of 2,000 redundancies in 1977 and two closures in 1978, only about 100 jobs have been lost over the past four years due to compulsory redundancies or closures. Moreover, in three cases local redundancy plans were withdrawn as a result of campaigns based on the Corporate Plan.

The Combine — and many outside observers — were convinced that the company wanted to cut back drastically on aerospace work in the UK. As a report in the *Investors Chronicle* put it on 29 November 1974:

> Lucas remains determined to concentrate all its major capital investment projects overseas and leave Britain more or less on a care and maintenance basis.

The Lucas Aerospace workforce was cut from 18,000 in 1970 to 13,000 in 1975 when the Corporate Plan was drawn up. Since then nearly 2,000 jobs have been lost through natural wastage. But it is widely believed that, if the company had had its way over closures and redundancies, this figure would have more like 5,000.

What was the importance of the Plan in this resistance to job loss? The Plan was an argument for action, a confidence-builder, a reason for believing that jobs could be saved and that they were worth saving. It provided counter arguments to those with which management justified the redundancies. It undercut the attraction of the offers of redundancy money which normally proves fatal to any redundancy campaign that is purely defensive in its arguments. Paradoxically then, the positive alternative provided by the Plan enabled the Combine Committee and the site committees to win defensive victories. Their plan for socially useful production enabled them to defend the *status quo* on jobs until an increase in orders for military aerospace systems reduced the immediate pressure for redundancies

Thus, even if the Combine has not achieved much in the way of direct influence over investment, product or technology policy, the development of the Plan and the subsequent campaign have at least delayed those of management's plans most harmful to the livelihood and security of workers at Lucas Aerospace.

Extending collective bargaining?

However, the aims of the Combine's alternative Plan were more than defensive. Indeed the plan was based on the idea of extending beyond conventional "defensive" trade unionism. By campaigning for an alternative production and employee training plan the Combine were attempting to influence the Company's corporate investment programme, recognizing that jobs could not be safeguarded unless collective bargaining was extended to cover "non-wage" issues such as investment policy and technological development.

In this, they were giving their own interpretation of the pronouncements about "industrial democracy" current at the time. Their emphasis was on direct shop-floor involvement and the extension of collective bargaining, as opposed to the introduction of "worker directors" or other forms of minority participation in management. How successful were they in this regard?

As we have seen, following the launching of the Plan in January 1976 the company refused to recognize the Combine's legitimacy and so was able to avoid detailed discussions on the Plan: James Blyth assured MPs at the House of Commons in March 1977 that although the company was "anxious to diversify", it "did not need the Combine Committee to tell them" (*Guardian*, 21 March 1977). Subsequently, however, with the involvement of the CSEU, management had at least to go through the motions of considering alternatives. This had the support of very senior technical managers with Lucas Industries but such support could not persuade the custodians of managerial prerogative, the senior financial and personnel directors, to reconsider their position. At site-level, strong joint trade-union organization achieved two breakthroughs in collective bargaining. At Hemel Hempstead management had to negotiate and concede defeat over the future of the industrial ballscrews; and at Burnley they agreed to negotiate over new products which led to a prototype of the heat pump. But as we have seen these breakthroughs were soon closed up again.

In 1979 the industrial ballscrew plant at Hemel was closed, and in Burnley the heat-pump project has remained at a prototype stage even though the technical tests went well. It could be argued, however, that the Plan had a more indirect influence on technological developments within the company. It is difficult to separate out the effects of the changing market place and the technological environment from the effects of the Plan. The Plan certainly proposed a number of products which have since been taken up by the company in some guise or other — mostly outside of the Aerospace Division. But the company might have done this anyway. Three developments must be distinguished. First, there was a defensive reaction on the part of the company reflected in the company's public relations. For instance, the company has taken pains in its publicity to emphasize any of its products which have a visible social usefulness. In 1978 they published a broadsheet to celebrate a hundred years of Lucas activity. This put heavy emphasis on the Lucas kidney machines (which, remember, they had tried to sell off in 1976), cardiac pacemakers (production of which has since been almost entirely run down) and their various electric vehicles, including the Lucas taxi and the Seddon minibus. On the ATV programme "We've Always Done It this Way" (September 1978) James Blyth boasted that Lucas Industries' "record of diversification and record of investment on new products and in new manufacturing capabilities bears comparison with most of British industry. And that is why fundamentally the Corporate Plan is not sensible for the Lucas organization".

At a subsequent press conference he pointed out: "We have diversified to a very large extent within our own field," and gave electronic fuel systems as an example. He added that Lucas were the "world leaders in electric vehicle development . . . we make kidney machines and we have done work on solar cells . . . wave energy and wind energy, on heat pumps". Lucas have also given rather overblown publicity to projects which are clearly socially useful but for which they were only partly responsible. For example, in November 1976 they announced that they were developing a four-wheeled electric car for the disabled, together with an electric-powered wheelchair, which in fact was being developed by Salford Corporation and Manchester Polytechnic with some parts coming from Lucas. A member of the Lucas research centre in Birmingham describes the Lucas input as "insignificant". At the end of the announcement the Lucas management found it necessary to point out: "there is no connection between the research we are doing on wheelchairs and the various demands for more socially useful products. We maintain that all Lucas's products are socially useful" (*Birmingham Post*, 5 November 1976). No more has been heard of the Lucas involvement in the project since.

The second kind of development concerns projects initiated by technical management of a sufficiently small scale not to come before the higher level management, whose judgements are governed by more administrative and narrowly commercial criteria. There is evidence that at the lower, small-scale level the Corporate Plan has been an encouragement to the technicians involved. For example a very small amount of work has been done since 1976 on developing a hybrid petro-electric vehicle in Birmingham. It is run on a shoestring by technical workers who work in the Electric Vehicles System Divison of Lucas Batteries.

The third area of development concerns substantial officially sanctioned diversification efforts. In the years following the launching of the Plan there were several of these which we will document below. However, the scope for diversification, even on a small scale, has narrowed considerably with changes in the Lucas board in 1980. The new chairman, George Messervy, has introduced a very restrictive commercial regime. Several diversification projects have already suffered. Research into medical electronics at the Shirley Research Centre, which was started in the mid-'70s, has now been abandoned. A research project at the Group Research Centre in Solihull developing an absorption heat pump has been stopped. In addition resources given to developing a small generator suitable for windmill applications have been cut. Lucas had exhibited this at the 1977 Energy Show. Finally the research programme on fluidized-bed coal combustion announced in 1978 has only very limited resources. This lack of resources for the fluidized-bed coal combustion project is especially surprising, since the concept looks very promising — both technically and financially. The basic idea is to replace conventional coal-burning "grates" in power plants with a system which uses *powdered* coal (and other combustible materials) mixed with sand and "fluidized" by blasts from gas jets — thus increasing combustion efficiency and reducing pollution. The NCB had been experimenting with fluidized-bed units for some time, notably with their Grimethorpe project, and the UK was the world leader in this area of technology. The government allocated £50 million to this area of development. In 1978, Lucas Aerospace Burnley manufactured a 10 MW unit in collaboration with the NCB, which was installed in the Lucas subsidiary Rist Wires and Cables in Newcastle under Lyme. Lucas's interest in fluidized bed was mainly on account of their experience with gas turbines and the idea — supported by the fourteen-man committee — of developing a coal-fuelled gas turbine. [1] The project was very much within Lucas's field of technical capability. As Blyth put it when asked why Lucas Aerospace Burnley had been able to get involved in what was not a directly Aerospace-linked area, "it happened to fit with the technology at Burnley." However, in spite of trade-union pressure, there is still only one person allocated to this promising and potentially job-creating project.

One of the few diversification projects to survive the first year of the new regime was in the solar-electric field, which featured in the Corporate Plan. In 1979 the company set up a separate Lucas Energy Systems division to develop and market various solar-power systems — using US-produced photo-electric cells bought in from, for example, the Solar Corporation of America. These solar systems are backed up by Lucas control equipment and also low-cost battery storage units developed initially by Lucas for their electric vehicles. The silicon wafers fabricated in the USA are actually encapsulated (to make complete cell units) at Lucas Aerospace's plant at Luton, using their experience of glass/plastic technology, but the headquarters of the new division is at the Lucas World Service Faculty at Haddenham, near Aylesbury — where the research and development teams are located. In 1980 the new company won a £1.2 million "Sundial" contract for supplying 2,550 solar-cell units to power the radio-telephone network in Colombia, South America,[2] and an £800,000 contract for a similar system for Algeria.[3] In February 1981 the company joined with British Petroleum in a joint solar research/marketing venture — Lucas BP Solar Systems — each company putting in an initial £250,000. One project that subsequently emerged was a large (80kw) electricity generating solar-cell array to be installed in 1982/3 at the CEGB's Marchwood Centre near Southampton. However, in March 1982 Lucas announced that it was withdrawing from this CEGB project.

In summary then, Lucas as a company has developed some of the ideas in the Corporate Plan in some form or another in the main outside the Aerospace division. But, with the exception of the electric vehicles, these and its other diversification efforts have not been backed with substantial resources — and most have now been wound up.

Technical obstacles to extending collective bargaining?

The reasons for these cutbacks have not been "technical". Rather they were a result of corporate priorities and financial objectives. This helps us to rule out at least one explanation of why negotiations did not take place over the Combine's Plan. Technical difficulties were not the main problem.

It is worth noting in connection with the technical feasibility of diversification that Lucas Aerospace is well used to changing product lines regularly — since it deals mainly with short-run batch production. While some plants may not initially be suited to longer runs, there does not seem to be any fundamental reason why the emphasis could not be shifted. A researcher on secondment to CAITS produced a detailed plan demonstrating how a new Liverpool plant could be developed for heat-pump production, using "integrated product teams" rather than conventional flow lines.[4]

Moreover, there would be a considerable potential for Lucas workers to carry out design and development work on new products, whose mass-production could be carried out in other firms. It was always the intention of the Combine that their alternative proposals should be "farmed out" where appropriate. So even if, as Lucas have frequently argued, the company is not suited to the assembly and marketing of complete systems like heat pumps, they could usefully produce components and do sub-contract and design work in the control systems area. In the case of the heat pump the Combine was in any case equally keen to develop *turbine*-powered heat-pump units, which would be much more in keeping with Lucas's traditional skills. Blyth himself openly accepted that technology was not the problem in the case of the heat pumps. At a press conference in 1978 he commented that "the problem with heat pumps is not the technology, it's a marketing problem".

Markets?

The second possible justification of the company's refusal to negotiate over the Corporate Plan is that the alternative products are not economically viable in terms of sales potential.

In the case of the heat pump at least this is hard to support. As noted earlier, even on conventional market criteria, the assessment (in 1976) produced by Frost *et al.* indicated that by 1985 there could be a UK domestic market of some £255 million, while the European market might be £897 million in the commercial sector. Subsequent reports by the Department of Energy have been particularly enthusiastic about the gas-powered heat pump of the type proposed in the Plan and developed, under pressure from the stewards at Burnley, in prototype form by the Open University Energy

Research Group.[5] Moreover, the market for conventional electric-powered heat pumps has, as predicted in the Plan, grown enormously — with 2,000 units a year being installed per annum by 1981.[6] Clearly then, the company could have no market grounds for resisting heat-pump development — indeed they have recently taken to portraying the Burnley project as their own idea. Many of the other products also seem likely to be profitable, though not necessarily leading to the rate of return desired by Lucas shareholders and creditors. For example, as we have seen, considerable interest has already been shown in the road-rail bus. The hybrid petro-electric vehicle idea has also been taken up enthusiastically elsewhere. In 1981 Dragonfly Research Ltd produced an initial hybrid petro-electric-engined bus for the Greater Manchester Passenger Transport Executive. A van was also being tested at Maidstone Borough Council. In the USA enthusiasm for hybrids is much greater — prompted by the 1975 "Electric and Hybrid Vehicle Research, Development and Demonstration Act" with the US Department of Energy funding major projects, including one with General Electric based on a Buick. Audi and several other car firms are also investigating hybrids. In addition, the whole field of renewable energy systems is expanding rapidly as predicted in the Plan — with wind and solar units of the types proposed in the Corporate Plan gaining increasing acceptability. The UK solar collector industry already has a £25 million annual turnover (including exports) and a number of major UK wind-power programmes were launched in 1981 involving industrial consortia led by GEC, Taylor Woodrow, McAlpine's and British Aerospace, including £5.6 million allocated to a 3MW unit for the Orkneys, likely to be the first of several large wind turbines for UK use.[7]

The aerospace industry in the USA has been increasingly involved with windpower: for example Boeing has produced three "Mod 2" 2.5MW windmills as part of the USA's ambitious wind-energy programme. With windpower looking very competitive with other sources of electricity (generating costs for Mod 2 are estimated at between 1.5–1.7 p/kwh) the windpower industry in the USA — and indeed worldwide — is booming. For example, two Californian utilities in 1981 ordered 105 MW of wind-electric capacity from US manufacturers and there are major wind programmes in Holland, Denmark, Sweden and many other European countries. In Britain it has been officially estimated that we could obtain about a quarter of our electricity from windmills — chiefly sited offshore, where wind speeds are higher and the environmental intrusion less. Thus several of the Combine's products could have been viable for an enterprise with an observant eye for future markets and not under pressure to produce a high rate of return on investments. Lucas Aerospace, however, is not in the habit of looking for new markets. In fact probably one of the main reasons why the company wants to stick with military aerospace is that it can then forget about "marketing", relying instead on profitable cost-plus defence department contracts.[8]

Inertia and bureaucracy?

There are probably other internal factors which reinforce this externally favoured inertia. Several studies have shown that, as companies grow in size, proportionately more resources are given over to administration and less to innovation. Creative technologists face more bureaucratic constraints from accountants and administrators; and work on technical innovation decreases status and career opportunities.[9] Not all large corporations suffer from these tendencies to inertia all of the time; there are also aspects of increased size which can favour innovation. Certainly Lucas has been more or less responsive to innovation at different times. But judging from the experience of the electronics workers and technical managers in Birmingham and the recent fate of several new diversification projects, inertia, fear of the unfamiliar and an unwillingness to take risks have all contributed to Lucas's response to the Combine's proposals. What the Combine's Plan did was ,to *move ahead of the market*, by identifying technical possibilities that met social needs in socially appropriate ways and preserved jobs and skills. It could be argued that this approach is likely to be more effective in throwing up original and innovative, as well as socially appropriate, ideas — in particular since it draws on a wider range of people than just company "new ventures" or R&D groups.

Social criteria?

Surely a more fundamental obstacle to negotiations about the Corporate Plan was the clash of underlying criteria for production decisions? True, several of the Combine's proposals could have been profitable for Lucas, but the criteria on which the Plan was drawn up were based on a social view of profitability, a view which took into account the social costs of unemployment and the consequences of products and the production process on the environment and people's health and safety. Here it is important to distinguish between these criteria of social efficiency and profitability being the *basis of all* production decisions and, on the other hand, these social criteria *affecting a small part* of the company's activity, subordinate to the overall objective of company profit maximization. Lucas management did in fact consider — we are not sure how formally — an option of the latter sort in response to the Combine's Plan. The idea was floated that the Combine should be given a factory in order to produce one more of their proposals. The motivation for this was partly that this would give the Combine enough rope to hang itself. Others in management argued against the proposal on the grounds that the inevitable failure of the Combine's factory would ultimately rebound on the company.

Such partial concessions to explicitly social criteria are not unusual in major corporations, particularly aerospace corporations. For instance, in the 1960s the US Aerospace Industry had, in the face of recession and retrenchment, launched upon an ambitious programme of diversification to "social technologies".

The 1960 US Aerospace diversification project
In the mid-1960s the US aerospace industry was in recession. At one point around 120,000 jobs were lost in two years in California and Seattle and 4,000 jobs were being lost every month nationally. American involvement in the Vietnam war had yet to expand and the USA space programme was nearing completion. In this situation diversification seemed one possible answer: the industry could switch from "spectacular and technically sophisticated products like weapons systems and space vehicles towards mundane but socially sophisticated products meeting primary human needs such as surface transport or water supplies"[10]

In the event, all that these companies could offer were "technical fixes" involving very sophisticated (and expensive) technology, much of it of dubious value and purpose: computer data files and analysis techniques for criminal records and crime-pattern analysis, electronic surveillance systems to combat crime, and so on. As Robert Boguslaw put it in 1972:

> Could we really expect technical élites nurtured on a diet of weapons system development, a criterion framework of time and cost efficiency, and a "free enterprise" management ethos, really to address themselves to the technological tasks involved in providing human dignity and a peaceful planet?

Ida Hoos has suggested that in the final analysis the purpose of these projects was simply to draw attention away from the companies' main continuing activities.

> Anxious to create an image reflecting the public good and demonstrate social responsiveness, companies, deeply engaged in the development of fighter bombers, missiles, and rockets wish to convey the impression that their prime focus in benevolent.[12],[13]

The challenge of the Lucas Plan
Returning to Lucas, just how "radical" were the product proposals in the Plan — how did they differ from those in the 1960s US programme and in what way were they "socially useful"? Any attempt to assess the political and social significance of a technology is obviously fraught with difficulties, since the strategic context changes continually. What is a radical demand at one time becomes a limited demand for reform in other situations.

To take one example. The idea of heat pumps is radical in the sense of challenging the existing pattern of wasteful fuel use. Typically a conventional heat pump will produce twice or three times more useful heat than if the same amount of fuel was burnt direct. There are, however, two basically different types of conventional heat pump — one uses electricity to power a compressor motor, as in a normal refrigerator, the other uses heat from a gas flame to drive an absorption system, without moving parts.

HOW TO CONVERT THE CONCORDE INTO 27,526,380 PARRAFIN HEATERS

There are some efficiency drawbacks with absorption systems and the electric heat pump is by far the most common — some 2000 units were installed in the UK in 1981. But how one values gas versus electric heat pumps depends to some extent on one's attitudes to electricity as a secondary fuel. Electricity is produced by burning fossil fuels (oil or coal) or nuclear fuels to produce steam to drive turbogenerators. The overall process is inherently only about 30 per cent efficient, which means about two-thirds of the energy in the input fuel is lost — mostly as heat rejected into the environment. Using an electric heat pump (with its 3:1 energy gain advantage) can compensate for these losses, but the use of natural gas as a fuel is much more attractive in overall energy efficiency and cost terms — there are virtually no losses in the process of extraction and distribution.

The system developed by the Lucas stewards and ERG was a unique form of gas heat pump using a conventional rotary (car) engine fuelled by natural gas to drive a standard compressor — thus exploiting the advantage of both types of heat pump.* This in itself was a radical idea — one that has now been taken up elsewhere. But it could be argued that the real "radicalness" in the proposal is evident in the choice of context for the use of the device — for providing cheap district heating for groups of council houses, rather than as a simple "technical fix" for the individual house-holder. Be that as it may, it could be argued that heat pumps or any other products could be absorbed into the pattern of consumerism and sold for

---

* As noted earlier the net overall primary energy efficiency of the gas-fuelled engine-driven pump is typically around 1.3 compared with 0.9 for an electric pump.

profit just like any other product. It might, *environmentally*, be better to introduce such systems on a wide scale, but would that really change society *politically*? Some alternative technology enthusiasts clearly believe so; the widespread use of such decentralized systems would, they believe, *enable* a more democratic form of society to develop. However, this would not happen automatically — the technology itself can only facilitate change.

A linked point is that, if left to conventional industry to develop, new potentially radical technologies may not be developed appropriately — the type of devices they would produce would reflect the priority of the individual company's profits, e.g. expensive planned-obsolescent solar collectors which fall apart in a few years, sold to gullible rich individual consumers, or giant centralized solar, wind or wave power units reinforcing the monopoly of big business and/or the state. So it is important to specify the technology and its use in detail. And of course the context can change; what might be "progressive" in one context (e.g. small-scale technology) might not be in another: the concept of social usefulness is a dynamic one.

As we have seen in the specific case of the heat pump, the Lucas stewards recognized these problems, and specified the precise type and use of the technologies, with the potential for local control clearly identified. The Plan then was careful to develop proposals for products (such as windmills and solar collectors) that could be of use not so much at the individual "self-sufficiency" level, but at the community level (e.g. in council estates).[14] The transport proposals were similarly progressive — calling for the development of a road-rail system designed to meet the needs both of Western countries and the Third World, with a flexible low-cost system that could run on simple rails without the need to avoid inclines. The hybrid petro-electric vehicle idea has obvious social and environmental implications — not least the improved fuel efficiency. The medical technologies were obviously desirable in general terms — although, as noted elsewhere, there was concern that they might become "technical fixes", diverting attention from preventive measures (i.e. social/health policies). In its energy proposals the Plan also challenged Lucas's more general commitment to the technological *status quo*. Lucas, like many other high-technology firms, are wedded to a nuclear-electric future. The renewable energy options (solar, wind etc.) proposed in the Plan implicitly challenge this — as does the proposal for gas-fired heat pumps and combined heat and power. To the extent that the top managers and directors in firms like Lucas share with their colleagues in the UKAEA, the Department of Energy, GEC and so on, a concern for the promotion of nuclear power and other similar high-technology options, the Lucas Plan proposals would be seen as a general threat. In some cases the conflicts are more specific. Certainly there is no shortage of evidence that the vested interests in nuclear power have led the fight to marginalize alternatives.[15]

In the same way, the automobile and petroleum industries, heavily committed to the internal combustion engine, have until recently fought against the electric car — buying up patents etc. But for firms like Lucas the challenge would seem to be more general — a question, for them, of defending the existing technological paradigm which allows them to continue to operate as they have done in the past.

Beyond the specific product proposals and general technological paradigms, there is the challenge that is implicit in the Plan to the way technological and industrial decision-making is carried out in society. The Plan's product proposals combine rational, innovative and environmentally appropriate technical ideas with an awareness of social needs — as distinct from market demands. Implicit in this approach was a criticism of reliance on the competitive market mechanism as a way of matching resources to social needs. Of course, in some cases the competitive market mechanism will eventually lead to some of these needs being met, although not always in the most appropriate way in social and environmental terms.

In general, as Brooks has argued, market competition "sometimes leads to excessive differentiation of products and services or built-in obsolescence for rather marginal social gains, and in doing so may divert a substantial amount of technical effort in directions having only marginal social return. . . . Also competition sometimes rewards the least responsible corporate behaviour, while exacting a large social cost in regulation and in alleviating the disbenefit".[16]

It was this misuse of resources and human skill that the Lucas stewards set out to challenge — not just by railing in an abstract way against market competition, but by identifying specific socially-needed products. And this took them up against the company's basic objectives.

As a 1971 study of twenty-five large British companies indicated: "None of the companies had any doubts that their primary objective was to be efficient and profitable and that being socially responsible would serve no useful purpose if it hindered these overall company goals".[17]

A clash of objectives?

Negotiations on the Lucas workers' Corporate Plan would lay these overall company goals and the criteria for efficiency and profitability open to question and debate by people other than company shareholders. This points to the crucial limit on collective bargaining and the crucial reason why serious negotiations over the Corporate Plan never started.

For top management, the right to manage does not simply mean the freedom to get on with the technical tasks of management without interference. It is the right to manage in the interests of the shareholders. Shareholders rarely intervene directly to assert their interests. Movements on the stock-market and the pressures of the banks are usually sufficient to guarantee these interests. However, ultimately the need for a competitive return on shareholders' capital and creditors' loans sets the parameters and the goals of company management. The job of senior financial and personnel management is to ensure that these goals are met by translating

them into specific plans and instructions which the technical and production management carry out. There are many forms of industrial
democracy which are compatible with this system. These include all forms
of minority participation on company boards which enable trade unionists
to discuss and even influence how the goals are *implemented*. Collective
bargaining, too, over the employment contract and employment conditions
is able to influence only how the goals are implemented. Even recent
extensions of collective bargaining to cover health and safety only influence
how the corporate goals are implemented. However, an extension of
collective bargaining to cover major investment and product decisions
opens up the possibility of *the goals themselves* being changed, and changed
in the interests of groups other than the shareholders. This would upset the
whole structure of company financing which itself is protected in company
law. Inroads might occasionally be possible within a single company on the
basis of exceptional trade-union strength or exceptional management flexibility but they could not be sustained without a radical change in the
ownership and control of financial institutions and the company law which
protects those institutions.

Such a change requires political reforms which will be possible only
under the pressure of many more Lucas-type trade-union initiatives and
political organizations who support them. The same applies to the content
of the new goals of production which would become possible with such
a transformation. Once the profit maximization of each individual company
is open to question and social criteria become explicit criteria in negotiations about production plans, then the question arises of how those social
criteria are to be decided.

The Lucas Combine Committee put forward its own interpretation of
social needs on the basis of admittedly *ad hoc* discussions with colleagues in
other industries, in the public sector and in the local community. But
clearly on a larger scale no single group of shop stewards, however representative of their own members, can determine the social needs to which
their skills and the available productive resources could be put. Neither
could the existing state machinery provide the basis for such decisions. A
new kind of democratic planning would be needed, based initially on
people's resistance to the failures of the present mixture of bureaucratic
state planning and an oligopolistic market.

> It is certainly not the assumption of this Corporate Plan that Lucas
> Aerospace can be transformed into a trail blazer to transform large
> scale industry in isolation. Our intentions are much more modest,
> namely to make a start to question existing economic assumptions and
> to make a small contribution to demonstrating that workers are pre-
> pared to press for the right to work on products which actually help to
> solve human problems rather than create them. (The Lucas Combine's
> Corporate Plan).

The Lucas stewards certainly fulfilled their modest intention, but where
will the questioning to which they have contributed lead? Will it lead to
further initiatives by workers and users aspiring, as the Lucas workers
aspired, to control economic forces rather than remain their victims? What
new economic and political possibilities would the spread of such initiatives
open up? Or has this been simply the tale of a "maverick combination"
which momentarily sparked the imagination, a tale that is interesting to tell
but of limited significance for the future of either the trade-union movement or the organization of production? In order to answer this let us first
summarize the general significance of the Lucas workers' alternative Plan;
let us also understand it in the context of movements growing in both the
workplace and the community since the late 1960s.

A challenge and a claim

The Lucas Combine's strategy of proposing specific and technically feasible
alternatives questioned the appeal to economic and technological necessity
with which management justify their decisions. By campaigning for
detailed proposals based on explicitly social considerations, the Lucas
Combine has exposed to discussion and evaluation the hidden values which
govern management's seemingly neutral, technical and "rational"
decisions. Their Plan undermined in a practical rather than purely theoretical way the legitimacy of a system of production that gives priority to the
competitive success and profitability of individual enterprises. And they
stimulated practical thought about alternative ways of organizing production which make their objective the meeting of social needs. Moreover,
their actions asserted a different claim to legitimacy: the claim of working
people in direct association with each other (rather than through an overbearing state) to control production for each other's well-being.

This claim has a number of implications. First it challenges management's prerogative to manage without accountability to workers. The
Lucas workers' experience of drawing up and trying to implement their
proposals led them to question whether a ruling or managing class was
necessary for the production of wealth. But it is not only managerial
authority which is challenged. So also are political and economic
parameters within which the labour movement has operated. For the Lucas

Combine's Plan implies much greater popular control over social and political decisions than is possible through the present British state. During the last fifty years working people have won the right and the power to register their preferences and to veto political options by rejecting the government party in favour of an opposition party. Trade-union action is similarly traditionally limited to this checking, vetoing role. However, positive power, the power to draw up solutions and plans, has been the monopoly of professional politicians and managers. This view of the limits of popular involvement has been accepted by the leadership of the Labour movement as well as by the ruling class itself. Beatrice Webb, whose views influenced and reflected the attitudes of leading members of the Labour Party and the trade unions in the Labour Party's formative years, sums up the more or less hidden assumption that sets these limits:

> We [Beatrice and Sidney Webb] have little faith in the "average sensual man", we do not believe *that he can do much more than describe his grievances, we do not think he can prescribe his remedies*.[1] [Emphasis added.]

The Lucas experience is one example of how the "average sensual man" and woman can no longer, if they ever could, be so easily pigeon-holed. The experience of exercising only a negative checking power — "describing his grievances" — has, especially in the post-war years of full employment and the welfare state, raised expectations that cannot now be met and has therefore produced frustrations and a growth of *ad hoc* attempts to exert a more positive power; that is, to "prescribe the remedies".

Prescribing the remedies

In recent years, the "work-in" at the Upper Clyde Shipbuilders in 1971 was perhaps the first such attempt in industry which had a national impact. The purpose of the work-in was defensive: to save jobs. However, rather than simply "describe their grievances" in the hope that some latter-day Fabian would prescribe the remedy, the UCS workers in a dramatic way proposed their own solutions based on their own definition of economic rationality. In doing so they transformed their institutions — the shop stewards' committees — into the basis for implementing that solution. Momentarily, one caught a glimpse of how such a workers' committee might extend its positive powers over working hours, over the movement of materials and equipment, over the safety and speed of work, over production plans, financial goals and over the appointment of managers. Even though the victory of the Clyde shipbuilders in the end was limited and in many ways short-lived, their work-in did express an upsurge in workers' confidence in their own capacity to run production democratically. It was followed by hundreds of further sit-ins and work-ins throughout the following decade and beyond.[2] Some nurtured the seed of workers' control more consciously and confidently than others. In several cases work-ins led to large-scale producer co-operatives, the *Scottish Daily News*, KME and

Meriden being the more well known. Although few of these co-operatives survived the adverse environment of an uncooperative economy, nevertheless the drive to start them reflected a qualitative leap in workers' confidence to devise collectively their own futures.

The workers' plans produced by the stewards at Lucas, at Vickers, in the power engineering industry and elsewhere, took this confidence further. Their proposals were not only concerned with who should run the factory or workplace, they put forward alternative industrial policies that concerned the wider economic environment as well as the workplace. They tackled explicitly some of the wider economic and political relationships on which the co-operative had foundered.

In the building industry, too, workers have been fighting against the priorities of capitalist restructuring. In Birmingham in the late 1970s members of the construction workers' union, UCATT, put their industrial strength behind a campaign of social planners, conservationists, and environmentalists to save a large Victorian post office from being knocked down for speculative office blocks and to turn it into a community centre. These and other UCATT members have fought hard to save and extend the scope of local authority Direct Works. Their slogan is "build for people not for profits". They have been inspired by the campaigns of the Builders Labourers Federation in Australia. The BLF, in alliance with environmentalist groups, had successfully preserved homes under the threat of demolition, curtailed the building of speculative office blocks, prevented property speculators developing bush land, and stopped the demolition of historic buildings which the surrounding community wanted to preserve.[3]

An important distinctive feature of all these workers' actions was that they pointed to a way out of the impasse that many trade unionists find themselves in when defending a declining industry against management's attempts to restructure and "modernize". Such a defensive stand has often been the only way to defend jobs, but in the long run it is a hopeless struggle in industries like the car industry where the market for the type of cars being produced is virtually saturated. Workers' plans are in effect proposing a form of restructuring, but a restructuring in the interests of labour rather than capital. They anticipate and identify new markets and consumption patterns, and by their political pressure they attempt to back social needs with the purchasing power of local or national government.

It is not only in industry that people, especially in the last fifteen years, have been doing a lot more than "describing their grievances". Many groups in the wider community also are not satisfied with defending the *status quo*. Among women, for example, there has been a strong emphasis on campaigning for, and in some cases creating, health-care provisions, nurseries and child-care facilities which more adequately meet women's needs. Women campaigning to defend the Elizabeth Garrett Anderson Hospital in 1977 gained widespread and enthusiastic support because they focused the campaign on imaginative proposals for how the EGA could be more sensitive and responsive to the needs of women. Similarly women have not been satisfied with simply defending the existing nursery facilities or even with demanding more of the same. Campaigns in many localities have fought for resources from the state to finance nurseries under the control of parents, supporters and in some cases trade-union representatives. The National Childcare Campaign, which co-ordinates this movement for community-controlled nurseries, is exemplary of a growing number of groups, particularly among women, who reject the Fabian notions of enlightened planners deciding about other people's welfare.[4]

In many other spheres of consumption and daily need, consumers and users have become organized to press for improvements which neither the market nor electoral politics adequately express. The growth of campaigns around health care, around housing provision and heating costs, the groundswell of feeling among parents, teachers and schoolchildren for more democratic control within the education system and the plethora of campaigns for better, cheaper public transport are all evidence of this.*

Earlier visionaries

The desire to project an image of the future in the course of everyday defensive struggles and the self-confidence to construct such an image has resurfaced on a wide scale only in the last fifteen years. But in the half-century or so following the industrial revolution, when people also, for different reasons, had a sense of a different social order based not on capitalist but on co-operative values, this was a central strand in socialist thinking. William Morris is perhaps the best-known socialist in this visionary tradition. In his essay "Useful Labour not Useless Toil" he paints a part of his vision:

> What amount of wealth we should produce if we are all working cheerfully at producing the things that we all genuinely want; if all the intelligence, all the inventive power, all the inherited skill of handicraft, all the keen wit and insight, all the healthy bodily strength were engaged in doing this and nothing else, what a pile of wealth we should have! How would poverty be a word whose meaning we should have forgotten! Believe me, there is nothing but the curse of inequality which forbids this.[5]

This statement could almost have come from the preamble to the Lucas workers' Plan! The difference is that Morris had to talk of his vision of the desired future in general terms and more often than not he was talking to fellow socialists. He was inspiring them to continue their sometimes lonely struggle. The Lucas stewards, by contrast, were in a position to express similar aspirations in terms of detailed proposals; and they gained an

---

* See "The Greening of Marx", *Agenor* No. 71, 1978, for further discussion of the growth of consumer environmental and amenity groups. A key point is that users of state-provided public services are beginning to organize collectively.

audience among many thousands who would not necessarily consider themselves socialists but who felt that somehow management and government were abusing and misusing people's creative powers. Morris was ahead of his time. When he was writing there were many improvements in the lives of working people which, for good or ill, professional politicians and administrators could carry out on their behalf. These remedies involved the reduction of absolute poverty, the universal provision of education, health and other social services through the welfare state. But this raising of material living standards and of educational standards only fuelled aspirations and expectations which by their nature could not be simply described, for somebody else to remedy; for these were aspirations for democratic control over work, wealth and the state itself.

The Lucas workers' Plan was not then a totally new initiative, in a world of its own. Rather it is a development of workers' past struggles for greater control over production; and it is an initiative which has parallels in campaigns over public services. However, the fact that the Lucas Combine spelt out in detail what workers' control over the company in which they worked could mean, and campaigned industrially and politically for their proposals, is a major development. And it is worth inquiring into the uniqueness of the conditions which made it possible.

i. Highly skilled workforce

There is among Lucas Aerospace workers both a particularly high proportion of design engineers, scientific and technical workers and a particularly high proportion of skilled workers on the shop floor (only about 10 per cent of shop-floor workers at Lucas Aerospace are in the category of unskilled or semi-skilled). Other industries have a similar proportion of design, scientific and technical workers, for example the computer and nuclear industries, and there are industries with a high proportion of skilled workers on the shop floor, for example the shipbuilding and parts of the heavy and mechanical engineering industries, but the only industry which combines high proportions of both is the aerospace industry. This kind of workforce was likely to be particularly responsive to the Combine's alternative Plan because it valued and made use of their skills. It could be argued from this that workers' plans depend for support on a highly skilled workforce; and more strongly, that workers' plans further the interests only of skilled workers.

ii. Versatile technology

A second factor favourable to the initiative of the Lucas Aerospace stewards was the versatile potential of the technology in the aerospace components industry. Aerospace components are produced in small batches to meet special orders; and to meet the specific requirements of each order the machine tools and the production process have to be adaptable. Most of the machine tools in Lucas Aerospace are what are known as "universal" machine tools, which can be used to carry out many different engineering jobs. By contrast, in industries based on mass-production the machine tools are purpose-built or "dedicated" to perform one job only. Mass-production is organized on flow-line principles, often with relatively inflexible conveyor-belt systems designed to maximize productivity for one specific product. It could be argued, therefore, that in mass-production industries alternative production options are not normally as easy to envisage as they are in the decreasing number of companies involved in small-batch production.

iii. Tradition of alternative production

Another favourable factor peculiar to the aerospace industry and industries involved in arms production is that there is a history of exploring alternative products as a result of the need to maintain the company's capacity in spite of the vagaries of government defence policies. We have seen the short-lived attempts by management to initiate diversification projects in the 1950s. There was also a brief and limited trade-union experience with which older Lucas stewards in the Midlands were familiar: in the first year or so after World War Two, Communist trade unionists in the aircraft industry in Coventry and elsewhere drew up proposals for converting their industry to peaceful, socially useful production. Their proposals were less detailed than those of the Lucas stewards, but some of their objectives were the same. Again there was a tradition on which the Lucas stewards were able to draw.

iv. A planned economic environment

Apart from these factors concerning the production side of the Combine's Plan, there are also specific features which concern the financing and purchasing side. Lucas Aerospace's main customers are governments or government-owned companies. In the case of the companies owned by the British government — Rolls Royce and British Aerospace — Lucas Aerospace has a near monopoly on the supply of several components.

Consequently the Combine Committee was in a more favourable position to put forward an alternative plan than trade unionists faced with more genuine competitive pressures. In effect the Combine already faced planned economic relations; the Combine Plan was merely challenging the content and the control of these relations. Since the government was already both subsidizing and purchasing from Lucas, the idea of a Labour government committed to defence cuts switching more of their purchasing powers to, for instance, medical and transport products, did not at first seem to pose insuperable problems. Moreover, when a company has such close relations and support from government, management's justifications for redundancies by reference to market forces lose much of their force. The need to consider profit and loss as part of a *social* balance that includes the cost of unemployment is a persuasive argument when much of the company's profitability comes from the tax-payer in the first place, and political considerations, albeit ones which the Combine considered antisocial, already determine the company's markets.

v. The Combine Committee: recognized but independent

Then there are the specific features that concern the means by which the Lucas workers drew up and campaigned for their alternative Plan. The vehicle of an elected, multi-union, multi-plant shop stewards' committee was very important to the character, the force and the impact of the alternative Plan. The Combine was able to draw on both the technical staff's analytic training and access to information and the craft skills and industrial strength of the shop floor. The combination is deeply subversive of management's power in several ways. An organization based on such a combination breaks down management's control over information by its very presence in every area of the company's activities and by its ability to piece together and make sense of each item of intelligence gleaned by its members. One source of central management's power is its overall view of production as against the fragmented and parochial view of each separate and normally isolated group of workers. The Combine represented a challenge to this monopoly of the overview. By providing workers' representatives with a means of gaining collectively their own overview of the company and its political and economic environment, the Combine provided the crucial condition for a *workers'* plan. In the past, the overview which planning requires has invariably been the monopoly of experts who may well on occasion *consult* with working people but who do not directly and closely *represent* them, as did the delegates to the Combine Committee.

However, the strength of this rare kind of shop-floor and office-based combine committee was favoured by special circumstances. Following the rapid spate of takeovers in 1968–70, Lucas Aerospace management was in at least as much disarray as the shop stewards' committees. One effect of this was that management, in the absence of its own communication systems with its workforce, gave effective recognition to the Combine Committee during its first, formative four years. It was not an institutionalized recognition involving procedures and agreements with management, but it enabled the Combine to meet with management virtually on request. In this way the Combine gained the credibility among the mass of workers which comes of having access to top management on the workers' behalf. Yet at the same time, because the recognition was not formalized, the Combine was able to retain its relatively open, flexible and self-determining structure. This latter point is important, for all too often formal recognition by management is achieved at the cost of separation according to union, restrictions on attendance to convenors only, and constraints on associations with other organizations outside the company.

The situation at Lucas Aerospace in the early 1970s provided an opportunity which is unlikely to occur in the same form again. Corporate management has learnt from its mistakes, in Lucas and elsewhere, and has considerably strengthened the resources and the tactical thinking put into industrial relations. Moreover, the vacuum in trade-union structure at a national company level which existed in the late 1960s is generally being

filled with some form of corporate — company-wide — bargaining arrangements. But these national arrangements are invariably separate for shop-
floor unions and for staff unions.[6] These developments do not preclude the
development of joint staff/shop-floor combine committees but they pose
problems for the relation of such joint combine committees to collective
bargaining. They are likely to be outside it, exerting pressure on it, and
requiring support and credibility from sources other than company recognition. Latterly this has been an unresolved problem facing the Lucas
Combine itself, but in its formative years it was able to have the best of
both worlds: recognition and independence.

vi. Political support

A final specific feature of the Lucas experience was the support which the
Combine Committee received and the confidence it gained from having, for
a brief moment, allies in government. Certainly, the Combine's traditional
trade-union tactics and policies against redundancies had reached something of an impasse and Combine delegates were already exploring new
ideas. However, without political support it is unlikely that the shop
stewards would have felt confident of selling something as bold as the
alternative Plan to their membership. The membership needed to believe
that there was a chance of success, only then would they support radical
proposals like the alternative Plan. This explains why in the first year and a
half of the last Labour government — while Tony Benn and Eric Heffer
were in the Department of Industry — numerous groups of workers came
forward with proposals, usually in response to an immediate crisis.* Yet
when the Department of Industry was under Labour or Tory ministers
who were reluctant even to meet shop stewards, let alone encourage them,
there were virtually no such confident workers' initiatives. It could be
argued that a government likely to give such encouragement and
confidence to workers' plans is not a realistic prospect in the short term and
therefore that the development of workers' plans is unlikely in the near
future.

Explanations not limitations

These factors certainly *explain* the Lucas initiative and the particular form
that it took, but that does not mean that they have to recur in the same
form for the ideas of workers' or popular planning to spread. One reason
for this is the Lucas initiative itself. It has broken down constraints on the
imagination by demonstrating possibilities which had not been thought of
before; possibilities which transcend the specific conditions that favoured

---

* The inquiry carried out into these first years of the Labour government by
Coventry, Liverpool, Newcastle and North Tyneside Trades Councils illustrates
that in every industry or company affected by the government's industrial
policies the shop stewards' committees drew up some form of plan or proposals
of their own while there was real hope of support from ministers in the
Department of Industry.

the Lucas workers' Plan, and which lead people to re-create similar conditions in another form. The following sections will discuss each of the conditions in turn. We suggest that in general these conditions are in *some form* necessary; however, we also argue that they need not take the particular form which they took in the case of Lucas Aerospace. We point to initiatives which already indicate the different ways in which these conditions are being met.

Overcoming the division of labour

In the first condition listed above, the skill and technical composition of the workforce, there is indeed a major problem: capitalist production has shaped a division of labour suited to its requirements. These requirements include a labour force appropriate for work on mass-production lines; that is a labour force in which the vast majority exercise very little skill. More generally the requirements of profit maximization tend towards the design of machines and production processes which continually reduce a company's dependence on the will, effort and ability of human beings. The result is that with every technological development under capitalist production, a reduction takes place in the capacity of the majority of shop-floor workers and increasing numbers of office workers to innovate and take control of their work.

This process is by no means smoothly successful. After all, human beings cannot be programmed. If they cannot express their creative abilities at work, they will seek other contexts. However, as work has become increasingly unskilled for the majority of workers, the trade unions have not, at least in the last twenty years, provided a means of building on people's creative abilities to challenge and present alternatives to the direction in which the division of labour is developing. Trade unions, who generally understand their role as being to get the best terms for the job rather than to question the nature of the jobs available, do not in general take up issues of skill and access to information. Even among craft unions the resistance to deskilling is a defence of the label of "skilled" and the wage levels which go with the label, rather than a defence of the content. There are few official trade-union institutions through which skills and information can be pooled to challenge management's or government's monopoly of the overview, or through which the talents and ideas stifled and unused at work can be harnessed to devise trade-union policies. However multi-union shop stewards' committees in industry and, increasingly, in the public sector, along with trades councils, have this potential and to varying degrees they have exercised it. These are two parts of the old institutions on which new institutions are being built, through combine, industry-wide and public-sector committees and through trades councils extending contact with shop stewards' committees, tenants' and other women's groups.

Combining skills to meet needs

To draw up and campaign for plans to meet the needs of different groups of workers and users clearly needs varying mixes of skills and information. For instance to redesign machine tools to make possible production processes which enhance or liberate human skills will require the skills of experienced and innovative designers in consultation with workers who may be completely unskilled from a conventional point of view but who certainly know what they want as far as working conditions, training and type of machinery are concerned. In this example one could imagine the designers involved in the combines in an industry with a high design content, like the aerospace industry, working with workers' committees in the car industry. There are other needs which do not relate to new products or to the hardware of the production process but concern for example the quality, price and distribution of a product; for instance, to fight the closure of a television factory, alternative policies might be based on the subsidized provision of televisions and a repair service for old-age pensioners. This policy would not require much technical skill to devise, rather it would require skills at social accounting, surveying community needs, and at investigating the company's business. Or take the issue of housing, where technical skills would be required to develop alternative policies on house construction, heating systems and repairs to meet tenants' needs. These skills would cover a wide range which are rarely brought together: architectural, engineering, decorative and construction skills. Moreover, there are often people with such skills who no longer have the chance to exercise them as a result of redundancy. This would require close contact between tenants' groups, building workers, sympathetic architects and organizations of the unemployed.

The problem is that of finding ways in which trade-union and community groups who have identified needs can work with people with the appropriate skills, from industry and from academic institutions, to develop alternative policies for collective bargaining and campaigning. So far, trade-union research and resource centres, either like CAITS or UDAP, with a technological emphasis, or like the Coventry Workshop with the involvement of community groups such as tenants' and women's groups, have helped to make these connections possible. For example the Coventry Workshop is engaged jointly with the trades council in encouraging and giving help to workers' and users' plans in Coventry. And in Newcastle the Trade Union Studies Information Unit is working with shop stewards in the power engineering industry, the local authority, trades councils and tenants' groups on a campaign for Combined Heat and Power systems, around the slogan "Jobs from Warmth". Organizations like the Joint Forum of Combines and the National Housing Liaison Committee also help to overcome the divisions of skill and the lack of access to information. The National Housing Liaison Committee brings together representatives of tenants' groups, building workers' and trades councils to co-ordinate campaigns for better housing and also to develop policies for better quality, more democratically controlled public housing.

Several Labour-controlled local authorities where socialists have a strong influence are also contributing to this process of sharing and pooling of skills and expertise. The Greater London Council's Economic Policy Group, of which Mike Cooley is now a member, is encouraging sympathetic technologists and engineers in London's polytechnics and universities to work with trade unionists in drawing up alternative proposals that will help to save or even create jobs. Thus people are finding ways to develop policies which not only challenge the existing division of labour — including divisions of labour and hierarchies of skill based on gender and race — but which begin to prefigure more fulfilling mixes of skill and ability, in the very process of drawing up the alternative policies.

Redesigning technologies

The second factor favouring the Lucas initiative was the particularly versatile technology in Lucas Aerospace. Just as we do not have to treat the present division of labour as an immutable constraint, neither need we accept existing mass-production technologies as presenting insuperable obstacles to alternative workers' and users' plans. We have indicated already that such plans are not exclusively about technology and products; but where they are, a pooling of design and technical skills can enable trade unionists working with very inflexible technologies to redesign them for the products or production processes they propose. In some cases this will mean much longer lead times than would have been necessary for the alternative Plan at Lucas Acrospace. And in some cases the existing equipment may not be appropriate for conversion. In these cases shorter-term policies such as work sharing, a shorter working week and retraining facilities will be more important for a time, while investment is made in new machinery. There will be other occasions where one part of a product does not require much change in the technology of the production process even if the product as a whole is a radically new design. For example, shop stewards facing the closure of one of the British Leyland factories at Speke on Merseyside considered campaigning to make the car body of hybrid power vehicles, while Lucas Aerospace workers in Liverpool would press to make the components for hybrid power systems. This need not have involved very radical changes in the technology of the Speke plant. Similarly the Leyland bus factories could make the body for the road-rail vehicle without requiring a long lead time.

Beyond the arms industry

Before the Lucas Aerospace experience, the arms industry was, as we have seen, the only industry where there was any tradition of alternative production strategies. However, now that product choice and the design of the production process has become the subject of trade-union policy-making, if only among activists at the base of the trade-union movement, then the arms industry is no longer the only area where there is some experience of discussion around alternative production strategies.

Another reason why workers' alternative plans have spread beyond the arms industry is because a semi-planned economic environment is no longer a feature only of the arms industry. We have pointed to the importance for the origins of the plan of a semi-planned relation between Lucas Aerospace — as part of the arms industry — and the government. This made the possibilities of following up and negotiating over the Combine's Plan with government support potentially much easier than in the case, for example, of a private clothing company selling to many private retailers. But this semi-planned economic environment applies in differing form to a large part of manufacturing industry as a result of nationalization, government finance or public purchasing at a national and local level. For instance, at least a third of all final transactions in UK economy involve public authorities as supplier and purchaser to and from the private sector, and most of the private sector receives significant funding and other forms of aid from the government. Even within the private sector many economic exchanges are between companies with a monopoly or near monopoly of the market. In effect relations between these corporations are planned rather than governed by free-market conditions.

Different forms of planning

Very few parts, if any, of contemporary capitalist economies conform to the criteria for a free market set out by those who theorize the market as the most democratic mechanism for economic decision-making. This does not mean that central state planning is the only alternative. The experience of the Soviet Union indicates that, for all the social improvements it has brought, centralized planning can be wasteful and inefficient in the way it allocates resources. A central government planning department, however well computerized, cannot handle efficiently all the millions of connections which, like a nervous system, make up the economy. Innovation tends to get stifled as much, if not more, than in the West, unless it comes through official established channels. Working people in the Soviet Union have few ways in which they can exert a democratic check on the waste, inefficiency and lost opportunities they see,[7] and no means by which to press collectively for improvements in their standard of living and quality of life.

The wrongs of Soviet-type planning, however, do not turn the wrongs of the disguised planning of the Western economies into rights. The initiatives of the workers at Lucas, at UCS, in the power engineering industry; of health workers and users defending hospitals like the EGA, and parents fighting for community-controlled nurseries, all point to another form of planning and economic decision-making, very close to Marx's notion of "associated producers rationally regulating their interchange with nature, bringing production under their common control instead of being ruled by it as by the blind forces of nature".[8]

In some interpretations of Marx, a central state has come to substitute and stand for such an association of producers, whereas in fact such an association can for many purposes be most appropriately based on localities or regions making up a federal system of self-managed enterprises.

Thus while aerospace and steel production might be nationally or internationally organized, some forms of vehicle production, furniture-making or food preparation might be most responsive to social needs if they were organized on a regional or local level rather than through national or multinational institutions. A national assembly would co-ordinate and set the framework for a wide variety of levels of association.

One reason why a centralized bureaucratic state has taken control in the countries where capitalist production has been eliminated is because this overthrow of capitalist production has only so far taken place in countries where an intricate, lively and resilient tradition of mutual association between working people had been unable to thrive. Autocratic regimes in Tsarist Russia, for instance, had prevented trade unions and working-class political parties and movements from gaining the experience and self-confidence that would be essential to sustaining truly democratic institutions of popular planning.

This book has illustrated some of the fragile but determined moves towards preparing such institutions. It has also indicated the tremendous opposition they are up against. How can these fragile connections and the ideas of popular planning which they express be sustained, and eventually become powerful?

This raises two problems: one concerns the limitations of trade unions, — usually established for defensive purposes — as the basis of a movement for popular planning. The second problem concerns the role of political parties and ultimately of government in supporting and implementing popular plans. The first problem brings us to the uniqueness, or otherwise, of the Lucas Combine Committee itself: its base in the factory trade-union committees and yet its independence from the often limiting procedures of collective bargaining.

The Combine Committee and the limits of trade unionism

The Combine Committee was in an ideal position for developing and fighting for a workers' plan. It had the benefit of a close connection with the shop-floor and office trade-union committee in each factory — a feature essential to the process of drawing up and fighting for popular plans, for without being based on the needs and attempts at control around which working-class people are organizing, planning will just be the work of a new group of experts making judgements about other people's needs. Without the backing of the factory organizations of collective bargaining there is no hope of overcoming the tremendous resistance which, as we know from the Lucas experience, such plans will undoubtedly meet.

The drawing up of the ideal structures of democratic planning must take account of the power of the existing state and the private corporations. To a considerable extent the institutions of popular planning will be developed in the course of resisting the decisions emanating from these centres of unaccountable power. Democratically drawn up alternative proposals are ways of strengthening such resistance. For these reasons, the drawing up of positive proposals and plans based on social need cannot be separate from the defensive institutions of collective bargaining (as they might be when popular planning and self-management have been achieved).

However, there is a strong case for some additional level of organization beyond but connected with existing trade-union organizations. This is especially true at a time when trade unions have been forced back to their most defensive positions. For example, delegates to the Lucas Combine Committee found that the day-to-day requirements of collective bargaining under the last year of the Labour government and the first years of Tory rule were of a very defensive kind. The confidence simply did not exist to put forward positive and radical policies of the kind they had developed in the Corporate Plan. However, the Combine believe that work should continue to develop the approach of the alternative Corporate Plan and to extend the network of organizations involved in similar initiatives, in preparation for more favourable conditions. Otherwise they and others would be unable to turn the opportunity of a radical Labour government, or at least an economic expansion, to their advantage and the cycle of dis-illusionment and demoralization, leading to another Tory victory, would once more be set in motion. This work will involve a conscious allocation of time and trade-union personnel to prepare discussions on issues of longer-term strategy; and to formulate the basis for positive bargaining positions on questions such as technology, government funding and corporate invest-ment plans, well in advance of the issues coming up in collective bar-gaining. This will involve the creation of some new structure, even if only extensions of existing trade-union organizations.

There are several arguments for this additional level of trade-union activity. First, the content of discussion and ideas in those organizations whose main function is collective bargaining is necessarily determined by the immediate tactical concerns of the negotiations at hand: on its own this is too narrow a framework to encourage ideas to develop about the future of the industry, the social needs which the industry could meet, and alternative products and technologies to press on management and govern-ment. Such a discussion needs stimulus and co-ordination outside of the procedures and agendas of collective bargaining. In the case of Lucas such a stimulus was provided by the Combine Committee when it sent out a questionnaire and thereby introduced a new dimension on to the agendas of the factory trade-union committees. The discussions at factory level stim-ulated by the questionnaire were in general more open-ended, more con-ducive to innovation and experimentation than the routine discussions con-nected with day-to-day negotiations.

A second reason for some additional level of organization concerns the fact that organizations whose main purpose is collective bargaining — including collective bargaining over proposals flowing from more broadly based workers' plans — need to *parallel* the power structures of the employers. By contrast the objective of developing alternative plans based on meeting the social needs of producers and users requires a form of association which *cuts across* different employers, and across the different but interdependent sectors of the economy. If workers' plans were produced only on an enterprise basis there would be a danger of including proposals that if implemented would simply put other workers out of work. There would also be a danger of implying that the producers alone had the right to determine what was socially needed. There would also be other, more strategic problems, concerning relations with the company, if workers' plans were simply focused on one enterprise: it would be harder to transcend the firms' economic boundaries, premises and priorities. For this reason negotiations on "planning agreements" with individual firms could degenerate into exercises in collaboration with management — as many trade unionists fear.

Clearly association with workers, and where necessary users, beyond the individual company and industry is needed. The Lucas stewards have tried to create such contacts with workers engaged on products related to those they proposed. In doing so they did not seek to replace or undermine more sectorally-based trade-union structures. Rather they sought to create associations of a very different kind. For example, arising out of their proposals in the medical field they, along with CAITS, called a workshop of workers and users connected with the health service.[9] However, such contacts and discussion could not be sustained without political support, particularly as they directly concerned government expenditure.

Planning for social need: some examples

Although in the early 1980s the confidence among the majority of trade-union members has been insufficient for them to become involved in drawing up positive proposals for their industry or services, an increasing number of trade-union activists are responsive to the idea. Evidence for this is in the growing interest in the discussions and local initiatives stimulated by four trades councils — Coventry, Liverpool, Newcastle and North Tyneside — around the idea of popular planning for social need. These discussions followed the trades councils' inquiry into the industrial policies of the last Labour government. The inquiry arose out of an anger and disillusionment with the way that Labour's industrial policies, promised in 1973 as a new radical departure from old-style nationalization, were transformed to allay the fears of the City, the Treasury and the IMF. The trades councils concluded that these "vested interests are too powerful to be overcome by politicians alone. We must create a movement in the workplaces and the localities around policies based on planning for social need, which can exert power for itself. Our inquiry concludes that it is only this grass-roots power which, with the support of a genuinely socialist government, can socialize and democratize production".

Since the publication of the inquiry, several other trades councils, notably Sheffield, Burnley and Nottingham, have become directly involved in exchanging ideas and experiences that give more specific meaning to the idea of a movement in the workplaces and localities around planning for on social need. Several of the combine committees involved in the Joint Forum have also joined these discussions. Together, the combine committees and trades councils have produced the declaration on "Popular Planning for Social Need — an alternative to monetarism from shop stewards' committees and trades councils." This declaration summarizes the basis on which trades councils and combine committees, with the help of trade-union and community resource centres, have begun to investigate the strategies of the multi-national corporations, the failings of the public services and nationalized industries and the needs which alternative policies must show can be met.

This concern with elaborating detailed alternative policies to be fought for through collective bargaining and extra-parliamentary campaigns is also apparent within the Left groupings of several unions. In the Post Office Engineering Union, for instance, the "broad Left" has already made a thorough investigation of the telecommunications industry, on an international level. Through workshops of activists across the telecommunications industry they too are developing policies to meet their members' needs. Moreover, by developing co-ordination between trade-union committees across competing multinationals, they are able to counter those arguments of managements which seek to identify workers' interests with the competitive success of the company.

The disarmament movement and the campaign against nuclear power have also stimulated and strengthened discussion among trade unionists for alternative plans. CND and END are beginning to work with trade unionists in the arms industry on plans for conversion. Activists in the anti-nuclear power movement have worked with members of many different unions affected by government energy policy, to develop a trade-union-based campaign for non-nuclear energy policies. This campaign has gained considerable support within the unions; at least ten major unions all oppose the nuclear programme.[10] The campaign has also had a considerable popular impact creating a very strong lobby for the development of alternative energy sources and conservation. The new approach to energy policy that is gradually emerging — albeit against fierce opposition — moves the emphasis away from a concern just with conventional energy *supply* technologies (for example, centralized electricity-producing power plants) to interest in local energy provisions (for example, solar energy and combined heat and power), and beyond that to a concern with the question of energy demand management, and energy conservation. Transport planning, waste recycling, urban planning, etc. — all very much the concern of local authorities — are increasingly being seen as relating directly to energy policy, which explains why public service unions like NUPE and NALGO are becoming much more interested in energy issues. This local government-level concern also offers more opportunity for involvement and initiatives by community groups, in relation, for instance, to local energy-conservation projects and community energy planning in general. There is a growing network of "Local Energy Groups" around the country concerned to find local job-creating alternatives to centralized energy provision.[11] Several Labour local authorities have also developed energy plans for their areas which emphasize local control and job creation. Given the existing alternative plans produced by power engineering workers, it seems that the basis for democratic planning linking users and producers is being created within the energy sector.

In these varied ways, networks are being created which feed into collective bargaining and campaigning but which have an independent momentum that enables them to see ahead of these day-to-day problems.

The shop stewards and trades council delegates involved in these networks are strongly motivated. They are not prepared, to leave economic policy-making and implementing to Labour politicians. It is this strong commitment to investigation and policy-making as a necessary part of trade unionism which keeps the networks going; for they have little support from the national trade-union body concerned with economic policy, the TUC. Rather than encourage and provide resources for these attempts to develop policies based firmly on working people's needs and skills, the TUC has made their development more difficult. The four trades councils who produced the report on "State Intervention in Industry" were at one point told that they could not meet with each other without permission from the TUC. Matters of government policy were not their concern, was the message. However, the TUC did not follow up the restriction beyond trying to discourage other trades councils from becoming involved. Nevertheless, the TUC has threatened this work in another way, by attempting to block the creation of two new trade-union research and resource centres in London and Birmingham — though the Birmingham centre has nevertheless gone ahead. As we have seen, such resource centres are a vital backup to the policy discussions of trades councils, combine committees, resource centres and other local and workplace-based organizations, however, cannot themselves sustain and implement these policies whether or not they gain official trade-union support. They need political support, both locally and nationally.

Political support

When talking about political support we cannot treat the state as a single homogeneous block, rather we must distinguish between the elected assemblies — that is Parliament and, at a local level, councils — and the permanent apparatus of the civil service, the Army and the judiciary. Action by socialist representatives in the former could be used to undermine the power of the latter in favour of the new institutions of popular power. These extra-parliamentary institutions in the workplace and in the locality in many ways prefigure a new kind of political system, but they will need the support of a government elected within the present system to achieve the transition to the new system.

The importance of political support from within the elected institutions of the present political system rests on two features of government in Britain — and parliamentary democracies in other modern capitalist societies. First, the government's role in the economy: the government controls either directly or indirectly much of the finance which at present enables capitalist industry to flourish but which could be used to support a move towards workers' self-management. Secondly, the elected government has a legitimacy in the eyes of the majority of people, over and above any particular economic institution or interest. And it can provide legitimacy for democratic organizations outside Parliament. A supportive government then is a potentially powerful ally for workers in industry with proposals for organizing their workplace to meet social needs. This is why the initial support of ministers of the Department of Industry was so important in helping the Lucas Plan get off the ground. Without this support the Combine delegates would have found it very difficult to gain support for the plan from their fellow stewards and trade-union members. The reverse of this dependence of the Lucas workers' Plan on government support for its implementation is that the hostility which the Combine later faced from the Labour government when the Plan was ready nearly destroyed the Combine Committee, and with it the alternative Plan.

The Labour politicians who treated the stewards from Lucas Aerospace and elsewhere with such indifference had little or no political commitment to the socialist aspiration of workers' self-management and social owner-ship. But even a party leadership which enters government with such a commitment will be under extremely powerful pressures to thwart and divert the wishes of workers struggling for control over production. For, in spite of a government's control over considerable funds, its legislative powers and its control over the exchange rate and other aspects of foreign trade, it is nevertheless finally dependent on those who control the production of wealth. When this control is securely in the hands of the management of multi-national corporations, even a well-intentioned socialist government can on its own do little against their will. It can only act against the major corporations and financial institutions if workers in those corporations, the real producers of wealth, have built up an internal challenge to management's control. What is needed, then, is an *alliance* between a socialist government and those workplace- and locality-based organizations which could create this counter power to the extra-parliamentary strength of capital. In the shorter run this applies to socialist-controlled local and county councils. In Sheffield, Greater London and the West Midlands, Left Labour councillors have taken the initiative to create such alliances. In doing so they are pushing against the grain of local government's corporate management in very unfavourable national political circumstances. It is too early to assess their success or otherwise.

The role of a socialist government

Comments on the possible contribution of government to such an alliance are bound to be speculative, for we are attempting to map out some of the political implications of popular planning at a time when the future of the Labour Party and the process by which a socialist government might be achieved are by no means clear. However, while over-deterministic prescriptions are of little relevance, the question of what types of political structures might be necessary cannot be avoided by rhetoric about "decentralization". We need to begin to think in detail about new forms of political organizaton. The possible role of a socialist government can be summarized under several categories. First it could play a *catalytic* role in bringing about direct association between the people, or the organizations representing them, connected with all spheres where existing market and planning mechanisms have failed to meet people's needs. The purpose of such direct associations would be to resolve conflicting needs, to arrive as

The market economy is insensitive to social needs...but this must be *seen* to be the case! Groups outside the factory — environmentalists, consumers, unionists in the service sector — can help by bringing pressure on public institutions *to order the alternative goods to meet obvious needs...*

far as possible at a common policy or several different but consistent policies and build the strength to implement these policies. For example in relation to the Lucas Plan the government ideally could have encouraged such direct contact between the different groups of workers and users who might have had an interest in, say, the road-rail bus: local authority representatives and purchasers, bus workers and transport users' committees as users, and Lucas Aerospace, British Leyland and Dunlop workers as producers.

Given British industry's close integration into the international economy, such direct association would need to be organized on an international level: between, for instance, workers in tractor companies or agricultural machinery producers in Britain and the agricultural departments of radical governments in the Third World, so that machinery could be produced with a design and a price to meet the needs of those countries by workers who would otherwise be made redundant in Britain.

This catalytic role in the process of developing the democratic organizations which could draw up and negotiate over alternative plans should not be limited to a socialist government. Indeed, the achievement of such a government will depend on progress made without it. Nevertheless a socialist government could play a vital role in strengthening and co-ordinating the process. Much of this co-ordination and association would take place at a local and regional level, but there would be a need for national co-ordination, perhaps through a national assembly, subordinate to Parliament, specifically concerned with deciding on the problems and conflicts arising from planning and self-management at a local and regional level that needed national and international resolution. Such an assembly would be based on representatives from workers' planning committees in the regions and within different economic sectors.* [12]

The role of a socialist government would not only be to provide resources and encouragement for the direct association through which plans could be drawn up, it would also *delegate powers* and legitimacy to the workers' committees formed in this process, where they were representative and democratically formed. These powers would be to monitor the implementation of policies decided nationally, regionally, or sectorally. In some ways this is like a radical extension of the powers at present delegated to shop stewards in health and safety legislation. Trade-union representatives have the power, backed by legislation, to monitor the implementation of the Health and Safety at Work legislation. On a far wider scale the same could apply to industrial policy. We saw in the Lucas case how, even

---

* The Polish movement, Solidarity, proposed an assembly along similar lines to be subordinate to their national parliament in terms of general economic principles, but to be responsible for co-ordination a system of self-management and democratic planning.

when agreement was reached in negotiations over a product proposed by the unions, that is the heat pump, management was able to inhibit progress or impose their own ideas. A civil service inspectorate could never adequately monitor such an agreement. It would require people with an intimate knowledge of the production process or the service involved. Workers' committees would need some power to carry out this monitoring, even when the company had been taken into some form of public ownership. This would be a step towards subjecting managers to election by workers and representatives of the local community.

A further role of a socialist government would be to *co-ordinate the funding* for the implementation of workers' plans. One of the first steps such a government would take towards socialization of the means of production would be the imposition of exchange controls, the nationalization of the banks and legislation for trade-union control over pension funds.[13] In addition a socialist government would back workers bargaining over proposals based on these plans, with financial and other sanctions on the companies concerned. Where this met with determined resistance, a socialist government would need to be prepared to socialize the company and/or industry, under workers' control. In several industries, depending on their strategic position and the strength of workers' organization, this socialization would take place in the first months of the government. This socialization would be very different from the kind of nationalization with which we are so depressingly familiar, because the workers would, in the process of extending collective bargaining, have developed a clear idea of how the resources of the company would be used and organized and would be prepared for self-management.

The joint worker/government plans might well propose breaking up the existing company structures. One principle of popular planning will be to identify the structures most appropriate to popular control, according to the kind of product or service concerned. The shape and structure of most major conglomerates — bringing together for instance newspapers and hotels and shipping lines under the same board — make nonsense for everyone concerned except the shareholder.

Finally, the government's role in supporting the new institutions of popular planning and self-management will be to set the overall framework of economic policy, including levels of taxation, exchange rates and the basis of international trading relations. Control of international trade would not necessarily or even primarily be import controls; rather the government's priority would be to identify trading arrangements with sympathetic governments which would be of mutual benefit.

Government measures of this sort would face considerable resistance from those with a vested interest in existing economic arrangements. But the extent and success of the resistance will depend on two conditions which can be influenced now, long before there is a real chance of such a government. First will be the political popularity of the government; in electoral terms, the strength of its parliamentary majority. Second will be the strength and popularity of union committees, community groups and local authorities who could counter the resistance. Both these depend on a political party, no doubt emerging in part out of the Labour Party — though not in its present form — which bases itself on encouraging people to develop and fight for detailed proposals for the future of industry and the public services. So that for instance in the case of the car industry the party would not stand simply for nationalization of the car industry; it would stand for proposals (for example) to get rid of planned obsolescence in car manufacture, to produce low-price, non-polluting city cars, to establish an extensive system for care and maintenance of long-lasting cars and to improve public transport. The emphasis would be not so much on nationalization for its own sake but on the industrial and social changes which workers in the industry have suggested and, especially important, have prepared for and gained popular support for, before public ownership is carried through. In these circumstances public ownership is seen clearly as the means of eliminating particular vested interests blocking popular demands.

This is a reversal of the traditional Labour view of state intervention, in which legislation for public ownership was understood as the first step towards socialism. Aneurin Bevan expressed this traditional approach clearly when he stated that "the conversion of industry to public ownership is only the first step towards socialism" and went on to say that the advance to full socialism depends on the extent to which workers in the nationalized sector "are *made aware* of a changed relationship between themselves and management" [our emphasis]. The argument in this chapter would imply a very different relationship between ownership and workers' power. Put it this way: the extent to which public ownership is an advance towards full socialism depends on the extent to which workers *create* a changed relationship between themselves and management in the course of achieving public ownership.

The failure of the traditional Labourist formula was a pressure that led the Lucas stewards to initiate a new approach. In doing so they, along with others, have illustrated, not only a new trade unionism but also a new politics, a politics not only *for* people but also *of* and *by* the people — not to be confused with another "new" politics, the politics of the SDP, which proclaims itself as a politics *for* people,[12] and which is a new form of the old élitist approach, in flimsy populist disguise.

What next?
There are many ways of becoming involved in shaping this new socialist politics. It does not take the form of a political party. Members of the Left of the Labour Party, the Communist Party, the Socialist Workers' Party and of no party are active in creating it. Rather its creation is taking place at the base of the trade union in parts of the women's movement, the movement against nuclear power and the disarmament movement. Since

this book has been only about one of the initiatives contributing to this politics the best way to end is with a list of useful literature and contact addresses which will enable you to find out more and hopefully to contribute yourself.

Resources – further information and contacts

On Lucas:

Lucas: an Alternative Plan, IWC pamphlet No. 54, Spokesman, Nottingham 1978 (20p). A shortened version of the full 1976 Plan.

Lucas Aerospace: Turning Industrial Decline into Expansion, Lucas Aerospace Confederation Trade-Union Committee, 1979 (£4.50). The CSEU "fourteen-man" committee report.

D. Elliott, *The Lucas Aerospace Workers' Campaign*, Fabian Pamphlet No. 46, 1979 (60p). A short account of the Lucas Campaign up to 1978.

The Diary of Betrayal, CAITS, 1980 (45p).

Addresses

CAITS, North-East London Polytechnic, Longbridge Road, Dagenham, Essex.

Lucas Aerospace Shop Stewards' Combine Committee, c/o Pete Flynn, 10 Chingford Bank, Burnley.

Other "workers' plans", campaigns and reports:

D. Elliott, M. Kaldor, D. Smith, R. Smith, *Alternative Work for Military Industries*, Richardson Institute, 1979.

Labour Party, *Sense about Defence*, Quartet, London 1979.

Trade-Union Strategy in the Face of Corporate Power: The Case for Multi-union Shop Steward Committees, Joint Forum of Combines, 1980 (25p).

State Intervention in Industry: A Workers' Inquiry, Coventry, Liverpool and Newcastle and Tyneside Trades Councils, 1980 (£2.00).

Popular Planning for Social Need, A declaration by combine commitees and trades councils (30p). Available from Coventry Workshop, 40 Binley Road, Coventry.

Workers' Power, CSE Engergy Group/AUEW-TASS Trafford Park (15p).

H. Beynon and H. Wainwright, *Workers' Report on Vickers*, Pluto Press, London 1979 (£2.40).

Jobs for a Change: Alternative Production on Tyneside, Newcastle Trades Council/Tyneside AWC/Tyneside for Nuclear Disarmament, 1982 (60p).

Dunlop: Jobs for Merseyside in a Trade Union Report, Speke Joint Shop Stewards' Committee, CAITS, 1979 (£3.95).

Also reports carried out by the Metal Box, Scotch Whisky, Thorn EMI combines, available from CAITS.

CAITS Conference reprints:

Alternatives to Unemployment: New Initiatives in Industry and the Community, CAITS, 1979 (£2.45).

Workers' Plans: Cutting Edge or Slippery Slope?, CAITS, 1980 (£2.25).

Other relevant CAITS material:

Workers' Plan for Better Health, 1980 (£1.50).

Trade Unions and Pension Funds, 1980 (45p).

Co-operation or Co-option 1980 (45p).

New Technology Information Pack, 1980 (75p).

Arms Conversion Information Pack, 1981 (£1.40).

Other relevant publications:

K. Coates et al., *Socially Useful Work*, Spokesman, Nottingham.

M. Cooley, *Architect or Bee*, Langley Technical Series, 1980.

H. Braverman, *Labour and Monopoly Capital*, New York 1974.

A. Glyn and J. Harrison, *The British Economic Disaster*, London 1980.

The Alternative Economic Strategy, A Response by the Labour Movement to the Economic Crisis, London 1980.

D. Massey and R. Meagan, *The Anatomy of Job Loss: The how, why and where of employment decline*, London 1980.

D. Albury and J. Schuartz, *Partial Progress*, London 1982 (forthcoming).

The Pluto Press series, *Arguments for Socialism*, contains many titles which elaborate the idea of production and services for need and the means of achieving them. M. Cooley and H. Wainwright are preparing a book for Penguin provisionallyentitled *Unemployment, Resistance and Alternatives*.

The New Socialist (150 Walworth Road, London SE17); *Marxism Today*, Central Books, 14 Leathermarket, London SE1 3ER; *Capital and Class*, 25 Horsell Road, London N1; *Socialist Review*, P.O. Box 82, London E2; and *New Left Review*, 7 Carlisle Street, London W1; all contain useful articles on issues related to workers' plans and socialist industrial strategy.

Films, slide shows, graphic material:
Two television film documentaries have been made in the UK on the Lucal initiative: ATV's *We've always done it this way* (50 mins), and the Open University/BBC's *Nobody Wants to Know* (25 mins), produced as part of the "Control of Technology" course. CAITS has a loan copy of the ATV programme and the OU/BBC programme can be obtained from the Open University, Milton Keynes, Bucks.

CAITS has produced a number of video tapes on the Plan, e.g. on the road-rail vehicle. The Lucas initiative also featured in the BBC "Open Door" programme produced by SERA – *Work not Waste*, available on video tape from SERA, 9 Poland Street, London W1.

A tape-slide show on The Plan is also available from CAITS, as is a range of exhibition and display materials, for example The Socially Useful Show, a series of ten posters expressing different aspects of the Plan.

Midland Design Collective, c/o Tony Fry, 23 Gordon Street, Leamington Spa, CV31 1HR.
The activity of this new design group is of spans contracted work, the development of socialist design process, practice and product, design research and design education. It works with other socialist and feminist organizations, especially those active in "bottom up" planning and economic/cultural production. So far it has worked on audio visual education materials, including a tape slide show on socially useful production.

Channel 4. *Science in Society*. Four programmes to be transmitted from November 1982, supported by a series of books to be published by Pan.

Contact addresses

On environmental politics, local socialism and alternative production:
SERA, c/o 9 Poland Street, London W1.
On alternative technology:
NATTA, Alternative Technology Group, Open University, Milton Keynes, Bucks.
On workers' health and safety, and radical science and technology:
BSSRS, 9 Poland Street, London W1.
On disarmament defence conversion:
Campaign Against the Arms Trade (CAAT), 6 Caledonian Road, London N1.
European Nuclear Disarmament (END), 11 Goodwin Street, London N4.
Campaign for Nuclear Disarmament (CND), 11 Goodwin Street, London N4.
On international trade-union contacts and joint campaigns/research:
Transnational Information Exchange, c/o 467 Caledonian Road, London N7, is on Science and Technology and the Alternative Economic Strategy.

Forums for discussion on socialist economic strategy:
The Conference of Socialist Economists, 25 Horsell Road, London N1.
SERA, c/o 9 Poland Street, London NW1.
Radical Science Group, c/o 7 Granville Road, London N4.
Groups of Alternative Science and Technology Strategies, c/o Ken Green, Dept of Liberal Studies in Science, The University, Manchester 13.

The Socialist Society, 7 Carlisle Street, London W1.
The Labour Co-ordinating Committee, 9 Poland Street, London W1.
Labour Briefing, 23 Leghorn Road, London NW10.

Local contacts on workers' and users' plans and local trade-union and community research:
UDAP (Unit for the Development of Alternative Products), Lanchester Polytechnic, Coventry.

Bradford ATEC (Alternatives
in Technology and Employment
Centre),
4 Grove Terrace,
Bradford.

Bradford Resource Centre,
93–95 Little Horton Lane,
Bradford BD5 OBU.
Tel: 0274–25046.

Bristol Resource Centre,
82 Bedminster Parade,
Bristol BS3 4HL.
Tel: 0272-667933.

Coventry Resource and Information
Service (CRIS),
Cox Street,
Coventry CV1 5LW.
Tel: 0203-56149/51884.

Coventry Workshop,
40 Binley Road,
Coventry CV3 1JA.
Tel: 0203-27772.

Lewisham Women and Employment
Project,
74 Deptford High Street,
London SE8.
Tel: 01–690–3550.

Manchester Engineering Research
Group (MERG),
c/o Salford Central Mission,
Broadway,
Salford 5.
Tel: 061-872 1869.

Hackney Trades Council,
Support Unit,
34 Dalston Lane,
London E8 3AZ
Tel: 01-249 8086.

The Junction Project,
248–250 Lavender Hill,
London SW11.
Tel: 01–228–1163/4.

Joint Docklands Action Group
(J-DAG),
2 Cable Street,
London E1 8JG.
Tel: 01/480 5324.

Leeds Trade Union and Community
Resource and Information Centre,
6 Blenheim Terrace,
Leeds.
Tel: 0532-39633.

Services to Community Action and
Tenants (SCAT),
31 Clerkenwell Close,
London EC1 OAT.
Tel: 01-53 3627.

Tyne and Wear Resource Centre,
2 Jesmond Road,
Newcastle-upon-Tyne,
Tel: 0632-811911.

118 Workshop,
118 Mansfield Road,
Nottingham.
Tel: 0602-582369.

West End Resource Centre,
87 Adelaide Terrace,
Benwell,
Newcastle-upon-Tyne.
Tel: 0632-732943/731210.

Notes

Chapter 1: A new approach
1. H.A. Turner, Garfield Clack and Geoffrey Roberts, *Labour Relations in the Motor Industry*, London 1967.
2. Interview in *Marxism Today*, October 1981.

Chapter 2: "Out of the white heat. . ."
1. Quoted in S. Young and A.V. Lowe, *Intervention in the Mixed Economy*, Croom Helm, London 1974. The powers which the IRC in fact used did not involve a major interference in the market. It lubricated rather than intervened in the market.
2. ibid.
3. H. Nockolds, *Lucas, The First Hundred Years*, London 1978.
4. ibid.
5. D. Massey and R. Meagan, *The Geography of Industrial Organization*, Progress in Planning Series, Pergamon Press, Oxford 1979.

Chapter 3: The failings of the old; the foundations of the new
1. Interview with author.
2. See R. Croucher, *Engines at War*, London 1982.
3. Another illustration of this is the initiative of shop stewards in the British Aircraft Corporation to produce proposals for workers' control when the aerospace industry was about to be nationalized in 1974.
4. In addition to the authors' interviews with members of the Lucas Aerospace Combine Committee, an interview with Ernie Roberts MP, who worked in the aircraft industry in Coventry during the 1940s and early '50s, provided much of the background information for this section.

Chapter 4: Roads leading to Wortley Hall
1. Engineering Industry Training Board, *Women in Engineering*.
2. In relation to women's lack of presence in the skilled sections of engineering, Cynthia Cockburn's article on a similar sexual division of labour in the print industry provides some helpful insights: C. Cockburn, "The Material Base of Male Power", in *Feminist Review* 9.

Chapter 7: Expertise and self-reliance
1. See R. Minns, *Pension Funds and British Capitalism*, London 1979.

Chapter 8: The origins of the alternative Plan
1. H. Nockolds, op. cit.
2. Interview with author.
3. John Elliott, *Conflict or Co-operation: The Growth of Industrial Democracy*.

Chapter 9: Drawing up the Plan
1. A spokesman for the US aerospace firm Boeing has commented with regard to the 2.5MW Mod-2 windmill, which is now being mass-produced: "I don't think a job like this can be done successfully except by an aerospace company." He added that the corporation's expertise in aerodynamics, electronics, control systems and programme management were essential (*Aviation Week and Space Technology*, 23 March 1981).
2. See for example S. Littler, "Perspectives on in-company technological innovation", in *Design Studies* vol. 1, no. 6, October 1980.
3. Mary Kaldor, *The Baroque Arsenal*, André Deutsch, London 1981.
4. *The Professional Soldier*, Free Press, New York 1960, page 8.

5. Professor Thring, *The Engineer's Conscience*, London 1980.
6. Professor Thring, "Machines for a Creative Society", in *Futures* vol. 2, no. 1, 1970.

Chapter 10: A positive alternative to recession and redundancies
1. *Lucas: an Alternative Plan*, IWC pamphlet No. 54, Nottingham 1976.

Chapter 12: Local victories — the Plan in action
1. *New Scientist*, 16 October 1976.
2. These fears have been confirmed by the announcement in February 1982 of 1,200 redundancies at Burnley as a result of a fall-off in orders from Rolls Royce.
3. The OU had filmed the Burnley "Teach-In" for a television programme on the Lucas Plan which formed part of the OU's Control of Technology course. Contacts made during this process led to liaison with the OU-ERG.
4. The initial plan, as agreed at a meeting of ERG, Lucas and MKDG representatives in February 1977, had been to seek funds from ETSU for the second (air-to-air) pump, while ERG and Lucas would share the cost of the first (air-to-water) machine. ERG would provide the design specifications and, subsequently, test and development facilities and staff, while Lucas would actually build the machine. MKDG would provide the test house and limited funds (£5,000 in the event).
As it became apparent that ETSU money would not be available, or at least delayed, the idea of the second (small) pump was dropped and funds were requested from ETSU for the development of the first unit. At the same time, however, the idea of a larger, more commercial-sized unit was considered — at least by ERG and the stewards — as a follow-up. ETSU in fact had been arguing that this was what was needed, rather than small units, which is why they were reticent about providing funds for ERG for the first unit, even though, as ERG pointed out, it was usual to develop small prototypes first.
5. See the OU-ERG *Evaluation of the Design, Construction and Operation of a Gas-fuelled Engine Heat Pump*, ER 034, October 1980.
6. Subsequently Ford developed a system based on a 150kw Ford Cortina engine.

Chapter 13: The Lucas Combine provides an example
1. Lorelies Olslager, *Financial Times*, 23 January 1976.
2. Harford Thomas, *The Guardian*, 9 January 1976.
3. *The Engineer*, January 1976.
4. *The New Scientist*, January 1976.
5. "Chrysler: the Workers' Answer to the Crisis", *Workers' Control Bulletin* No. 32, May 1976. For further details of the Chrysler stewards case see *State Intervention in Industry: A Workers' Inquiry* by Coventry, Liverpool, Newcastle and North Tyneside Trades Councils.
6. See H. Beynon and H. Wainwright, *The Workers' Report on Vickers*, Pluto Press, London 1979.
7. See "Alternatives to Building a Chieftain Tank", by the Vickers Combine Committee, in *The Right to Socially Useful Work* (ed. Ken Coates), 1978.
8. The equivalent of about 80 million tons of coal is lost each year as waste heat from power stations — much of this could be reclaimed by CHP
9. Since the Parsons and Clarke Chapmans workers first drew up their alternative proposals they, with the Trade Union Studies and Information Unit in Newcastle, have started a concerted campaign for combined heat and power focused on the slogan "Jobs from Warmth".
10. See *Sense about Defence*, London 1975.
11. Godfrey Boyle quoted in "Windmill Builders Become Political", in *New Scientist*, 8 April 1976.
12. See Peter Harper, *Undercurrents*, 6 March 1974.

13. The term "Green Ban" was used to describe the refusal of the building union in Australia to work on environmentally and socially objectionable projects. For more details see K. Coates (ed.), *The Right to Useful Work*, Spokesman Books, Nottingham 1978.

14. Newcastle Trades Council, Tyneside Anti-Nuclear Campaign and Tyneside Campaign for Nuclear Disarmament have since produced a pamphlet suggesting the outlines of a plan for socially useful production for Tyneside: *Jobs for a Change*, Newcastle 1982. Also see Martin Spence, "Nuclear Capital", in *Capital and Class* No. 17.

15. *Peace News*, for example, had produced one of the first news stories on the Lucas campaign in August 1975.

16. Anthony Darling, an industrial chaplain in Kent, wrote an article, "Lucas — whose side are we on?", questioning the supposed "independence" of industrial chaplains.

17. The *New Statesman* provided a particularly detailed coverage; see especially C. Hird, 7 July 1978, and P. Wintour, 27 May 1977 and 20 January 1978.

Chapter 14: An idea come of its time

1. See Mike Noble's introduction to the American edition of Mike Cooley's *Architect or Bee*, South End Press, Boston 1981.

2. M. Polanyi, *The Tacit Dimension*, Routledge, London 1976.

3. See R. Bhaskar, "Scientific Explanation and Human Emancipation", in *Radical Philosophy* 26, Autumn 1980, for further critical discussion of the work of Polanyi.

Chapter 15: Up against institutions whose time is past

1. Letter to Jeff Rooker, 13 December 1976.

2. Interview with authors.

3. 24 November 1977.

Chapter 16: A lost opportunity

1. G. Kaufman, *How to be a Minister*, London 1981.

Chapter 18: Making connections

1. *Trade Unions in the Face of Corporate Power*, Joint Forum of Combines, 1979.

2. *Combine Committee's Handbook*, Joint Forum of Combine Committees, London 1982.

3. *Trade Unions and Pension Funds*, CAITS, London 1980.

4. *Handbook on New Technology*, JFCC, London 1982.

5. S.E.P. Thompson, *"Warwick University Ltd"*, Harmondsworth 1970.

6. *State Intervention in Industry; A Workers' Inquiry*, Coventry, Liverpool, Newcastle and North Tyneside Trades Councils, Coventry 1980.

Chapter 19: The limits of collective bargaining

1. According to *The Engineer* (7 Sept 1978) Lucas was interested in fluidized bed "because of the suitability of combustion chambers based on gas turbine technology for fluid-bed preheaters". It added that Lucas Aerospace's current interest was in the newer concept of pressured fluid-bed combustion, an important step in the development of the coal-fuelled gas turbine — a concept which, it will be remembered, the fourteen-man CSEU committee also favoured. According to *The Engineer*, talks on a pressurized bed fired by a 90 hp gas turbine were "being held with ETSU with a view to possible state funding".

2. See *Electrical Review*, vol. 203, no. 15, 19 October 1979; *IEE News*, July 1980.

3. See *Financial Times*, 18 February 1981.

4. "Lucas Heat Pump Factory — Liverpool" — Alan Schwartz, Polytechnic of

North London; Mario Andrade of Middlesex Polytechnic also contributed to this project.

5.   See *New Scientist*, 15 December 1978, p. 704, and the review of gas heat-pump technology by D.T. Strong, *Chartered Mechanical Engineer*, June 1979.

6.   See "Rising energy prices fuel heat-pump boom" in *Electrical Review*, vol. 208, no. 11, 20 March 1981.

7.   See *Electrical Review*, 9 January 1981, for a review of the programme.

8.   For a general review of Aerospace diversification options "Energy and Aerospace", Proceedings on an Anglo-American conference organized by the Royal Aeronautical Society and the American Institute of Aeronautics and Astronautics, December 1978.

9.   There is a growing literature on the corporate "barriers to innovation", mostly from a managerial perspective — emphasizing internal organizational blockages, departmental conflicts and other disincentives facing creative individuals or groups within the firm. For example see D. Littler, "Perspectives on in-company technological innovation", *Design Studies*, vol. 1, no. 6, October 1980, which points out that given corporate fear of risks associated with new products and new markets and given the not untypical "climate where preference for traditional thinking and practices may prevail" . . . "the ability to persist enthusiastically with an innovative concept" is not at premium.

10.   N. Calder, *Technopolis*, McGibbon & Kee, London 1969.

11.   R. Boguslaw, "The Design Perspective in Sociology", in *The Sociology of the Future*, W. Bell & J. Man, Russell Sage 1971.

12.   *Systems Analysis in Social Policy*, ILEA 1969.

13.   See D. Elliott and R. Elliott, *The Control of Technology*, Wykeham 1976, for further details of the 1960s US diversification programme.

14.   *Defence Cuts and Labour's Industrial Strategy*, CND 1976.

15.   See, for example, David Ross, "Power Politics" in *Alternative Technology: an assessment of technical, environmental and institutional problems*, NATTA 1982.

16.   Harvey Brooks, "Science policy in the '70s", in *Science, Growth and Society: A new perspective*, OECD 1971

17.   Barbara Shenfield, *Company Boards*, Allen and Unwin, London 1971.

Chapter 20: A new trade unionism in the making?

1.   B. Webb, *Our Partnership*, entry for 29 December 1894, London 1948.

2.   Ken Coates, *Work-ins, Sit-ins and Industrial Democracy*, Nottingham 1981.

3.   For further details see *Trade Unions, Technology and the Environment*, Unit 9 of the Open University Course Control of Technology; and the contribution of Peter Carter (a UCATT official in Birmingham) in Eric Hobsbawm, *The Forward March of Labour Halted*, London 1981.

4.   See Edinburgh Weekend Return Group, *In and Against the State*, London 1980.

5.   "Useful Work Versus Useless Toil", in *Political Writings of William Morris* (ed. A.L. Morton), London 1979.

6.   See W. Brown, *The Changing Contours of British Industrial Relations*, Oxford 1981.

7.   See H. Dobb, *Problems of Socialist Planning*, London 1970, and O. Large, "Soviet Political Economy", in *New Left Review*.

8.   Karl Marx, *Capital*, vol. 3.

9.   See the CAITS "Health Pack", *Workers Plan for Better Health*, which contains the papers from this workshop.

10.   *Trade-Union Policy and Nuclear Power*, Technology Policy Group, Open University 1981.

11.   *Community Action and Alternative Technology*, NATTA 1981.

12.   See Tim Wholforth's interesting article on the role of Parliament in a socialist society in *New Left Review* no. 130.
13.   See R. Minns in *New Statesman*, 1981.
14.   S. Williams, *Politics is for People*, London 1981.

Technical Glossary

alternative technology: socially and ecologically appropriate technologies using wind, solar and other natural "renewable" energy sources.

heat pump: electricity or gas-powered device which pumps heat into a building. Works like a refrigerator in reverse.

hybrid engine: electric motor powered by batteries charged by a conventional petrol engine.

fluidized-bed coal combustion: system for burning powdered coal using gas jets to agitate the coal mixture and ensure efficient combustion with less pollution.

fuel cell: device for producing electricity from hydrogen and other gases: works like electrolysis in reverse. Widely used in spacecraft.

combined heat and power (CHP): a way of reclaiming some of the waste heat otherwise rejected at power stations, e.g. for use in district heating networks. Widely used on the Continent.

solar cell: photo-electric device for converting sunlight into electricity.

solar collector: roof-mounted device for absorbing solar heat to provide hot-water for domestic (or industrial) use.

telechiric device: system for remote precision control of some tool or equipment, enabling people to perform hazardous or inaccessible job at a distance.

renewable energy: naturally replenished energy sources (such as solar radiation, winds, waves or tides) which are inexhaustible in the sense of not being based on the use of finite reserves (like coal, oil, gas or uranium).

kidney machine: device for performing dialysis of blood for people with kidney failure.

ballscrew: device for transmitting motion precisely used in aircraft flying-control systems (flaps, etc.) and for machine tool controls. Essentially a species of "actuator".

servo-mechanism: a mechanical, electrical pneumatic or hydraulic system for transmitting or relaying control movements (e.g. via liquid pressure) to some other system. Usually to amplify human efforts — as in servo-assisted brakes.

Union Names

APEX:	Association of Professional, Executive and Computer Staff.
ASTMS:	Association of Scientific, Technical and Managerial Staff.
AUEW:	Amalgamated Union of Engineering Workers.
CSEU:	Confederation of Shipbuilding and Engineering Unions.
EETPU:	Electrical, Electronic, Telecommunications and Plumbing Union.
GMWU:	General and Municipal Workers Union.
NALGO:	National and Local Government Officers' Association.
NUPE:	National Union of Public Employees.
POEU:	Post Office Engineering Union.
TASS:	Technical, Administrative and Supervisory Section AUEW.
TGWU:	Transport and General Workers Union.
UCATT:	Union of Construction Allied Trades and Technicians.

Index

AEI (Associated Electrical Industries), 20–21, 34, 39

Allen, Jack, 30

alternative energy technologies, 101

Amalgamated Union of Engineering Workers. *See* AUEW

Amalgamated Society of Engineers, 26

APEX (Association of Professional, Executive and Computer Staff), 29, 41, 73, 79, 132, 134; response to Plan, 152

Asquith, Phil, 10, 46, 88, 187, 195, 197

Association of Professional, Executive and Computer Staff. *See* APEX

Association of Scientific, Technical and Managerial Staff. *See* ASTMS

ASTMS (Association of Scientific, Technical and Managerial Staff), 29, 49, 72–4, 179, 188, 213; response to Plan, 152–3

Aston University, 227

AUEW (Amalgamated Union of Engineering Workers), 26, 28, 36, 41, 45, 63, 67–8, 191, 203, 210, 218; response to Combine, 30, 42, 44, 212–13; response to Plan, 141, 148–9, 178–9

AUEW-TASS, 37, 48, 73, 121, 146, 149, 151, 178, 180, 184, 202, 206, 230; conflicts within, 151; organization in Lucas Aerospace, 29; relation to Combine, 121; response to Plan, 149; role in Mike Cooley's sacking, 208–12

Australia, 12, 159

Barker, Jane, 170

Barrett, Henry George, OBE, 28

Basnett, David, 149

BBC (British Broadcasting Corporation), 11, 167

Benn, Tony, 1, 7, 8, 12, 82–7, 113, 119, 136, 177, 250

Best, Dr David, 227

Bestwick, Lord, 131

Big Flame, 158

Birdshaw, Councillor, 224

Birmingham University, 228

Blyth, James, 124, 183–4, 187, 193–5, 232, 234–5

Boardman, John, 218

Boguslaw, Robert, 238

Booth, Albert, 173

Boxer, The, 223

Bradford College, 226

Bradford Telegraph and Argus, 140

Bradley's, G.E., 20, 40, 85, 101, 117

Brassington, Mr, 128

Bryer, Robert, 227

Brazil, 18, 199

Bristol Siddeley, 19

British Aerospace, 210–11, 217, 236, 248

British Gas, 138

British Leyland, 123, 176, 195, 208, 217, 219, 224, 253, 262

British Petroleum, 234

British Rail, 106, 240

British Shipbuilders, 217

British Society for Social Responsibility in Science (BSSRS), 80, 158

British Thompson Housman, 39

Broomhead, Danny, 94, 200

BSSRS. *See* British Society for Social Responsibility in Science

Builders Labourers Federation (Australia), 245

Burnley Express, 141, 159

Burnley strike, 64–9, 75

CAAT. *See* Campaign Against the Arms Trade

Cadbury Trust, 226–8

CAITS (Centre for Alternative Industrial and Technological Systems), 139, 157, 205, 207, 225, 227–8, 230, 235, 252, 257; formation of, 153, 168–71; and

Joint Forum, 218–23; method of work, 189; relations with Combine, 214–16

Callaghan, James, 172, 182

Campaign Against the Arms Trade (CAAT), 157

Campaign for Nuclear Disarmament. *See* CND

Canada, 159, 209

Castle, Barbara, 76, 79, 80

Caudwell, Anne, 124–5

CBI (Confederation of British Industry), 182

China, 151, 159

Chrysler, 142, 172, 181, 195

Clarke Chapman's, 145

CND (Campaign for Nuclear Disarmament), 10–11, 258

Communist Party, 36, 45, 59, 86, 151–2, 248, 264

Confederation of Shipbuilding and Engineering Unions. *See* CSEU

Conference of Socialist Economists (CSE), 143

Conroy, Danny, 9–10, 45–6, 59, 67, 76–7, 80, 87–8, 137, 148, 168

Constitution of the Combine, 56–8

Cook, Steven, 227

Cooley, Mike, 7, 59, 85–8, 116, 131, 164, 169, 187, 205, 253; relations with TASS, 29, 150–52; role in Combine, 37, 53, 80, 86–7, 159, 161–2; sacking, 196, 207–12

Cooley, Shirley, 196

Cooney, Jim, 37, 48, 53, 87, 88, 110, 117–18, 120, 203–4

Cooney, Mick, 8, 46, 67, 68, 136, 167, 190, 193, 204

Coop, Mr, 68, 116, 118, 119

Corley, Sir Kenneth, 19

Crossman Pensions Bill, 76

Cryer, Mona, 79

CSEU (Confederation of Shipbuilding and Engineering Unions), 29, 64, 67–8, 81, 190–5, 197, 208, 213, 215, 232; response to Combine, 83, 84, 178–81, 185–7, 200, 201; response to Plan, 153, 178–81, 204–5; structure, 26–8

Daily Mail, 140

Daily Mirror, 140

Daily Telegraph, 23, 70

Darke, Chris, 208

Darwin, John, 146

Deane, Alf, 132, 152

Deaton, Bill, 10

Denmark, 159, 236

Department of Employment, 113, 173, 192,

Department of Energy, 113, 135, 136, 235, 240

Department of Industry, 1, 7, 113, 131, 172–3, 176–7, 182, 187, 191, 193–4, 197, 250, 260

Director, The, 177

Dodd, Bob, 43, 125, 128

Dougan, Albert, 9

Dragonfly Research Limited, 236

Duffy, Terry, 41–2

Dumas, Lloyd, 160

Duncan, Dally, 41, 49

East Europe, 18

Easton, Dennis, 203

Economist, The, 79

Edwards, Michael, 219

EE. *See* English Electric

EEC *See* European Economic Community

EEF. *See* Engineering Employers' Federation

EEPTU (Electrical, Electronic, Telecommunications and Plumbing Union), 37, 48, 73, 187

Elizabeth Garrett Anderson Hospital, 245

Elliott, David, 95–6

Elliott, John, 86

Energy Research Group (ERG), Open University, 135–8

Engineer, The, 115, 140, 186

Engineering Employers' Federation (EEF), 26–7, 29, 67–8, 213

Engineering Voice, 45
English Electric (EE), and Special Products Group (SPG), 9, 20, 29, 34–5, 39–41, 44
Entwhistle, Steve, 141
ERG. *See* Energy Research Group
Europe, 12, 16, 18
European Economic Community (EEC), 18, 24, 82, 99
European Youth Conference, 159

Fabian Society, 227, 244, 246
Ferranti's, 84
Ferry, Alex, 191, 197
Financial Times, 86, 140
Flemming, Jim, 69, 135, 213
Flemming, Sid, 64
Fletcher, Richard, 95–6, 103, 169, 179, 224
Flynn, Peter, 210
Ford, 161
Ford, Terry, 88
France, 24
Free University of Berlin, 159
Frost, 137
fuel cell technology, 102
Future Studies Centre, 154

GEC (General Electric Company), 19–20, 23–4, 29, 34–5, 39, 48, 143, 217, 219, 236, 240
General and Municipal Workers Union. *See* GMWU
General Motors, 99
George, Mike, 170, 223
Germany, Federal Republic of, 24, 162, 164, 209
Gill, Ken, 151, 180–1, 184, 186, 209
GMWU (General and Municipal Workers Union), 44, 52, 63, 76, 149, 191, 203, 213
Golding, John, 198
Goodman, Robert, 238
Gough, Dave, 44, 203
GPO (General Post Office), 123
Grantham, Roy, 197
Greater London Council (GLC), 253

Green Party, 162
Guardian, 140
Gunter, Jack, 7, 43, 86, 88, 95, 110, 148

Haddon, Chris, 42
Hartman, Chick, 38, 86, 111, 130
Hawker Siddely, 19, 142
Hearsay, Arthur, 68
heat pump, 91, 93, 102, 135–9, 232, 235, 238
Hemel Hempstead, Industrial Ballscrew Division dispute, 128–9, 183, 232
Herbert's, Alfred, 84
Hill, Tom, 59
"Hobcart", 94, 101
Hobson's H.M., 20, 40–2, 72–3
Hobson's Integral, 21
Hodson, Albert, 81
Holland, 159, 209, 236
Hoos, Ida, 238
Horrocks, Brian, 141
Howe, Geoffrey, 141
Huckfield, Les, 173, 178, 181
Hughes, Howard, 48
Hulme, Jim, 79
Hunt, Ernie, 43, 148

IAM (International Association of Machinists and Aerospace Workers), 159, 161, 209
I.G. Metall, 159, 162, 209
Industrial Reorganization Corporation (IRC), 16–19, 21, 23, 25, 34
Institute for Workers' Control, 99
International Association of Machinists and Aerospace Workers. *See* IAM
Investors Chronicle, 231
Isaksson, Harry, 209

Janowitze, Morris, 92
Joint Forum of Combine Committees, 218–19, 223, 230, 258
Joint Production and Consultative Committee, 30
Joint Works Council, 133
Joseph Lucas Limited, 16

Joseph Pensions Act, 76

Kaldor, Mary, 92
Kaufman, Gerald, 113, 126–8, 173, 177, 179, 180, 184, 186, 191, 193–4, 196
Keaton, Lord, 17
Kelly, Stan, 44, 60, 86, 203
Kenny, Mike, 220
kidney machines, 40, 93, 101, 149, 229, 232
Kimball, Dexter, 165
KME co-operative, 244
Korea, 199

Labour government, 11, 76, 82, 172, 181, 184, 197, 199, 248, 256–7, 260
Labour Party, 76, 82, 87, 119, 132, 143–4, 151, 153, 156, 198, 244, 261, 264
Labour Weekly, 158
Lanchester Polytechnic, 228
Layko, Tom, 120
Lea, David, 175
Lee, Richard, 221, 223
Liverpool Evening Echo, 140
Lowe, Brian, 228
Lucas Aerospace sites:
    Birmingham 43–4, 46, 73–5, 122–8, 226;
    Brackwell, 41–2;
    Bradford, 39–40, 36;
    Burnley, 45–6, 64–9, 131–9;
    Coventry, 39;
    Hemel Hempstead, 37–9, 128–31;
    Liverpool, 44–5;
    Luton, 40–41;
    Morden, 38–9;
    Neasden, 40–41;
    Willesden, 36–7, 46, 205–6;
    Wolverhampton, 41–2, 72–3
Lucas CAV, 16–17
Lucas Electrical, 16–18, 123, 199, 208
Lucas Girling, 17, 106, 199, 208, 210
Lucas, Joseph, 16, 17, 20

McFadden, Dave, 160
McIntosh, Alex, 146
McSharry, Pat, 8, 43, 61, 74
Manchester Polytechnic, 233
Mann, Tom, 26
Marsh, 67
Marshall, Jim, 219
Marx, Karl, 254
Mason, Brian, 9, 42, 85, 118–19
Mason, Roy, 156
Massachusetts Institute of Technology (MIT), 165
Melman, Seymour, 160
Meriden, 245
Merseyside, 44–5
Messervy, George, 233
Middleton, Roy, 46, 76–7
Mid-Peninsula Conversion Project (California), 160
Militant, 158
Milton Keynes Development Corporation (MKDC), 135
Ministry of Defence, 16, 19
Ministry of Health, 101
Ministry of Supply, 44–5
Mogg, Clifton, 69–70
Moran, Terry, 11, 46, 112, 137, 157, 164, 205
Mottram, John, 202–3
Mowforth, Dr Edwin, 106
Muirheads, 21, 39
Monopolies Commission, 20
Morris, William, 246–7
Multi-Role Combat Aircraft (MRCA), 162
Murdoch, Bob, 146
Murphy, Ron, 143
Murray, Jim, 143–4, 219

NALGO (National and Local Government Officers' Association), 146–7, 258
Napiers, 41
National and Local Government Officers' Association. *See* NALGO
National Childcare Campaign, 246
National Coal Board, 82, 234
National Council of Aerospace

Shop Stewards, 32
National Economic Development Office. *See* NEDO
National Enterprise Board, 126–7, 153, 176–7
National Health Service (NHS), 146
National Housing Liaison Committee, 252
National Union of Public Employees. *See* NUPE
Nebel, Kurt, 210
NEDO (National Economic Development Office), 28, 174–5
New Products Committee, 134–7
New Propellor, 32
New Scientist, 136, 140
Newcastle Trades Council, 145–6, 257
Nicol, A.J., 78
Noble, David, 165
Nockolds, Harold, 20–21
North-East London Polytechnic, 103, 170, 223
Norton Villiers, 123
Norway, 159
NUPE (National Union of Public Employees), 146, 258

O'Neill, Jim, 48, 117
Open University (Technology Faculty), 95, 236
Orloff, George, 128

Parry-Evans, Mike, 94
Parson, John, 166
Parson's, C.A., 145–7
Part, Sir Anthony, 177
pensions, 76–80
Pilling, Trevor, 46, 66, 68
Plowden Commission, 19
POEU (Post Office Engineering Union), 258
Poland, Ernie, 43, 52, 74
Polanyi, Michael, 169
Post Office Engineering Union. *See* POEU
Premier Precision, 20, 39, 41–2, 117

Press coverage:
left, 158;
local, 22, 140–41, 159, 233;
national, 22–3, 70, 86, 106, 119, 140, 175
Price, Chris, 173
Punter, Brian, 42, 72, 73

Quakers, 157
Queen Mary College, London University, 95–6
Quirk, Tommy, 52, 188

Radical Science Journal, 158
Rendall, Walt, 152
Reuther, Walter, 160
Reynolds, Mike, 9, 203
Right to Fuel Campaign, 147
Rivett, Mr, 126
Robinson, Derek, 217, 219
Robles, Ricardo, 229
Rolls Royce, 16, 19, 122, 123, 134, 210, 217, 218, 220, 225; crash of, 21–2, 42–4, 52, 73, 213
Rooker, Jeff, 13, 174, 178, 181
Rotax, 20–21, 29–31, 34, 36–40, 90, 129
Routley, John, 201, 215
Rowntree Charitable Trust, Joseph, 170, 226

Saab, 162–3
Salisbury, Brian, 44, 112, 167, 207, 226
Scanlon, Lord, 148
Scarbrow, Ernie, 9, 11, 42, 51, 61–2, 90, 95–7, 114, 116–18, 126, 130, 140, 172–5, 181, 185, 212; attempt to sack, 196, 205–8, 217; role in Combine, 37, 48, 53, 55, 88, 205–7, 216
Science and Technology Committee, 80, 95
Science for the People, 158
Scott, Sir Bernard, 70, 82, 119, 159, 175
Scottish Daily News, 244
Scragg Limited, Ernest, 141
Seager, Barry, 29

SERA. *See* Socialist Environment and Resources Association
Shaiken, Harley, 161–2
Sharp and Company, Albert, 20, 24
Sheet Metal Workers' Union, 45
Shirley Research Centre, 233
Shutt, Jim, 229
Silverton, Cyril, 38, 93
Skelland, Dick, 54, 149
Smith's Industries, 59
Socialist Environment and Resources Association (SERA), 147, 155
Socialist Medical Association, 80, 124
Socialist Review, 158
Socialist Worker, 158
Socialist Workers' Party (SWP), 158, 264
solar cell technology, 102
Solar Corporation of America, 234
South America, 234
Soviet Union, 151, 254
Spain, 199, 209
Stone Platt Industries Limited, 141–2
Sugden, Gordon, 187, 200
Sullivan, Mr, 137
Sun, The, 140
Sunday Telegraph, 119, 175
Sunday Times, 106
Swarbrick, John, 152–3, 188
Sweden, 99, 159, 163–4, 209, 236

Taliazuchi, Pino, 209
Tate, Phil, 130
TASS (Technical, Administrative and Supervisory Section AUEW). *See* AUEW-TASS
Taylor, Frederick Winslow, 100
Taylorism, 100
Tedstall, Geoff, 72–3
TGWU (Transport and General Workers Union), 27–8, 41, 72, 153, 156, 178–9; response to Plan, 148
Thatcher government, 197
Third World, 103, 124, 143, 163, 240, 262

Thring, Professor, 95–6
Tierney, Sid, 126–7
Titchen, Fred, 220
Transport and General Workers Union. *See* TWGU
transport technologies, 103
Treaty of Rome, 18
Tribune, 158
TUC (Trades Union Congress), 76, 81, 111, 156, 175–6, 185, 221, 259
Turner, H.A., 13
Tyne Shop Stewards' Conference, 144
Tyneside Socialist Centre, 155–6

UAW (Union of Automobile Aerospace and Agricultural Workers), 159–61
UCATT (Union of Construction Allied Trades and Technicians), 245
UKAEA, 240
Undercurrents, 154
Union of Construction Allied Trades and Technicians. *See* UCATT
Unit for the Development of Alternative Products, 228–9, 252
United States of America, 12, 24, 75, 90, 92, 94, 99, 103, 159–62, 165, 209
Urwin, Harry, 27

Vactric Controls Equipment, 20–21, 39
Varley, Eric, 172, 174
Vickers, 19, 143, 153, 217, 219, 220, 245
Vietnam War, 160
Voice of the Unions, 158

Walesa, Lech, 14
Walker, Ron, 48
Ward, Peter, 210
Warwick University, 227–8
Weaver, Eddie, 39
Webb, Sidney and Beatrice, 27, 244
Webber, Ernie, 53, 60

Weber, Willi, 162
Weinstock, Arnold, 34–5, 219
West Midland County Council, 229
West Midlands Enterprise Board, 79
West Somerset County Council, 224
Whitely, Ron, 29
Whitney, Alan, 118–20, 174, 187, 197
Weiner, Norbert, 165
Williams, Bill, 114, 128

Williams, G.F., 134
Williams, John, 176
windmills, 102
Wimpisinger, William, 161, 209
Wise, Audrey, 175, 198
Wood, Frank, 43
Wortley Hall, 236
Wilson, Harold, 16, 184
Wyton, Tony, 61

Young, Mike, 38, 129